Compact Guide to Word®

About the Compact Guide Training Series

Computer training has become a billion-dollar business and a major problem for end users, workers, and corporations. Beginning training courses typically cost between $100 and $500. With this is mind, we at AP Professional decided to attack the problem and offer the best in training at a fraction of the cost. The goals were simple. We wanted to create a program that would

- teach the subject quickly and easily
- provide the in-depth training that users expect
- be easy to use at or away from the computer.

It seemed that an interactive CD-ROM, combined with an excellent book, would provide the most reusable and flexible training program. We decided to look at all of the best CD training products on the market. After looking at the competition, we concluded that the LearnKey, Inc. products offer the best interface and use the best instructional methodology. Each instructor on the LearnKey videos is an excellent teacher. Each is also effective on camera. LearnKey was quite gracious in adapting the content of the CDs to meet our needs.

With the LearnKey CD, we had the leverage to get some of the top writing talents in the computer business. The result is the best in CD/book training at an affordable price.

Now that you have bought this package, enjoy the CD, read the book. . . whichever! When you are done, you can loan them to a friend, share them with your co-workers, or put them on your shelf so they can be used again and again.

You may also want to purchase other books in the Compact Guide Training Series, including

Compact Guide to Excel
Compact Guide to Windows 95
Compact Guide to Visual Basic 4

(We'll be doing many more, so watch for upcoming titles!)

For special deals on bulk orders, call (619) 699-6477. Order five or six for your office lending library!

For instructions on the CD, see Appendix A. If you need technical support, you may contact LearnKey at (520) 717-1733.

We at AP Professional and LearnKey, Inc. hope you will enjoy this exciting new package.

Jeffrey M. Pepper
AP Professional
Vice President, Editorial Director

Compact Guide to Word®

Tom Badgett

AP PROFESSIONAL
Boston San Diego New York
London Sydney Tokyo Toronto

This book is printed on acid-free paper ∞

AP PROFESSIONAL
1300 Boylston Street, Chestnut Hill, MA 02167
World Wide Web site at http://www.apnet.com/

An imprint of ACADEMIC PRESS, INC.
A Division of HARCOURT BRACE & COMPANY

United Kingdom Edition published by
ACADEMIC PRESS LIMITED
24–28 Oval Road, London NW1 7DX

ISBN 0-12-513835-0

Printed in the United States of America
95 96 97 98 IP 9 8 7 6 5 4 3 2 1

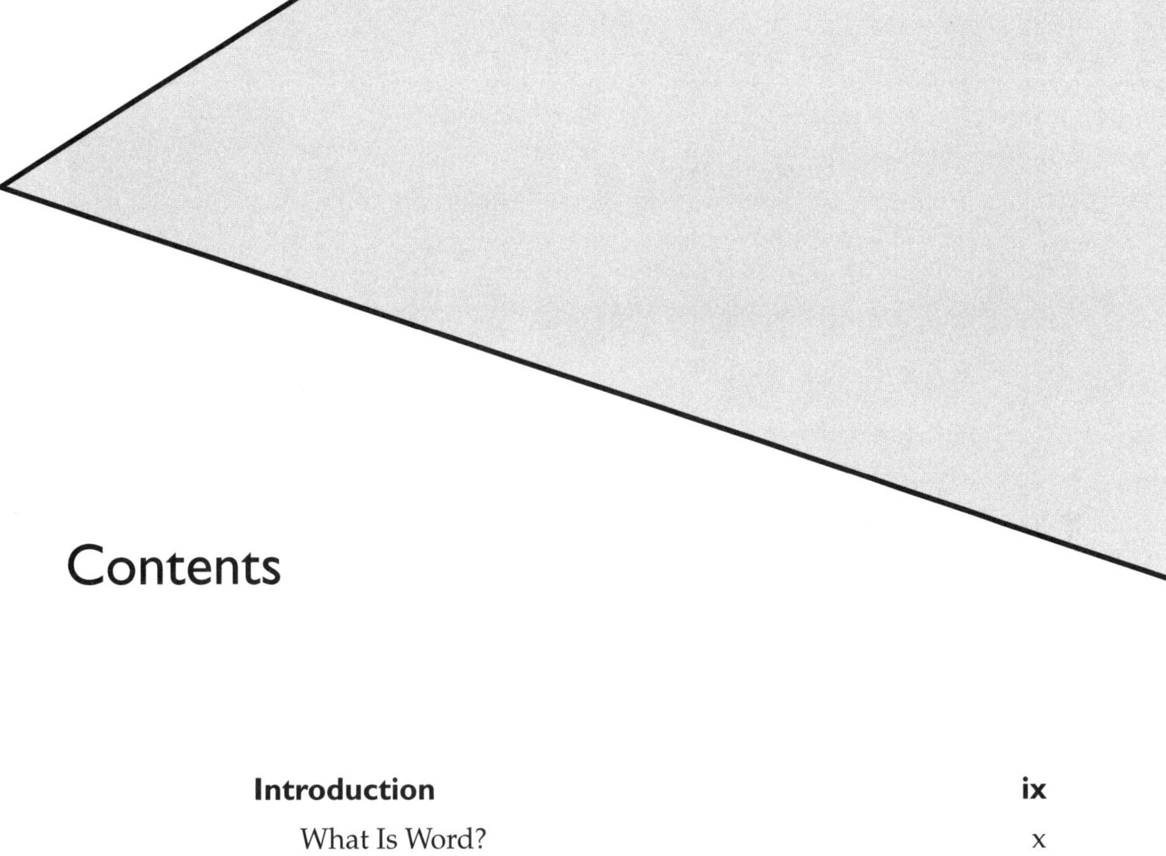

Contents

Introduction

Microsoft.

That one word evokes a myriad of images as diverse as your own experience and perspective. But whatever else it means, Microsoft has become synonymous with high-end, Windows-based business applications. Indeed, with the product marketing posture taken by this international software giant, you hardly see or hear one of their software packages named without the corporate association: Microsoft Windows®, Microsoft Office®, Microsoft PowerPoint®, Microsoft Excel® and, of course, Microsoft Word®. Indeed, Word, perhaps more than any other single product, is tied inexorably with the Microsoft corporate name.

Word is gaining popularity in the word processing world, both because of Microsoft's strong corporate presence and because of the product's strong performance on the desktop and on the road in countless laptop and notebook computers. If you already have some experience with Word, then you know what I mean. If you're just getting started with Word, you'll soon learn about its strengths—I'll point those out throughout this book—and you'll become acquainted with its weaknesses. I'll show you how to work around these few little "gotchas" in this book as well.

What Is Word?

Microsoft Word is, at the baseline, a word processor, a software tool that helps you type, edit, and format text on the printed page. Word processing with products such as Word has been among the top one or two computer applications since computers appeared on individual desktops some 15 years ago. Word processing software has changed a lot during those years, of course. And, as part of this evolution, Microsoft Word has become much more than just a word processor.

In addition to manipulating text, Word helps you create and insert graphics images into documents, design creative page layouts, make use of a variety of fonts and colors, and work interactively with other applications such as spreadsheets, presentation software, email managers, schedulers, and more. In fact, Word is integrated into the Microsoft Office and general Windows environment to the point that many users consider Word their single interface into many, if not most, of the other applications they use.

The Word 6.0 Environment

Microsoft Word is a Windows-based product that uses the Windows interface, object linking and embedding (OLE), and networking to build an overall environment that is creative, functional, and relatively easy to learn and to use. Word is much more than a standalone word processor. It is an integrated publishing and writing tool with strong links to other applications. And, because Word is available for Macintosh and other platforms, it can form the basis of a broad-based office environment.

What Is in This Book?

By today's standards, this is an unusual book. In addition to the text and screen shots, drawings and examples you would expect to find in a book about computer software, you'll also find a comprehensive, interactive video about Word on the CD-ROM that accompanies this book. You'll find several books on the shelves these days that include a CD-ROM, but I challenge you to find a book with an interactive video CD-ROM. This book, and others in this series, holds a unique place on bookstore shelves, in corporate America's reference libraries, and on the desks of home users.

There's a brief description of what's on the CD-ROM and how to use it at the end of this book, but you can explore the disc easily by inserting it in your CD-ROM player and using the File, Run command from the Program Manager to execute the setup program. You'll find video demonstrations, animated examples, audio descriptions, and a whole lot more to help you practice the concepts you read about in this book.

The book and the video concentrate on Microsoft Word Version 6.0. This is the most popular and most used of the current Word versions, and it is the first version of Word that significantly upgraded program features from previous releases. I'll show you how this version of Word is different from other versions and I'll also discuss briefly the important features of Word 7.0, the version of Word that ships with Office 95, the Windows 95 version of Microsoft Office.

If you plan to step up to Windows 95, you can still run Word 6 and its associated applications, or you can upgrade to Office 95 and use Word 7 instead. Either way, the information in this book—along with the detailed, interactive instructions on the CD-ROM—will prepare you to get the most out of the Word release you have.

I've summarized below the major topics you will find in this book.

Introduction

That's what you're reading now.

Chapter 1: Starting Word 6.0

This chapter gives you an overview on launching Word and accessing the basic Word features. You'll learn how to start Word from the Program Manager or File Manager, and how to make Word your default Windows operating environment. I'll also give you a detailed look at the Word screen, so we can agree on terms and what the on-screen Word objects are called and what they do. And, I'll show you how to use the mouse and your keyboard to issue commands and control Word.

Chapter 2: Important Word 6.0 Features

Word 6.0 was a significant upgrade from the previous Word 2.0 for Windows that formed the mainstay of so many word processing desktops. Word 6, and the newer Word 7, include a number of features that experienced word processor users had been asking for and that even neophytes will learn to appreciate. In this chapter I show you the salient features that are new with Word 6 and try to relate these features to your real word processing world. I hope this will help you understand a little more about the design of this product and, more importantly, help you learn how you might use its extended features to your best advantage.

Chapter 3: Creating Your First Document

At its simplest level, Word is a simple program. If you understand the Windows environment and the concept of word processing, it should be very easy for you to create a document in Word. In this chapter I show you how to handle the basics, but I also discuss a few of Word's extended features, such as Wizards and Templates, to help you move quickly beyond the simplest beginnings. There's also a section in this chapter that shows you some typing and editing basics, and I introduce the beginnings of document formatting.

Chapter 4: Formatting a Document

The good news with Word is that the software handles most of the basic document formatting for you. In fact, if your document is fairly basic and requires only the simplest of formatting, you need do little more than type on the keyboard. If, on the other hand, you'd like to learn about the use of fonts, character attributes, type styles, paragraph formatting, and special techniques such as creating dropped capitals, then the information in this chapter is what you need. I also show you how to use some of Word's advanced features such as AutoCorrect and AutoFormat, I discuss the spell checker tool, and a whole lot more.

Chapter 5: Page Layout

Character- and paragraph-level formatting are only part of the Word document story. You also need to know how to use Word elements to create an overall page design. That's what I cover in Chapter 5. You'll learn how to create and format columns, how to set page margins, how to use headers and footers, what to do with page breaks, and how to save your work.

Chapter 6: Printing Documents or Envelopes

Unless you are using Word to present information on-screen, or you're using it as a production front end to a page layout program such as Quark or PageMaker, the ultimate object of creating a document in Word is to print it out. After all the editing and creating, you want to commit the words to paper so someone else, or lots of someone elses, can read what you have written. In this chapter I'll show you how to hook up your printer, how to configure Word to use your specific printer, how to format documents for your printer, and how to print your documents. I also discuss some specialty printing tasks such as printing on an envelope and printing mailing labels.

Chapter 7: Searching for Data

Among the really useful features of a word processing software package is the ability to search for specific kinds of information, including text, format codes, paragraph codes, and more. You can also tell the program to change each occurrence of a word or phrase to something else, an excellent facility for making global changes to a document. In this chapter I show you how to use the Word search tools, including the Find File utility that is part of Word's intrinsic file management features.

Chapter 8: Using Tables

Even if you've used Word a good bit, I'll almost bet you haven't used tables very much. Word tables are something that many users seem to avoid, either because they don't understand the need for tables, or can't figure out how best to use them. In this chapter I'll show you, step by step, how to create and use your own Word tables and explain why you'd want to.

Chapter 9: Using and Creating Styles

You should never consider any letter or memo, manual or report a standalone document. Chances are that at some point you will want to use elements of one existing document in a new document you are creating. Think, too, about a corporate image for publications. Many companies agree on document formatting for all in-house writing so there is a common layout and appearance. This makes it easier for everyone to create new documents and for those who must read them to understand what they are reading. All of these processes are made easier with Word styles. In this chapter I'll show you what a style is and describe how you can use existing Word styles and create your own for personal or corporate applications.

Appendix A: The Word CD

You can use this book alone; you can use the CD alone; you can use the two together. In this appendix I describe the CD, summarize what is on it, describe how to install the software and tell you how to use it. The good thing about CD-ROMs is that they include a lot of online help and step-by-step instructions. Once you get the operational CD software installed, you won't need much additional help in using the video. This appendix will offer a handy quick reference to get you started, however.

Appendix B: Word 7.0 and Windows 95 Overview

As this book is written Microsoft Word 6 and Windows 3.11 are widely used products. However, Windows 95 and Word 7 are gaining popularity and are apparently being accepted by the user public. In this appendix I'll show you how Word 7 is like Word 6, how it is different, and suggest how you can make the transition to the new operating environment, if you want to.

Chapter 1

Starting Word 6.0

As part of the Microsoft Windows environment, Word launches from the Program Manager or Windows 95 desktop like any other Windows-compliant application. Just where the Word icon appears and how you start the program differs slightly from installation to installation. There also are some simple tricks you may want to try to help you launch Word easily and automatically if Word is your primary operating environment.

I'll discuss these options in this chapter, and, in the next section, I'll show you some basic Windows navigation techniques and define some terms just to make the rest of this chapter easier to understand.

The Windows Screen

Microsoft Windows provides a *graphical user interface*, sometimes called a *GUI*, for your computer data and applications. The main Windows interface is the Program Manager or Windows 95 desktop screen, which consists of several application windows or program icons (the exact number depends on how many applications you have installed). Inside each application window is a group of icons that represent programs or utilities within that application group. Figure 1.1 shows a Program

Figure 1.1 Windows Program Manager with Main and Accessories Windows

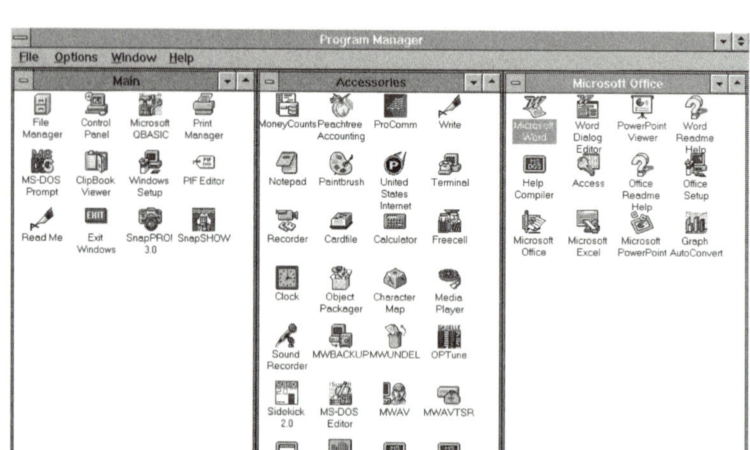

Manager screen with basic Windows components, including the Main and Accessories application windows.

Windows Navigation

As a graphical user interface, it looks as if moving around, choosing files, and conducting other tasks in Windows would be intuitive and extremely easy. Once you understand a few basics, it is. In the beginning, however, just understanding how to use the mouse or how to use some of the other navigation features of Windows can be difficult and even frustrating.

The mouse is a great improvement in computer interaction, and it seems so easy and natural when you watch someone with some experience use it. When you first sit down with a mouse, however, it is a pretty awkward experience. I can't teach you to feel comfortable with the mouse. That comes only with some experience. I can offer a couple of hints that make using the mouse easier, and I can share a couple of terms that you'll see throughout this book.

First of all, as you move the mouse pointer around the screen, notice that the shape of the pointer changes depending on the type of object under the pointer. When the pointer is over an object that can be selected, the pointer is an arrow point. When the pointer moves over a part of the screen that can hold text, on the other hand, the pointer changes to an I-beam. This is the *insertion point* and it shows that you are pointing to a text portion of the screen.

If you click on the screen with the I-beam showing, a text insertion point is fixed and I-beam changes to a blinking vertical line (a blinking vertical line indicates the insertion point). The next text you type will appear at that location.

NOTE: If you run out of desk before you have moved the mouse pointer where you want it, simply pick up the mouse and move it over to give you room to move.

NOTE: You can resize some Word objects by moving the mouse pointer to the edge of the object until the pointer changes to a double-ended arrow. Press and hold the left mouse button and drag the edge of the object to the new position.

NOTE: As you move the mouse, keep your wrist on the desk and move the mouse with your hand. If you try to move the mouse by moving your whole arm, you will have less control and get fatigued easily.

Your mouse probably has two buttons, usually termed left and right. Some mice have three buttons. The button in the middle is almost never used. The left mouse button is the main one. When I instruct you to click or to double-click or to hold down the mouse button in this book, I mean the left button. Some applications don't use the right button at all, but in Word you can use the right button to display additional menu choices. For example, if you press the right mouse button after selecting a block of text, you will see a pop-up menu with six frequently used selections on it (see Figure 1.2).

If you place the pointer within one of the displayed toolbars and press the right mouse button, you'll see another menu for customizing the toolbar displays (see Figure 1.3).

When I tell you to *click* on a Word object, I mean to move the mouse pointer over the object and press the left mouse button momentarily. *Double-click* means to place the mouse pointer over an object and press the left mouse button twice in quick succession. A double-click operation can be a little complicated for some users. For one thing, there is sometimes

Figure 1.2 A Right Button Command Menu

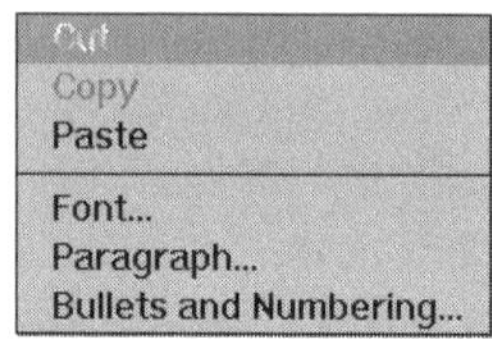

a tendency to move the mouse pointer between clicks. This moves the pointer off the object you are trying to select, so the double-click doesn't take effect. In addition, you need to double-click with a close-spaced rhythm. If you leave too much time between the clicks, you won't make the selection you want.

Sometimes you want to select a menu item without actually executing it. When a double-click is required to start a specific menu item, you can use a single click to highlight or select the item. You can also drag a highlight cursor or selector by holding down the left mouse button while you move the cursor. A menu or dialog box selection that requires a single click will be executed when you move the highlight bar over the choice and release the mouse button.

When you are working with text, you can generally select a portion of text by placing the mouse pointer at the beginning of

Figure 1.3 A Right Button Toolbar Menu

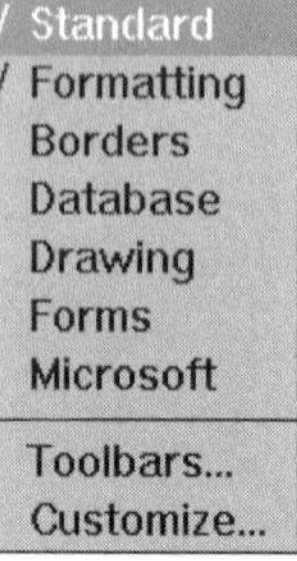

the block of text you want to select, holding down the left mouse button, and moving the highlight across as much text as you want to select. Once selected, the text can be manipulated as a unit or block.

You may want to point to an item without selecting it, as when you want to view the ToolTips for a toolbar button. To point to a screen object, simply move the mouse pointer over the object and pause without pressing any mouse button.

In the next section I'll describe the most common ways for starting Word, then we'll look at some more menu and navigating tips.

Starting Word from the Program Manager

For most of us, starting Word from the Program Manager or by using a Windows 95 shortcut icon on the desktop is the easiest and most common method for starting the program. The Windows Program Manager is the default operating environment for Windows users. It is the section of Windows that holds all of the program groups that provide access into Windows applications (refer to Figure 1.1).

Your Program Manager screen may not look just like the one in Figure 1.1, but it will be similar. The difference comes with what applications you have installed in Windows and which application groups you have open. An *application group* (or application window) is a collection of programs, note files, or documents, each represented by an icon. Related icons are grouped into a window so you can launch them easily by double-clicking on the desired one.

Look again at the sample Program Manager screen in Figure 1.1. Open application groups shown in this illustration include Main, Accessories, and Microsoft Office. You may have other groups such as Games, Network, Internet, or whatever other applications you have installed on your computer. In addition, you probably have other application groups that are not open. They are shown as small, gray icons at the bottom of the Program Manager screen.

If you have installed Word as part of Microsoft Office, then the Word icon should be located in the Office group. In addition, you will see a Word icon on the Office toolbar that is probably in the upper-right corner of the Program Manager display.

The Word icon—which you will find in the Office or other group window or on the Office toolbar—is shown by itself in Figure 1.4.

To launch Word from an application group, first open the group, if it is not already open, by double-clicking on the icon that represents the group. Once the group window is open, locate the Word icon and double-click on it to launch the program.

To launch Word from the toolbar, single-click on the Word icon.

NOTE: The Office toolbar provides an interesting feature that is not available when you launch applications from inside an application group. You can launch a program from the toolbar by single-clicking on the icon. If you launch a program from an application group, then you must double-click on the desired icon. In addition, when you click on an icon on the Office toolbar, the Office application first searches open programs to find out if the program you selected is already running. If it is, then it is given the focus (brought to the top of the Windows display). If you double-click on a toolbar icon, a new instance of the chosen application is launched, even if a previous instance is already running. When you double-click on a program icon inside a program group, a new instance of the program is started every time. You can't start a program from inside a program group by single-clicking on it.

Starting Word from the File Manager

The File Manager is a Windows application or utility you can use to browse your local or network disks. The File Manager displays all available disk drives, directories, and files. You can use it to create new directories, remove existing directories, copy and move data, and to execute programs. (Use the Explorer in Windows 95.)

Figure 1.4 Word Icon Close-up

To launch the Word application from inside the File Manager, double-click the File Manager icon in the Main application group to display the File Manager screen shown in Figure 1.5. The File Manager icon looks like a small file cabinet.

Open a directory display for the disk drive that holds the Word application (probably drive C), then display the subdirectory that contains the Word program. If you installed Word as part of Microsoft Office, the executable Word file likely is in the C:\msoffice\winword directory.

Open this directory with the File Manager and locate the **winword.exe** program file. Double-click on winword.exe to launch Word.

Starting Word Automatically

Particularly if you use Word as your main operating environment while in Windows, it might be a good idea to launch Word when you open Windows. You can do this in a couple of ways.

Figure 1.5 The File Manager Main Screen

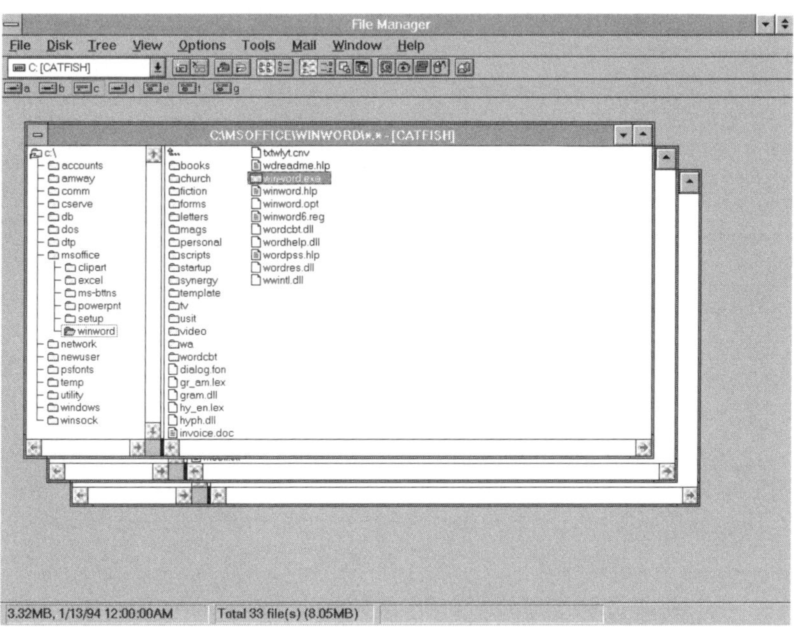

If you are comfortable with DOS, simply add the **winword.exe** file name to the command line that you use to launch Windows. If Windows opens automatically when you boot your computer, it probably means there is a **win** command in your autoexec.bat file. Locate this line and use a text editor such as DOS Edit to add the Word argument to the **win** command line:

```
win c:\msoffice\winword\winword.exe
```

With this command to launch Windows, the Word application will come up inside Windows as soon as Windows starts.

You can also add the Word application to the Windows Startup group. This causes Word to load automatically inside Windows after the Windows user interface opens. You can do this easily by opening the msoffice group (or whatever group holds the Word application), locating the Word icon, and dragging it onto the startup icon or into the Startup group, if this window is already open.

The Word Screen

However you launch Word, you should see a basic opening screen that contains certain components that you can use to manipulate the Word application.

Like Windows itself, Word presents a dynamic screen. There are basic components that appear pretty much anytime you open the Word application. Within that basic framework you can add or remove objects, customize objects, and so on. Figure 1.6 shows the basic Word screen with components labeled.

The basic function of Word is to manipulate words, of course. But this program includes a number of additional, really useful features that help you format a document. We'll get into some of those later in this book (and there are plenty of examples on the accompanying video CD-ROM). For now, let's look at Word navigation and manipulation basics.

Understanding Menus

Any program that runs under Microsoft Windows has a menu scheme that is similar to the Program Manager menu system and to most other Windows products. Although menus are how we have accessed program features for years, Microsoft

Figure 1.6 The Basic Word Screen with Components Labeled

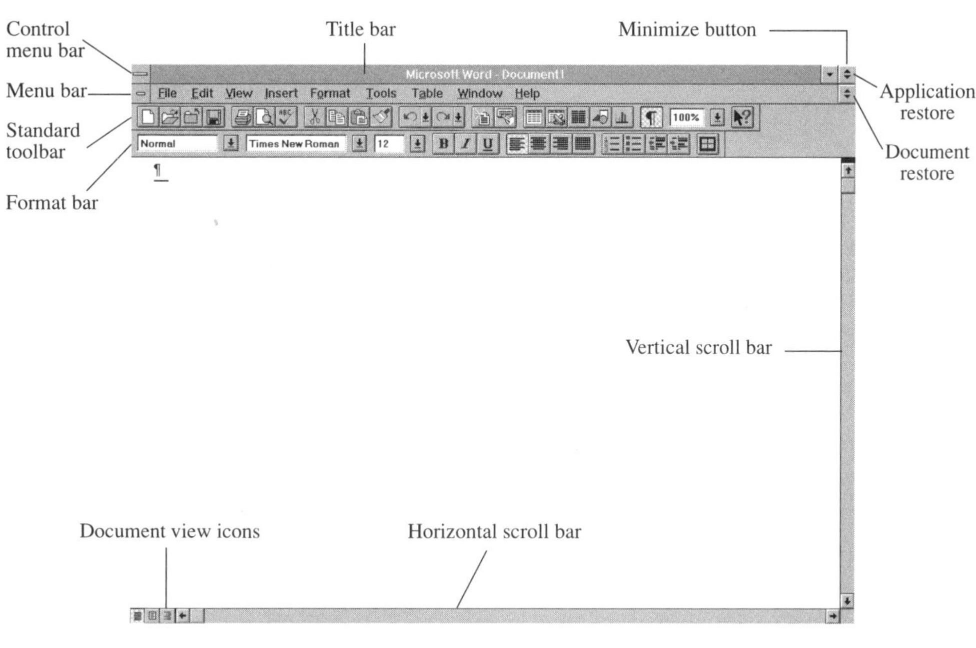

reports that only about 24 percent of users manipulate Word with the menus. More people use the *toolbar,* which I'll talk about in the next section. Figures 1.7 and 1.8 show the basic Program Manager menu bar and the Word menu bar.

Notice the similarity between these menus. They are arranged in a horizontal fashion (similar to the style first used by spreadsheets like Lotus 1-2-3). When an application is active, you are working in the main part of the screen. You may be entering information into a spreadsheet, typing in a word

Figure 1.7 Program Manager Menu Bar

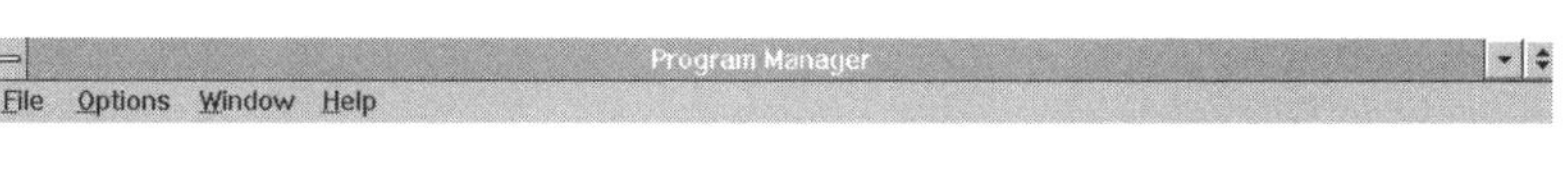

Figure 1.8 Microsoft Word 6 Menu Bar

processor, or, in the case of Word, inserting text or graphics into a document. When you want to use a menu selection, you can access it in two ways:

- Use the mouse to point to the menu item and pull down the list.
- Press and release the Alt key to activate the menu, use the cursor movement keys to highlight the item you want, and then press Enter. You can also activate the menu with Alt, then press the underlined character in the menu name to pull down the menu. In the Word menu in Figure 1.8, for example, you can access the View menu by pressing the V key after you press the Alt key to activate the menu bar. Figure 1.9 shows the Format pull-down menu.

Note that some menu choices give you additional feedback about the way they work. A selection followed by three dots (. . .), for example, means that a dialog box will be displayed if you select that menu item. Once the dialog box is displayed,

Figure 1.9 The Word Format Pull-Down Menu

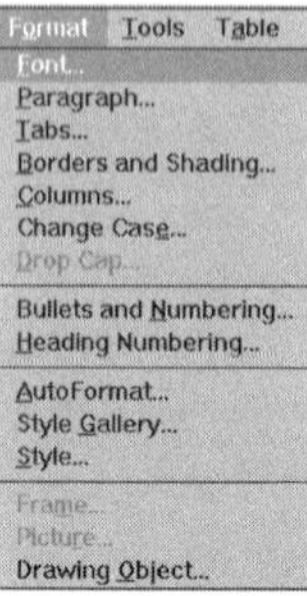

Figure 1.10 The Word Edit Menu

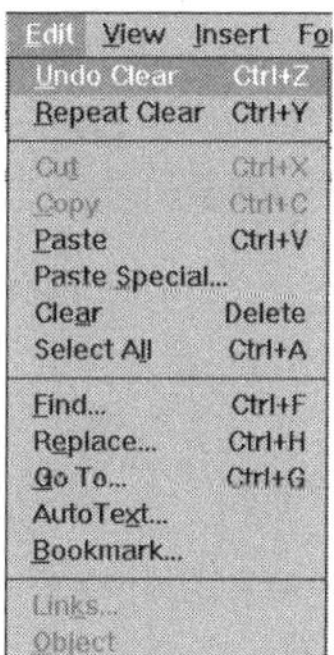

you can provide additional information or answer questions to get the desired results. (See the discussion of dialog boxes later in this chapter for more information.)

Some menus in Word prompt you with the *hotkeys* to execute some of the individual commands. Figure 1.10 shows the Word Edit menu that includes these hotkey prompts.

Notice that the choices on a pull-down menu also have one character in each selection underlined. After you pull down the menu, you can either use the mouse to highlight and choose a selection, or you can simply press the keyboard character that is underlined in the selection you want. You don't have to press the Alt key in combination with the keyboard key in these submenus.

Understanding Toolbars

With a full-featured application such as Word, the menu structure can become extremely complex. Remembering where each choice is and how to use it can be difficult. That's why Word uses additional ways to get into its features. One of these is the toolbar. The last data I have available from Microsoft shows that about 59 percent of Word users access program features with toolbars. That should give you an idea of the usefulness of this feature. The Word toolbar is located directly under the menu bar. It consists of 22 standard buttons with pictures to help you understand what each button does.

To access a Word command or feature from the toolbar you just have to click on its button. The button is a visual representation of a menu choice, a macro, or internal command. If you frequently use commands other than the ones supplied on the standard toolbar, you can easily customize the display to include buttons for the features you want.

Understanding Dialog Boxes

A *dialog box* is an interactive pop-up display that asks for more information before conducting the operation selected from a menu. Figure 1.11 shows a typical Word dialog box.

Notice that there are several features of this dialog that are common to most dialogs. The dialog box is definitely a separate entity from the rest of the display, for one thing. It is well defined and it carries a title.

Along the right side of the dialog are several buttons. Which buttons appear depends on the function of the dialog, but you are almost certainly sure to find a Help button, a Cancel button, and an OK button. If there isn't an OK button, there will be a button that says Go On or Execute. For example, if you display the Style dialog (Format, Style...), the selection to close the

Figure 1.11 A Typical Word Dialog Box

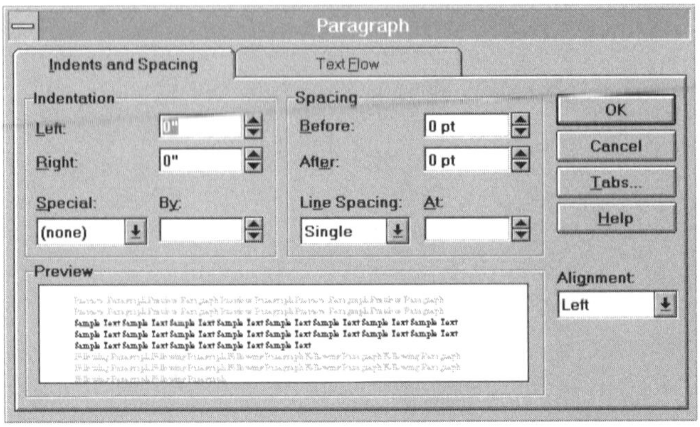

dialog and continue is Apply. This is obvious, given the title of the dialog box and the menu choice you made to display it in the first place.

In addition to these buttons, most dialogs include one or more areas for user input. You may be asked to specify a disk drive, a directory, or a file name, or to make selections by clicking on buttons. A button is a (usually) round object that is selected or deselected by clicking with the mouse. When a button is selected it is colored dark, or, in the case of three-dimensional buttons, appears to be depressed. These are *toggles*. The first time you click on it, the button is selected. On the second click it is deselected.

Understanding Scroll Bars

Most of the time you work with a Windows application, all you are seeing on the screen at any one time is a portion of the total display. In Word, for example, you can see only a portion of one page of the document.

To see other parts of the document you can use *scroll bars*, the gray horizontal and vertical devices at the bottom and side of the screen. Notice the vertical scroll bar in Figure 1.12. Click on the upward-facing arrow to move up in the document; click on the downward-facing arrow to move down in the document.

In addition, there is a small box between the arrows on the scroll bar. This shows how far you are from the top or bottom of the file. You can grab this box with the mouse and drag it up or down on the bar to move rapidly across several pages.

Scroll bars frequently appear in dialog boxes as well, to let you select an item in a window that contains too many items to appear in the dialog at one time.

Arranging Windows

As a Microsoft Windows product, Word supports some *multitasking*. That means you can work on more than one document at a time, copy or move information from one document window to another, and view multiple documents simultaneously to compare them.

Figure 1.12 Word Screen with Scroll Bars

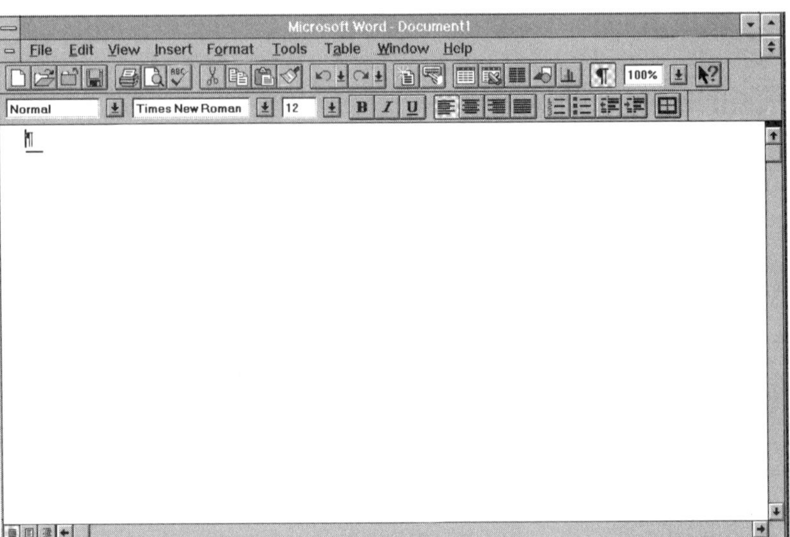

As you work with multiple Word windows you may need to rearrange the open windows to make them easier to view, to move one out of the way, or to access a different document. There are, several ways to display multiple Word windows. Each time you open a new document, Word overlays the latest window over the previous ones. After you have three or four of these ope, , it will be impossible to see previous displays. Use the Window, Arrange All menu sequence to have Word shrink these windows and place them on the screen where you can see them all at once. Figure 1.13 shows a screen with three documents open.

Even with just three document windows open at once, however, it can be difficult to see detail in the screens. You can use this type of display to show you what windows are open so you can select a document. Click on the up-facing maximize arrow on the window you want to edit to move the selected window to the forefront and the remaining windows to the background.

Another way to display multiple windows is to split a single document into two windows. This lets you view two parts of the

Figure 1.13 Word Screen with Three Open Documents

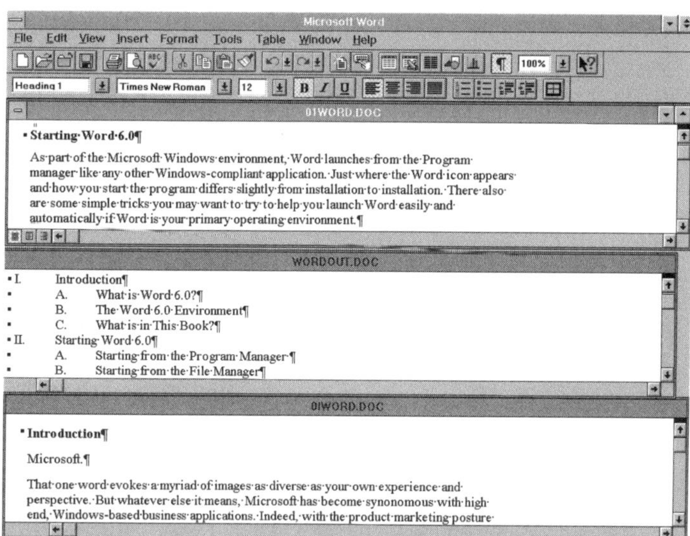

same document simultaneously. To do this, simply select the Window menu and choose Split. A line will appear across the middle of the current window. You can move the line up or down to specify how much of each split window will be displayed.

You can activate any of these cascaded windows by simply clicking on the title bar of the one you want. Then you can enlarge the display by clicking the restore button (the upward-facing arrow) at the far top right of the window. When you want to go back to another of the windows, first shrink the current document by clicking on the double-ended arrow on the right of the menu bar. Then you can click on the title of another document window and enlarge it as before to work with it.

Summary

Whether you are new to Windows or have a lot of experience with other Windows programs, you shouldn't have much trouble getting up to speed with Word. After a little practice manipulating the Word menus, toolbars, and document screens, it should feel very natural. Just remember that the Windows user interface provides a standard of data presentation and manipulation that is similar across all major Windows programs, including Word.

In the next chapter I'll point out some of the major features of Word—a tour of Word features and facilities—so you can start getting more out of this most basic and yet full-featured program from the Microsoft stable.

Chapter 2

Important Word 6.0 Features

Microsoft Word is among the industry's most popular word processing packages. This is true partially because Microsoft is a huge company that spends huge amounts of money promoting itself and its products. But Word also is popular because it is good! It is full-featured, relatively easy to learn and to use, and it has everything you need to produce simple documents or complex publications.

And Word is getting better all the time. Each new release includes extended features that make Word more desirable and more functional. In this chapter I will point out some of the new features that make Word 6 and later versions particularly useful and user friendly. We'll build on these basic features throughout this book to help you produce your own Word-based documents.

Expanded Help

Online, context-sensitive help is a standard feature of Windows-compliant software. In Windows-based applications you can click on Help on the main menu to display an online manual that lets you search for specific topics. Many dialog boxes also contain a special Help button that displays help about the particular operation you are trying to perform.

Different manufacturers carry out this online help theme better than others. Some programs offer in-depth electronic documentation; others provide only minimal online help. Microsoft Word does a creditable job of providing standard Windows online help. But Word 6 has added some extended features to help you with the transition from other products and to help you get the most out of the standard features Word provides.

Help for WordPerfect Users

One of the difficult parts of changing from one software product to another is learning how the new product handles some of the standard tasks that you already know how to use. In its effort to capture as much of the word processing market as possible, Microsoft has included online, interactive help for users of WordPerfect, for years the number one or number two word processing software package on the market.

Whether or not you are a WordPerfect user, you might be interested in this level of online help intrinsic to Word. To try it out, click on Help on the main menu bar, and choose WordPerfect Help.... You will see the dialog shown in Figure 2.1.

Figure 2.1 WordPerfect Help

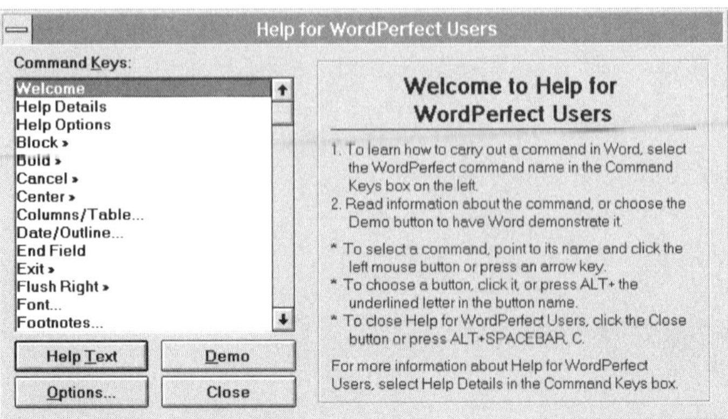

To get standard text-based help, simply click on a topic on the left side of the dialog and read instructions to complete the task on the right side.

Notice there are additional buttons on the bottom of the dialog. You can configure the WordPerfect help system by clicking on Options... to display the dialog shown in Figure 2.2.

Use this dialog to tell Word what type of WordPerfect help you want to receive. You can tell Word to provide constant help text, or demo help, for example. If you choose Help Text, you'll see text boxes that pop up to tell you how to compete the current operation.

If you choose Demo help, you will see animated screens that step you through the chosen operation. With WordPerfect help enabled, each time you issue a WordPerfect command, Word demonstrates how to complete the command in Word.

Examples and Demos

Still another way to get interactive help in Word is the Examples and Demos section. Click on Help on the main Word menu bar and choose Examples and Demos. You will see the screen in Figure 2.3. Choose the topic you'd like to explore

Figure 2.2 WordPerfect Help Options Dialog

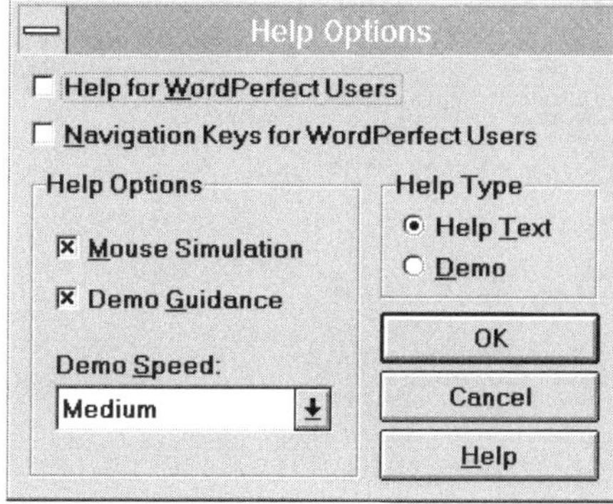

Figure 2.3 Main Examples and Demos Help Screen

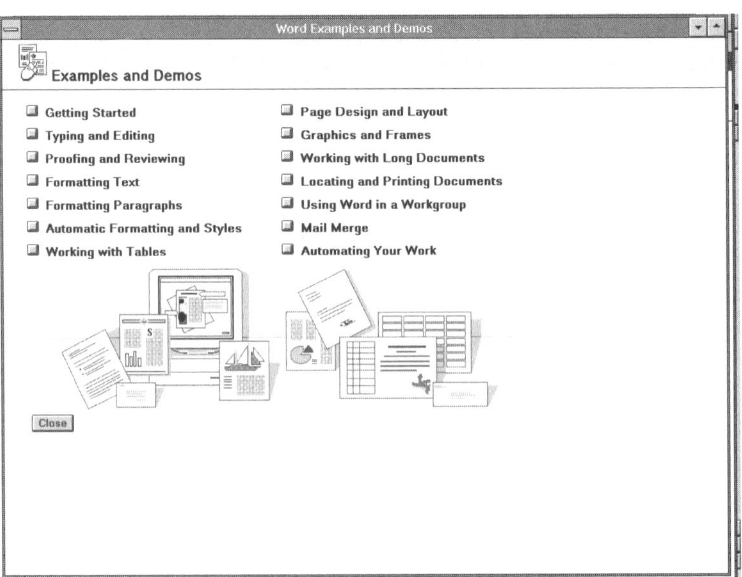

from this list, and watch as Word animates the description of completing the selected task.

Wizards

Word *Wizards* go a step beyond the examples and demos help. They give you interactive help, stepping you through the tasks required to complete certain operations. A Wizard basically asks you questions through a dialog, then uses your answers to finish the task you are trying to complete. There aren't Wizards for everything you may want to do in Word, but there are Wizards for many tasks.

For example, if you want to create a new document to prepare a meeting agenda, click on File, choose New, and then Agenda Wizard. You will see the dialog shown in Figure 2.4.

Figure 2.4 Opening Agenda Wizard Dialog

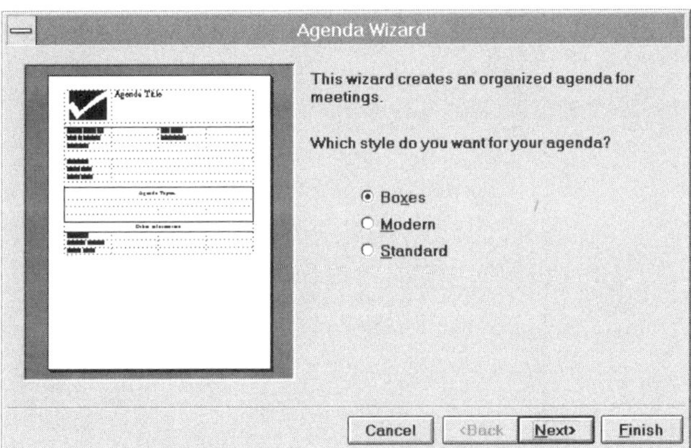

Select from this dialog the type of agenda document you want to create, then click on the Next button to display the next dialog in the Wizard.

All Word Wizards operate similarly. Initiate the Wizard process by choosing a task you want to complete, then fill out the required information on each dialog until the Wizard is finished. You can use Word Wizards for a number of tasks, including several types of new document (use File, New and choose any templates that include a Wizard).

Table Wizard The Table Wizard is one of the new Wizards that help you create the proper look and feel to each document. Using tables in general is very easy in Word, but with the table format Wizard you can give your tables a special look.

To use this Wizard, place the insertion point anywhere inside the table you want to format, then click on Table on the main Word menu and choose Table AutoFormat... to display the Table AutoFormat Wizard dialog shown in Figure 2.5.

Use the scroll bars on the left of this dialog to select different table styles. The format associated with each style is shown in

Figure 2.5 Table AutoFormat Wizard Dialog

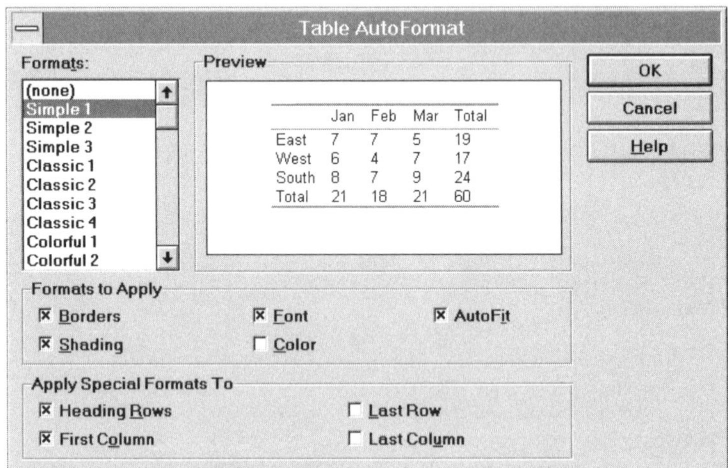

the Preview window. When you have the style you want to use, click on OK to format the table.

TEMPLATES

Word 6 includes a number of preformatted documents stored as *templates*. A Word template is a special type of document that includes built-in page and text formatting. Any document you create with the File, New command or by clicking on the New Document tool on the Word toolbar is based on a template. The default template is Normal, and includes a number of basic formatting features, such as the default text style for headings, paragraph spacing, fonts, and so on.

In addition to the Normal template, however, Word includes templates for special documents, including brochures, fax cover sheets, letters, and more. To use a template, start a new document with the File, New command, and choose the template you want from the template list, shown in Figure 2.6.

Figure 2.6 Word New Dialog

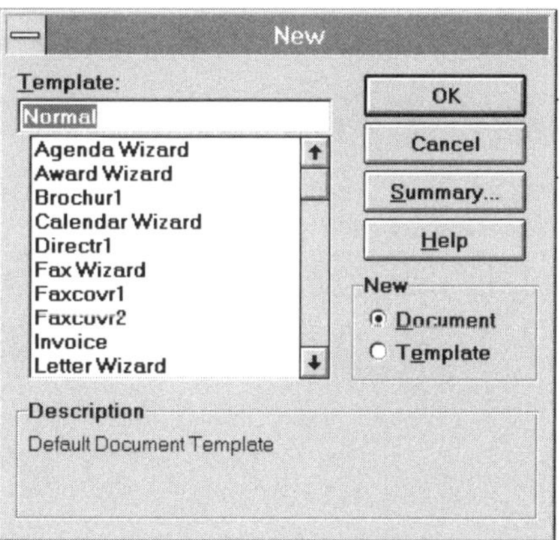

AutoCorrect

The original appeal for electronic word processing was the ability to change or correct text automatically. The traditional method is to determine a word or phrase you want to change, then start a search and replace utility. Or, you can run a spell checker that locates any word that doesn't appear in the electronic dictionary.

Word 6 expands this basic capability with the AutoCorrect utility. With AutoCorrect you tell the program what words to look for and Word automatically changes misspellings to the correct form.

For example, you may find that you frequently type *bake* instead of *back*. You can enter this pair in the AutoCorrect lookup table. Now when you type *bake*, Word automatically changes it to *back*. Obviously, when working with common words like this, you must use caution, because if you want to type *bake* instead of *back*, you'll have to enter *bake*, let Word correct it to *back*, then erase the correction and enter the word you really want.

Figure 2.7 AutoCorrect Dialog

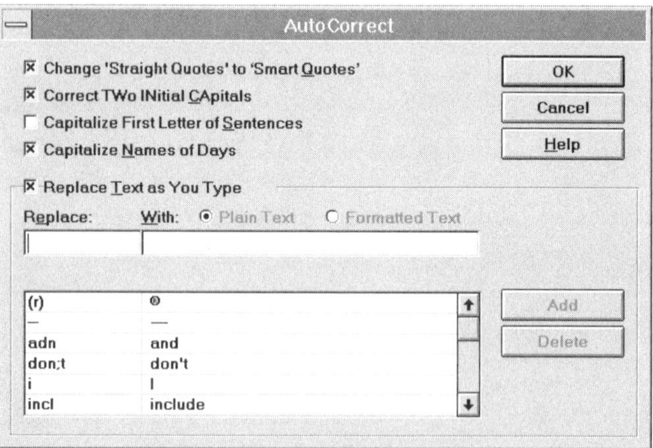

But for common typing mistakes, such as *adn* instead of *and*, or *teh* instead of *the*, the AutoCorrect feature can be a real time saver.

Word ships with a number of words already installed in the AutoCorrect lookup list. You can see what they are by clicking on Tools from the main Word menu and choosing AutoCorrect. The dialog in Figure 2.7 is displayed.

Enter your own typing mistakes and corrections by entering the common mistake in the left part of the table and the word you'd like it to be on the right.

In addition to correcting mistakes, the AutoCorrect feature can be used to automatically type words you use frequently. For example, as I wrote this book, I entered the letter *W* in the AutoCorrect table to translate to *Word*, and the letter *M* to translate to *Microsoft*. Use this feature anytime you enter repetitive words during the course of preparing your documents. This could include your own name, the name of your company, and so on. This feature is particularly useful when you are preparing contracts and other legal documents that tend to frequently repeat the names of the individuals or companies involved.

NOTE: Use AutoCorrect to place any entry that is 31 characters or less and that does not contain any spaces. For more complex entries, use the AutoText feature, described below.

You can even use AutoCorrect to insert a graphic object into the current document. Simply copy the graphic (a company logo, for example) onto the Clipboard, launch the AutoCorrect utility, type the abbreviation you want to use in the Replace: field of this dialog, click in the With: field, and use Edit, Paste to place the graphic into this field.

AutoText

AutoText is another approach to entering text or other document objects automatically. Whereas AutoCorrect is designed primarily to correct typing mistakes or to substitute words or phrases for short abbreviations you enter from the keyboard on the fly, AutoText replaces text only when you tell Word to do it.

In general you use AutoCorrect to insert items you must type frequently, such as a company name, whereas AutoText is used to insert items you use less frequently, such as an Excel spreadsheet fragment or complex graphic.

NOTE: If you are familiar with earlier versions of Word, the AutoText feature was called the Glossary.

To enter text or a graphic into AutoText, first select the object using the mouse or by holding down Shift and moving the cursor with the arrow keys. If you want to include formatting with the text, be sure you select the paragraph mark along with the text. Now select Edit and choose AutoText or click on the AutoText icon on the standard toolbar to display the dialog shown in Figure 2.8.

Accept the name Word suggests in the Name: field of this dialog, or type a name of your own. If you are inserting text, the name Word selects is the text or part of the text. You'll probably want to shorten the name because this is what you'll type to enter this object into your document later. Click on OK to store the abbreviation and the object you inserted into AutoText.

Figure 2.8 AutoText Main Dialog

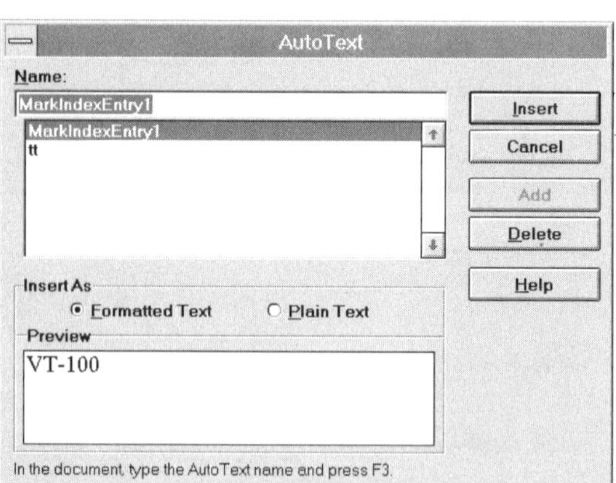

To use AutoText, type the abbreviation you specified into your document and add one space after it. Then click on the AutoText icon on the standard toolbar. Word replaces your abbreviation with the previously stored substitution text or graphic.

You can also insert AutoText objects into a document from the AutoText dialog. Use Edit, AutoText to display the dialog and choose the object you want to insert from the list. Click on Insert to place the selected object into the document at the location of the insertion point.

AutoFormat

Word does an excellent job of coordinating with other software applications. The AutoFormat feature is one way Word supports integration with other applications. Suppose you import a text document from a file you downloaded from an online service or exported from a spreadsheet. Each line of text ends with a carriage return, and there is no formatting (boldface, underline, and so on).

With Word's AutoFormat utility you can remove the end-of-line carriage returns, allowing auto-wrapping of the lines, and insert some document formatting. For example, Word automatically selects heading styles for text it interprets as a heading.

To use AutoFormat, just make the document you want to format the current document, then click on the AutoFormat icon on the standard toolbar or use the Format, AutoFormat... command sequence to display the AutoFormat dialog. If you click on OK, the utility formats the current document. If you click on Options, you will see the Options dialog shown in Figure 2.9.

Make any changes to the AutoFormat check boxes on this screen, then continue the AutoFormat by clicking on OK to close the Options Dialog, then OK again to close the AutoFormat dialog and start the AutoFormat process.

You'll probably find that this AutoFormat feature is pretty good, but it won't solve all of your document formatting problems. You'll find heading styles where you intended a single line of text, and other problems, but overall, using AutoFormat

Figure 2.9 Word AutoFormat Options Dialog

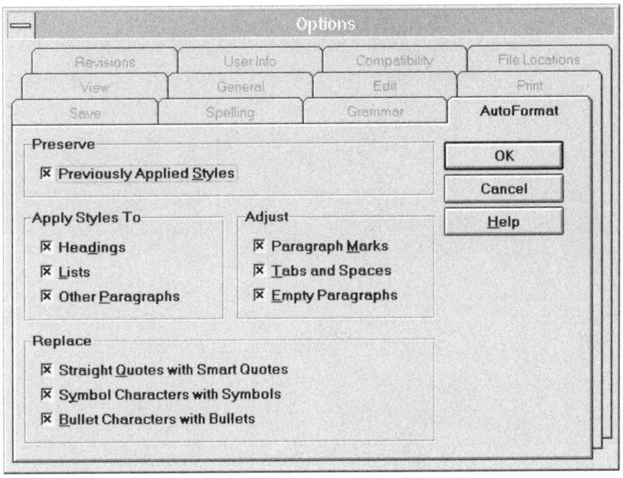

will save you a lot of time in formatting straight text documents over trying to do it from scratch.

AUTOMATIC MULTILEVEL BULLETS AND NUMBERS

Another of Word's strengths is its ability to format bullet lists and numbered lists automatically. You can create a bulleted or numbered list by simply typing the items you want in the list, selecting the list, and clicking on the bullet list or number list icon on the standard toolbar. This toolbar utility generates only a single level bullet or numbered list, however.

To generate multilevel lists, you need to use heading styles. An item in a list that will appear as a top-level entry should be formatted with a Heading 1 style, the second level items get Heading 2 style, and so on. Next, select the text you want to format as a list, and use the Format, Bullets and Numbering... menu sequence to display the Bullets and Numbering dialog. Click on the Multilevel tab to display the dialog shown in Figure 2.10.

You can see from Figure 2.10 that you have several choices for multilevel formatting, including several number styles and styles that include bullets. Choose the one you want and

Figure 2.10 Bullets and Numbering Dialog

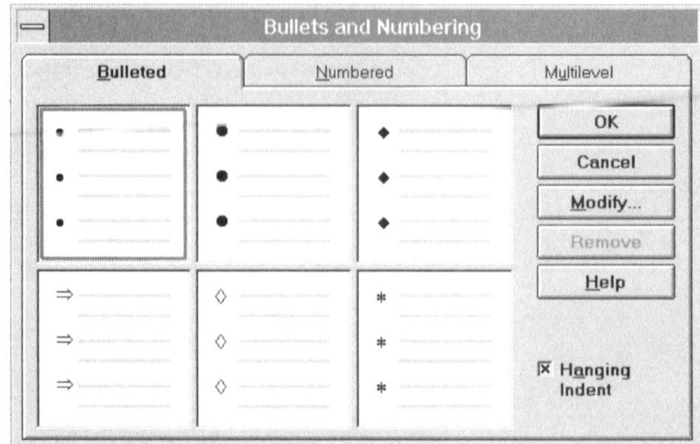

click on OK to apply the chosen style to the selected text in your document.

AutoCaption

In addition to text, Word does a pretty good job of handling graphic objects integrated into your documents. And the newer versions of Word include an AutoCaption feature to make it easier to track illustrations and to provide captions for them.

To use AutoCaption, click on an object you want to caption to select it, then use Insert, Caption... to display the dialog shown in Figure 2.11.

Word automatically identifies the selected object as Figure 1 or Figure 2 or Figure 3 and so on, depending on the order in your document. You can edit this default entry or change it entirely, if you want.

In addition to this more-or-less manual caption feature, Word includes an AutoCaption utility that automatically provides a sequential caption to all items of a particular type in your document. If you tell Word that all .BMP files are figures, for example, then each time you add a new .BMP file to your document, Word gives it a new figure number. You can also identify spreadsheet objects, scanned images, and so on, telling Word how you want them labeled.

Figure 2.11 Caption Dialog

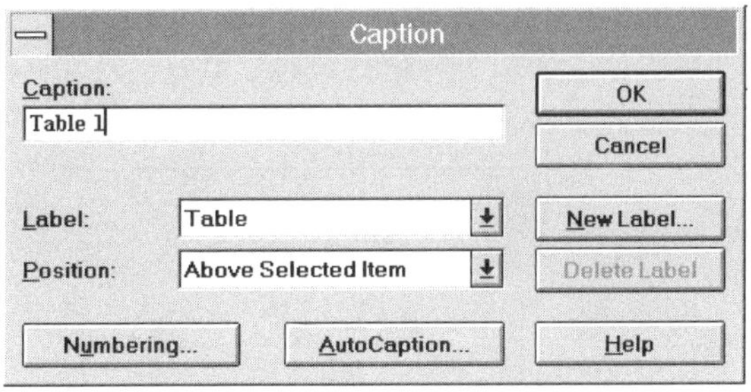

Figure 2.12 AutoCaption Dialog

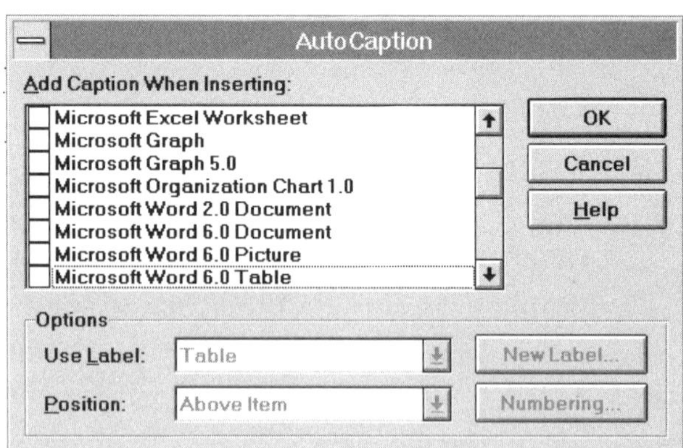

To set up the AutoCaption feature, display the Caption dialog shown in Figure 2.11, then click on the AutoCaption button to display the AutoCaption dialog, shown in Figure 2.12.

If you specify how you want Word to handle each of the object types you are likely to insert into the current document when the document is first created, it will make the management of text boxes, tables, graphic images, and the like easier and more consistent.

Cross-Reference

To make it easier to actually use Word's excellent object-management features, the Cross-Reference utility supports in-text references such as "See Figure 2.11 on page 123." In fact, you can include such cross-references that refer to other documents as well as to the document in which the cross-reference appears.

In addition, once you have entered a cross-reference you can update it automatically if the order or location of the figures changes.

To create a *bookmark* you must mark the text that will be referenced. Text that appears in a heading, a footer, a caption, or an endnote is already marked appropriately for a cross-reference. To include other text in a cross-reference, mark it as a bookmark.

To create a bookmark, select the text, then use the Edit, Bookmark... command to display the Bookmark dialog, shown in Figure 2.13. Type a name for the bookmark and click on OK to create it.

Then, to create a cross-reference to the bookmarked text, or to other marked text (a title, footnote, etc.), position the insertion point in the document where you want the cross-reference to appear and type the reference text, such as, **To learn more about how this feature works, see "** (include the quotation mark). Then select Insert and choose Cross-Reference... to display the dialog shown in Figure 2.14.

From this dialog specify the type of marked text you want to reference (a bookmark, endnote, and so on). Next, choose the specific reference that must already exist in your document in the For Which... window of this dialog. Finally, tell Word what part of the marked text to include in the reference. This may be the bookmark name, the heading text, the page number, or all of this information.

Click on OK to complete the reference. Word completes the previously entered sentence by placing the reference text you just specified after the quotation mark in the cross-reference you typed before calling up the Cross-Reference dialog.

Figure 2.13 Bookmark Dialog

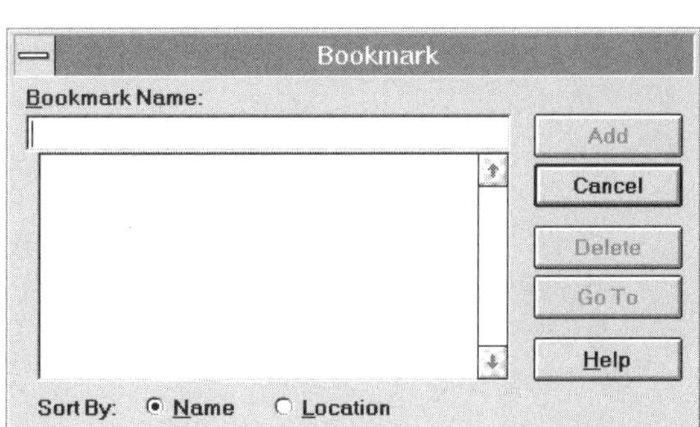

Figure 2.14 Cross-Reference Dialog

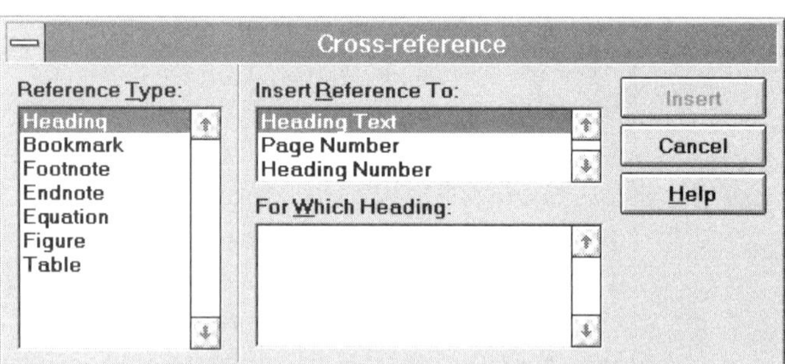

Editing Features

The ability to edit text is the main reason you are using a word processing software package in the first place. You'll find that Word includes a number of enhanced and useful features to make this chore easier and more flexible.

I've already mentioned the AutoCorrect utility that automatically helps you correct typos or misspellings as you enter text. While not strictly an editing tool, AutoCorrect helps you reduce your editing tasks by helping you keep data entry as accurate as possible in the first place. The AutoText utility works in a similar fashion to help maintain accuracy and consistency.

In addition, here are some other editing features you probably will find useful.

Multilevel Undo

Word keeps track of your most recent typing and editing activities, even storing the complete keystroke and mouse sequence. This enables you to undo not only the most recent typing or editing you have done, but a series of changes to your documents.

To reverse the most recent editing change, just click on the Undo button on the standard toolbar (that's the left-facing circular arrow), or use the Edit, Undo menu sequence. You can undo a sequence of steps, but you must undo them in the reverse order in which they were conducted. You can't conduct five editing steps, for example, then undo step two. You must undo step five, then four, then three, and finally step two can be undone.

You can use the Undo feature to help you evaluate formatting changes, for example. Simply make the change you want to evaluate, then click Undo. You can click the Redo button (or use the Edit menu to choose Redo) and have the new formatting reappear. Click Undo/Redo several times until you decide which way you want to leave the document.

Be aware as you work with your documents that you can't depend entirely on Undo to correct your mistakes. You can't unsave a document, for example.

Smart Cut and Paste

Cut and paste refers to the process of removing a piece of text or other document object from its original location and pasting it into a new location within the same or a different document. You use standard Windows procedures to do this in Word. Select the text or object you want to move, click on Edit and choose Cut (Alt+X) to remove the object and place it on the Clipboard.

Next, position the cursor (insertion point) at the new location and use Edit, Paste (Shift+Insert) to copy the item from the Clipboard into your document at the new location.

This basic procedure is nothing new. However, Word includes some nice little features to help make the process as painless as possible. For example, if you cut the last word in a sentence, a space is left after the next-to-last word and the ending period. Word is smart enough to know you don't want this extra space to appear and so removes it, closing up the line. The same thing happens when a line ends in a parenthesis or other punctuation.

Drag and Drop across Windows

Drag and drop refers to the ability to mark a block of text or another object, then use the mouse to drag the selected object to another location. Word has supported drag and drop to another location within the same document for some time. Now, however, you can drag an object from one Word window to another. You might want to do this to move an illustration or paragraph from one document to another, for example.

You can also copy a Word object to another document. Just hold down the Ctrl key while you select the object and while you are dragging it between windows.

Enhanced Find and Replace

You can use the Edit, Replace menu sequence to enter old and new versions of text so Word will scan the document, replacing every occurrence of original text with whatever you specify as the replacement text. You may want to do this after finishing a document for X-Y Z Corporation and you discover the correct name is A B C Corporation, for example. This kind of global find and replace also helps you create "boilerplate" documents that can serve as quotes or other documents that you can customize for each client.

Now you can also search and replace items that have traditionally been hard to correct in word processing software.

NOTE: I will discuss the search and replace procedure in this section. The same techniques apply if you want to simply find something in your document without replacing it.

To find and replace almost anything within your document, click on Edit and choose Replace to display the Replace dialog. To locate formatting commands, for example, click on the Format button at the bottom of this dialog and choose from among Font, Paragraph, Language, and Style.

When you choose one of these formats to find, Word displays the standard dialog associated with that document feature. If you choose Font, for example, the standard Word Font dialog is displayed, but it is labeled Find Font. Choose the feature you want to find from the appropriate dialog and click on OK. Then repeat the process in the Replace With: field of this dialog.

Likewise, you can search and optionally replace other special document features such as paragraph marks, a field, a manual page break and so on. To do this, click on the Special

Figure 2.15 Pop-Up Special List from the Replace Dialog

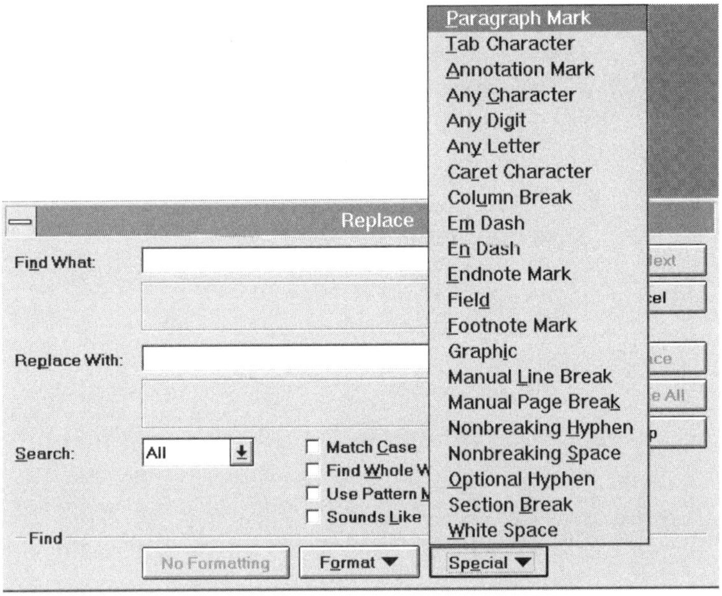

button at the bottom of the Find dialog to display the pop-up list shown in Figure 2.15.

Choose what you want from this list and click on OK. The rest of the find or find and replace procedure is the same as if you were looking for straight text.

Formatting and Style

I've already discussed some formatting features available in Word. Here are a few special ones you can use to make your task of creating consistent, attractive formats a little easier.

Format Painter

The Word standard toolbar includes a small icon that looks like a paintbrush. You can use it to "paint" the format of one block of text over another block of text. Just place the insertion point inside the block that contains the format you want to copy. Next click on the Format Painter icon. The pointer changes to a small paintbrush.

Now select the text to which you want to give the format you have captured in the Format Painter paintbrush. When you release the mouse button after selecting the text, it will contain the format of the original text.

NOTE: If you want to format more than one paragraph or block of text, double-click on the Format Painter icon after you have chosen the text with the source formatting. Select the text blocks, one after the other, to give them the same format as the source text. Click again on the Format Painter icon when you want to disable format painting.

Dropped Capitals and Other Symbols

A *dropped capital* is a special format that is sometimes applied to the initial letter in a chapter or document. The initial character is formatted considerably larger than the rest of the text in that paragraph, and it is moved slightly out of line with the remaining text on the initial line.

Now, instead of having to manipulate a lot of formatting and movement tools to create a dropped capital, you can have Word do it automatically. Simply select the character you want to format as a dropped capital, then select the Format menu and choose Drop Cap... to display the Drop Cap dialog shown in Figure 2.16.

You can see from the samples displayed in this dialog how you can have Word format the dropped capital. Click on the format you want and click on OK to effect the formatting. You can also choose a different font to use for the dropped cap if you wish by selecting the font from the Font field of this dialog.

When you return to your document, the dropped cap character will be inserted with a frame around it. This lets you grab it and fine-tune the placement of this special object, if you wish.

Word includes support for other special symbols as well. To insert a symbol, position the insertion point where you want it to appear, select Insert and choose Symbol. You can choose from among a number of fonts and special symbols in this dialog.

Figure 2.16 Drop Cap Dialog

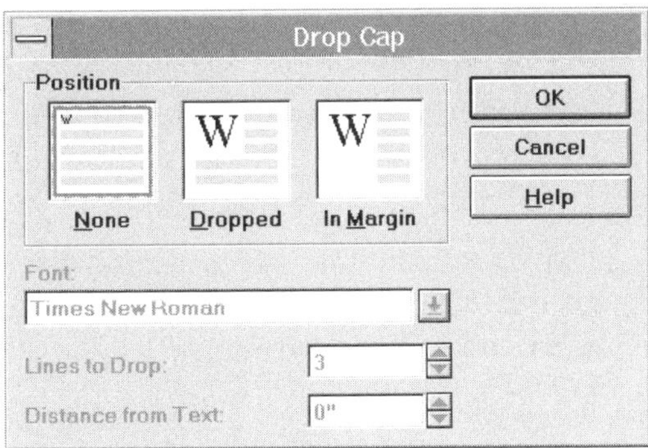

Borders Toolbar

The borders toolbar is just one of many toolbars Word supports. You can display it by clicking on the borders symbol at the far right of the standard toolbar. When you do, the toolbar shown at the bottom of Figure 2.17 is added to the Word display.

To place a border around a paragraph or other Word object, display the borders toolbar, place the insertion point in the object you want to format with a border, and choose the type of border you want to use.

The icons in the middle of this toolbar specify where a border line will appear: top, bottom, left, or right, for example. You can also use this toolbar to insert borders around all of the

Figure 2.17 Word Borders Toolbar

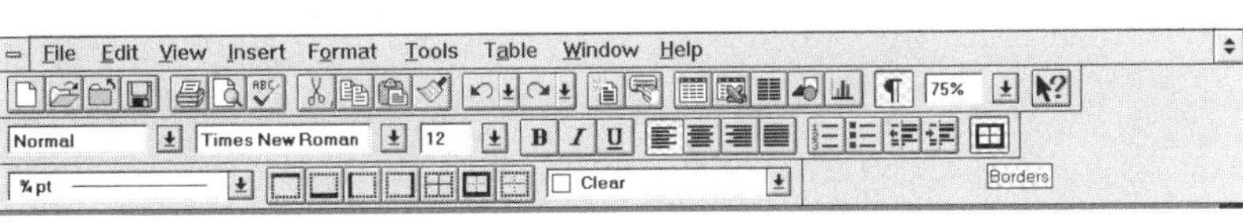

cells in a Word table by choosing the third icon from the right. Place a border all the way around the selected object by choosing the icon second from the right, or remove borders by choosing the border icon on the far right.

Specify the weight (thickness) of the border by selecting a line from the window at the extreme left of this toolbar, and choose a fill color from the pull-down list on the far right.

To remove the borders toolbar, click on the Borders icon on the standard toolbar.

Character Styles

A *style* is a set of text attributes you can use to format a document. Styles make formatting easier than using discrete formatting because you can specify different styles for each type of text, then to change the overall appearance of a document or even a collection of documents, you simply modify the style.

There are two types of styles: styles at the paragraph level and character-level styles. Use a paragraph style to specify formatting that applies to an entire paragraph; use character styles to emphasize a character, word, or part of a word.

Character styles hold any of the format information found in the Format, Font dialog, shown in Figure 2.18. This includes the type style, size of text, and text attributes such as boldface, underline, and italic.

Word is supplied with a number of intrinsic styles that you can apply by choosing a style from the style list on the format toolbar, or by choosing Style from the Format menu. The format toolbar normally is positioned just below the standard toolbar and includes style and font pulldowns, as well as tools for boldface, italics, underline, and other text and paragraph formatting.

To apply a character style, select the text you want to format, then pull down the style list from the format toolbar. Normally you will see only a subset of the available styles within a given template. (All documents are based on a template, remember. Unless you specify a different template, new documents use the Normal template.) To view a more extensive list of available styles, issue the Format, Style command to view the dialog shown in Figure 2.19.

Figure 2.18 Font Dialog

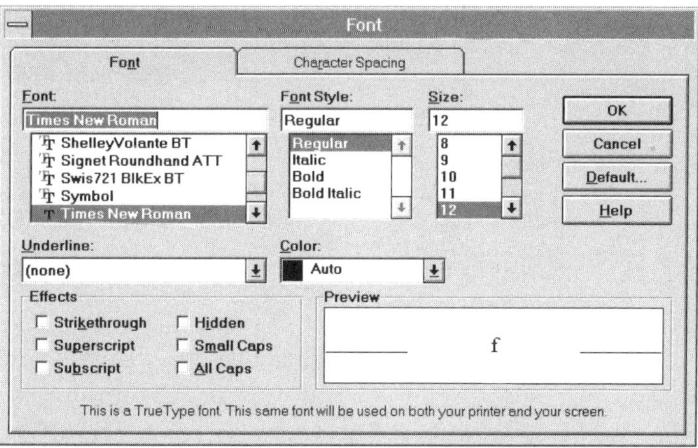

Pull down the list of styles in the List field of this dialog, and choose All Styles. You will see a list of all of the available styles in the current template. Your list may be slightly different, but a typical list is shown in Figure 2.20.

Figure 2.19 Style Dialog

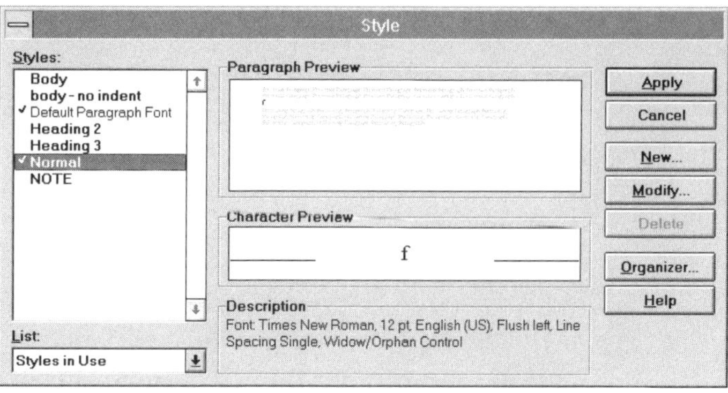

Figure 2.20 Typical All Styles List from Style Dialog

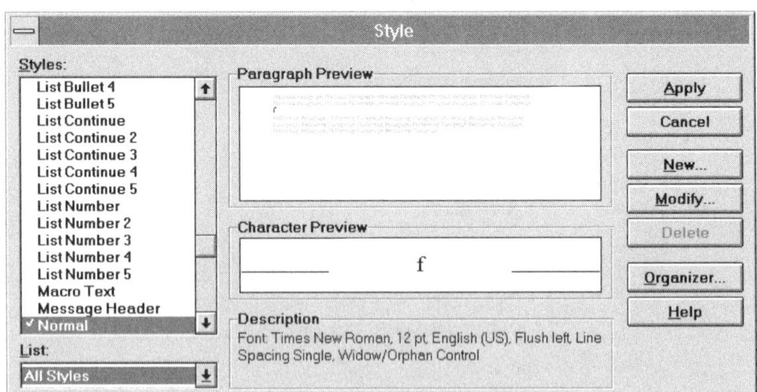

You can select a style and view the results in the Character or Paragraph Preview window of this dialog. When you have located the style you want to use, highlight it and click on Apply to enable the chosen style within your document.

Character Spacing and Automatic Kerning

Normally, as you type characters into a Word document, built-in software features determine the spacing between characters. Character spacing depends in part on the font in use, in part on the order of the characters and other settings. How characters fit together on a line is called *kerning*. Word includes automatic kerning that moves some characters closer together to improve the appearance of the text on the page. Kerning takes advantage of the fact that some characters require more room on the page than others.

For example, the letter l (lowercase L) obviously doesn't require as much space as an uppercase M, or even a lowercase m. If character spacing were fixed, there would be apparent gaps between some character pairs. This special character spacing works on any proportional typeface, but it doesn't apply to fixed-space fonts such as Courier.

Figure 2.21 Character Spacing Tab of the Font Dialog

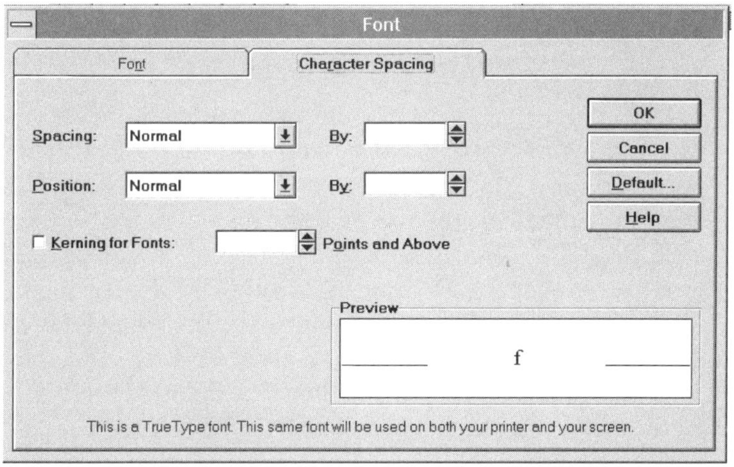

In addition to this automatic character spacing, Word supports user-defined spacing so you can compress or expand selected text for emphasis or to make text fit into a specific space. To adjust character spacing, select the text you want to modify, then select Format from the main menu and choose Font. In the Font dialog, click on the Character Spacing tab to display the Character Spacing dialog shown in Figure 2.21.

You have a wide range of control over character spacing from this dialog. For example, compare the next few lines of text to see sample spacing adjustments:

This line uses normal spacing

This line uses 3-point expanded spacing

This line uses 1-point compressed spacing

This line uses normal with these words raised 5 points

Use such special character formatting for emphasis or simply to help you place all of the text you want in a specific area. However, use caution, because too much compression or expansion makes text difficult to read, and when you change spacing you change where page breaks occur, changing overall document formatting.

Organizer Dialog

Word designers tried to include a number of helpful features to make using basic word processor features, and customizing your documents, as easy as possible. One feature that can help, even if you use it only occasionally, is the Organizer dialog. The Organizer dialog shown in Figure 2.22 is displayed by selecting Format, choosing Style, and then clicking on Organizer. It gives you an overview perspective of template styles and other items so you can add them to the current document or template, move them, or delete them.

On the left side of this split display is a list of items available in the template on which the current document is based. On the right side of this dialog is a list of Normal template items. If the current document is based on the Normal template and you haven't added, deleted, or changed anything at the template level, then the two sides of the dialog are the same.

Figure 2.22 Organizer Dialog

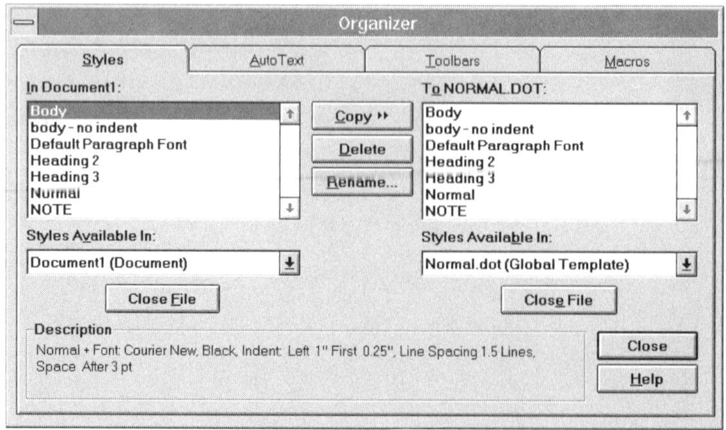

If, on the other hand, you created macros, AutoText objects, styles, or anything else as you worked with the current document, then you may want to copy one or more of them to the Normal template or to the template attached to another document.

Simply highlight the object you want to copy to the right side of the dialog and click on the Copy button in the middle of the dialog.

To change the files displayed in this dialog, click on the Close File button, which then changes to Open File. Click on Open and choose a file from the file list.

Page Layout

Modern word processors such as Microsoft Word include many page layout and desktop publishing features. New page layout features provide a great deal of flexibility in document design. Here are a couple of layout features that will help you achieve a professional document design.

Unequal Newspaper Columns

Newspaper columns—sometimes called snaking columns—are used in newsletters and other publications. Creating multiple columns in Word is easy. Just select Format and choose Columns... to display the Columns dialog shown in Figure 2.23.

You can establish columns of almost any width, but Word includes a number of preset column configurations. The first three preset buttons give you one-, two- or three-column configurations. The last two presets let you specify two-column formats with unequal column widths.

The Left preset creates a newspaper column format with a narrow left column and a wider right column. The Right preset creates a newspaper column format with a narrow right column and a wider left column.

You can also specify column widths by placing the insertion point in the column you want to adjust, then entering the column width in inches in the Width field of this dialog.

Figure 2.23 Columns Dialog

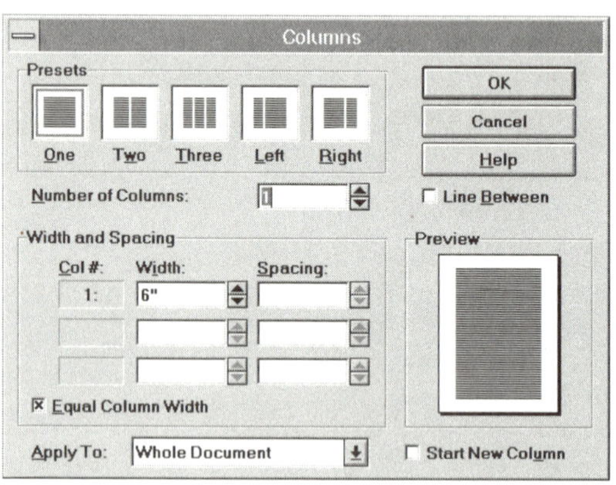

Enhanced Print Preview

Word is basically a *WYSIWYG* (what you see is what you get) editor, but you can get even a better view of how a document will print with the Word Print Preview facility. When you view a document in Print Preview, you can see the entire document on a single screen, or view multiple pages side by side. Particularly when precise pagination information is important, or when your document includes graphic images, Print Preview is an important part of the document preparation process.

To use Print Preview, make the document you want to view current and click on the Print Preview button on the standard toolbar (the icon that looks like a folded page with a magnifying glass on top of it). Or, you can use the File, Print Preview command to preview your document.

Notice that when you display a document in Print Preview mode, the pointer changes to a magnifying glass. Click with the glass on the document to shrink or expand the preview document. Use the Print Preview toolbar that appears at the top of your screen when a document is in Print Preview mode to display the document full screen, to specify the amount of zoom (by percent of full-document size), to display multiple pages, or to close the Print Preview screen.

Mail Merge

Mail merge is the ability to merge a letter with a series of names and addresses, or to merge a customer statement with a file that details charges, or any merging that lets you match a single standard document with a variable list. Word supports mail merge very well. I'll show you later in this book how to create a mail merge project. Here I'll point out some of the strong mail merge features supported by Word 6.

Improved Form Letter Creation

To use mail merge you need a master document and a document that contains the variable information. Word calls the common document, the one that holds the information that goes to everyone, the *main document*. The document that supplies the variable information is called a *data source document*.

An example of a main document is a form letter. You can use an existing document as the main document or you can create a new document.

Once you have a main document, you must create a data source (or establish an existing document as the data source). Later versions of Word help with the entire process by providing menus and instructions.

Click on Tools and choose Mail Merge... to display the Mail Merge Helper dialog shown in Figure 2.24. From this dialog you can step through the process, following Word's instructions as you go.

Improved Label Printing

Word 6 and later also makes it relatively easy to print labels of all kinds: mailing labels, product labels, disk labels, and more. You can create your own label design, but more than likely the built-in list of label formats will handle most label printing needs you have.

The labels in Word are listed by Avery number (Avery is a national manufacturer of labels). You can start with a standard Avery design and modify the measurements if you wish.

Figure 2.24 Mail Merge Helper Dialog

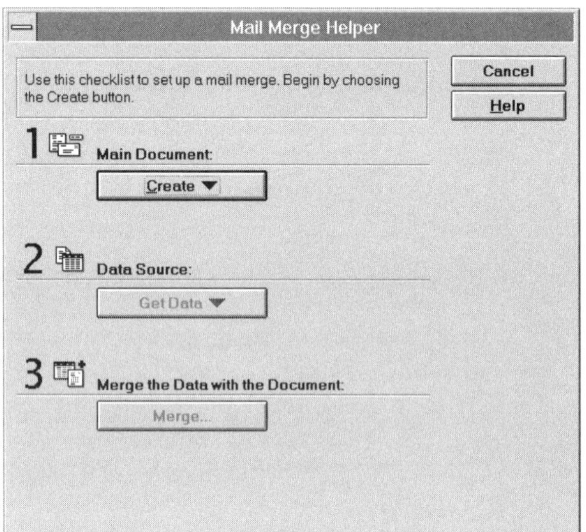

To view Word's label support dialog, click on Tools and choose Envelopes and Labels. Click on the Labels tab of this dialog to see the screen in Figure 2.25.

You have two basic choices for printing labels in the chosen format: one set of data on a whole page of labels, or different information on each label on the page. You can also print only a partial page from this dialog.

Improved Envelope Printing

The difficulty of addressing envelopes with a computer is probably the single most influential factor that keeps companies making standard typewriters. Now with Word, the process is easier. You can print letterhead envelopes with preprinted return addresses, or include a return address on each envelope you print.

Select Tools and choose Envelopes and Labels... and click on the Envelopes tab to display the dialog shown in Figure 2.26.

Figure 2.25 Labels Tab of the Envelopes and Labels Dialog

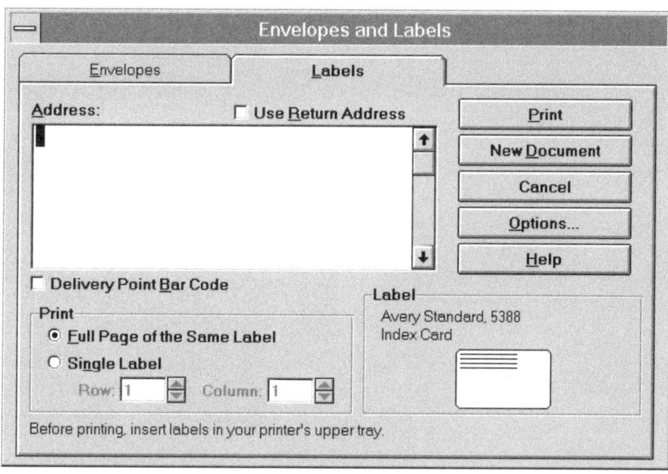

Figure 2.26 Envelopes Tab

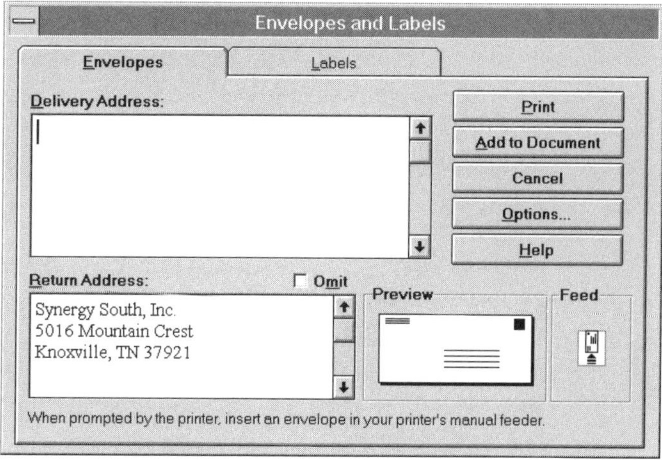

If there is information at the top of the current document that Word can interpret as an address, then that data is inserted in the Delivery Address window of this dialog. If this information is not correct, type the delivery address you want.

Your return address is shown in the lower window. This information comes from previously entered information in your user profile. You can change this data as well.

Choose the type of envelope you will be addressing, then click on OK to start printing. It really is *that* simple!

Support for Bar Codes and FIM Codes

You can also include bar codes in your address information. After you've entered the delivery address in the Envelope dialog, simply click on Options to display the Envelope Options dialog shown in Figure 2.27.

Click on the bar code button to include a bar code for the delivery address on the envelope. In addition you can click on the FIM button below the bar code box to also include Facing

Figure 2.27 Envelope Options Dialog

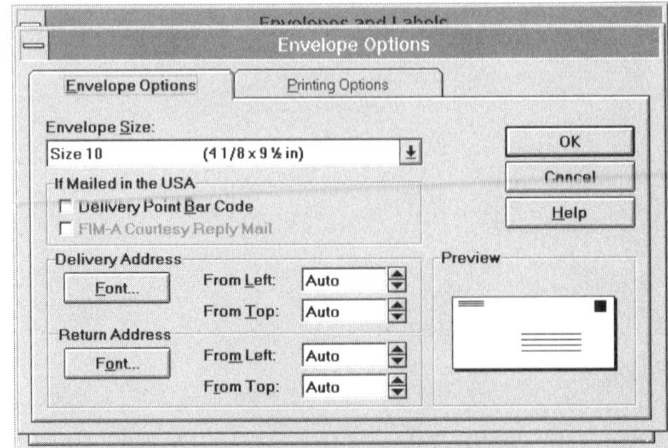

Identification Marks on the envelope to identify the front of the envelope during presort processing at the post office.

User Interface

The entire Microsoft Office suite of products includes a series of user-friendly features that makes it easy to use individual software packages and to transition among various products. These common elements are particularly important parts of the Word and Office user interface:

Toolbars

I've discussed toolbars previously. There are several included in Word. They mirror most of the Word menu commands, making it easy to conduct even somewhat complex operations by clicking on an icon.

ToolTips

As helpful as toolbars are, it can sometimes be difficult to tell exactly what a particular icon does. That's where ToolTips come in. By moving the mouse pointer over on-screen Word objects and pausing briefly, you will see a short pop-up label that describes the selected object.

Shortcut Menus

In addition to ToolTips, Word includes a number of pop-up shortcut menus to help you accomplish a number of tasks. Just move the pointer over an object and press the right mouse button to pop up a special menu.

Full Screen Views

With all the toolbars, menu bars, and other on-screen help, the Word screen can sometimes get a little cluttered. If you want to see your document without other distracting objects, select View and choose Full Screen. To return to standard view, click

Figure 2.28 Customize Toolbar Dialog

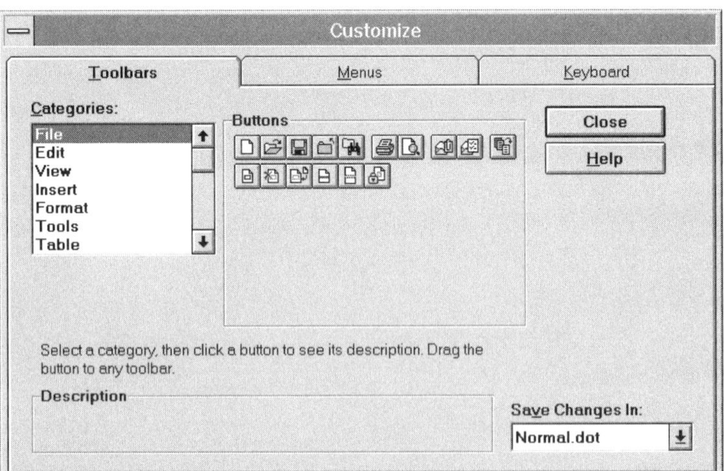

on the button that appears in the Full Screen icon that appears on the full-screen display, or press Esc.

Customizing Word

The standard features included with Word will be good enough for most of us. However, when you want to change the look or operation of certain Word tools and features, you can do that too.

Drag Buttons to Customize Toolbars

For example, you can change the position of toolbars by dragging them anywhere you want on the screen. And you can change the position of the toolbar buttons when you switch to Customize mode. Point to a toolbar and press the right mouse button. Choose Customize to present the display shown in Figure 2.28.

You can also add new icons to a toolbar by grabbing an icon from among those displayed in this dialog and dragging it to the toolbar. You can display additional tools by selecting different commands from the list on the left of the dialog.

Tabbed Options Dialog

Among the more interesting and useful cosmetic changes to these new versions of Word are the tabbed dialogs. With a dialog that displays various screens as tabs, like a stack of file folders, it is much easier to choose which set of options you want to access in a given dialog.

WORKGROUP FEATURES

Beginning with Word 6, Microsoft began incorporating network, document sharing, and workgroup features. This support for networked computing and shared documents makes it easier for people working together on a project to share ideas and to coordinate changes.

Master Documents

Word's Master Document feature lets you combine several documents into a single document for editing, indexing, or generating a table of contents. You can use this feature to combine various chapters or sections of a document, for example. Even if many people across a network have created separate portions of the large document, you can combine the components over the network into a master document for viewing and editing.

To create a master document from existing documents, open a new document by clicking on the New Document icon on the standard toolbar or by using the File, New command. Then establish master document view by selecting View and choosing Master Document. You will see the outline toolbar at the top of the document, which you can use to display various levels of the master document when it is complete (see Figure 2.29).

Now, insert individual files into the master by inserting subdocuments (the existing component documents). Click on the Insert Subdocument icon. Specify a directory and file name,

Figure 2.29 Master Document Toolbar

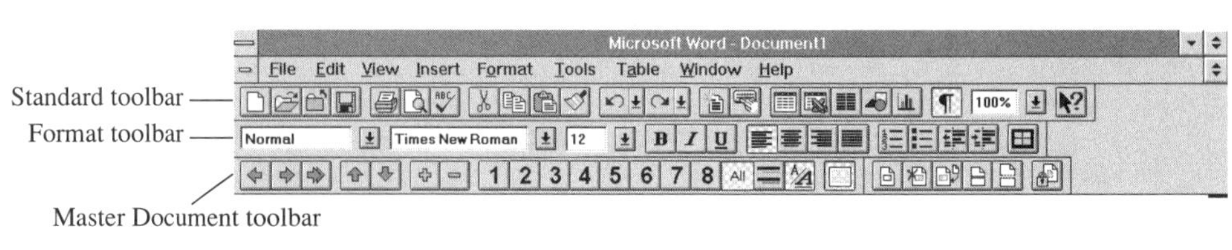

and Word inserts a marker for the specified document into the master file.

Repeat this process until you have built a master document that consists of all of the individual documents that make up the whole. Now you can expand the document to pull in all of the text from each individual document. From there you can build a combined index or table of contents. You can view the master at various levels by selecting the level of detail you want to see from the outline toolbar.

Review/Revision

Use the Revisions dialog to view or make changes in a document. You can use this dialog to track changes and comments from multiple reviewers as well. Word assigns a color to each reviewer, making it easy to tell who made particular changes in a document.

To turn on revision marks, select Tools and choose Revisions to display the Revisions dialog box, shown in Figure 2.30.

Click on the Mark Revisions While Editing check box to enable continuous revision tracking. You can make suggested changes, send the document to someone else to make their changes, and so on. Then after the final review, you can tell Word to make the changes permanent.

Forms Support

Like envelope printing, printing on forms with a word processor has never been particularly easy. With Word 6 and later, the task is easier. You can create forms within Word that you can fill in, and you can design print routines that will fill in pre-

Figure 2.30 Revisions Dialog

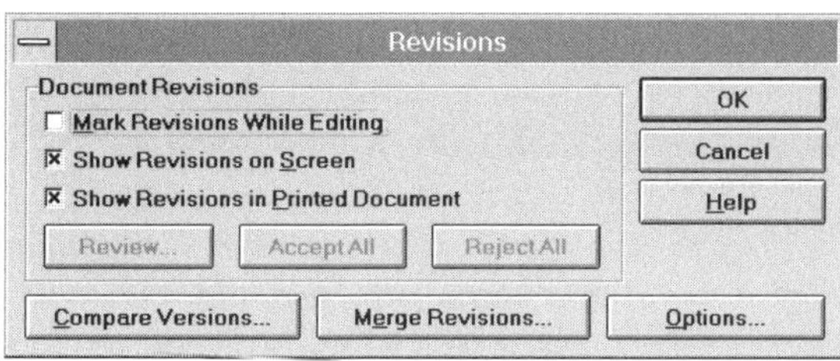

printed forms. I'll show you later in this book how to manage Word forms.

SUMMARY

I've shown you some of the newer features in Word 6 and later, just to get you started with some of the enhanced features Word contains. This isn't all, of course. Word 6 and later contain a large number of enhanced features. Whether you use all of them or not depends greatly on the type of work you do with Word. Chances are you will use only a small portion of the capability built into Word. But you can see from this chapter that this is a powerful program that can handle just about any word processing need.

In the next chapter we'll start using some Word features by creating a document. I'll show you step by step how to use Word to create and edit a basic document.

Chapter 3

Creating Your First Document

One of the interesting things about Microsoft Word is its multifaceted nature. On one hand Word is a powerful word processor with enough features to handle light to medium desktop publishing and page layout tasks. At the same time it is a basic editor with a friendly interface that anybody with a reasonable amount of computer experience can learn quickly and use easily.

Because of the way the program is designed, you can use as much or as little of Word's power and features as you need for the current project. And that's the way you should learn to use Word with this book. Start with the basics, using only what you need right now, but remain flexible, willing to add to your knowledge and skills as needed.

In this chapter I'll discuss some basic document creation, editing, and formatting skills. This is for Word beginners, enough information to help you feel comfortable with the program and to serve as a good starting point for the more in-depth knowledge that you'll pick up in later chapters and by studying the included CD-ROM video. As we go along, you'll see the associated topics on the CD video highlighted.

Starting a New Document

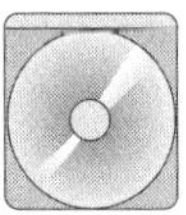

Choose Word Features from screen 2 of the CD video's directory screen, then click Create a Document.

When you open Word from the Program Manager, a blank document is opened. You can start typing immediately, just as you would if you had slipped a blank sheet of paper into a typewriter. You can use Word's extended formatting and layout features—but you don't have to. Just type the text you want (a personal letter, a To-Do list, business correspondence, a grocery list, whatever). Press Enter (Return) only when you want to start a new paragraph, not at the end of each line. Use the Tab key to indent the first line of paragraphs or to line up items in a list. And, remember to save your work regularly.

NOTE: Delete existing text by pressing the Backspace key once for each character you want to remove to the left of the insertion point or by pressing the Del key once for each character you want to remove to the right of the insertion point.

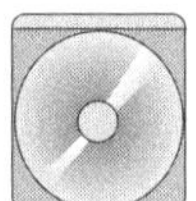

Choose Save/As from the Create a Document screen.

To save the text you are typing in Word, click on the diskette icon on the standard toolbar or select File and choose Save As. Either way the Save As Dialog shown in Figure 3.1 is displayed.

Don't wait until you have finished the document to save it. After you have entered only a few lines of text, save the document. This creates a disk file for it, provides a name for the document, and helps protect against loss of data. If you wait until the document is complete, you run the risk of losing information. In addition, by saving a document early, you make it easier to save the file regularly.

After a document has been saved once, you can use the Ctrl+S shortcut to save any changes to the file. As you work with a document you should save it at regular intervals. I have the habit of saving documents when I start a new paragraph. Many people would call this excessive, but using the shortcut key makes the process easy; you don't even have to move your hands off the keyboard. I've heard another simple guide for how often you should save your work: How much are you willing to do over? I think a paragraph or so is about all the work I want to do over. But if you don't mind doing a whole document over, then wait to save your work until you're finished.

NOTE: You should also develop the habit of saving your work to a backup disk. I use a second networked hard disk and a floppy. I save my documents as I work back to the primary local hard drive, then when I am finished for the day, or when I switch projects, I save all the documents I have created or changed since the last backup to a floppy and a second hard disk. Excessive? How much time do you have to do your work again?

So here's the basic new document process: type what you want and save your work often. Word at this level is a basic program: simple to use, functional, and straightforward. For much of what you do with a word processor, this type of usage is all you need to know.

However, there is obviously more to Word than this. In the rest of this chapter we'll explore other ways of creating a document and of editing and formatting it.

Figure 3.1 Save As Dialog

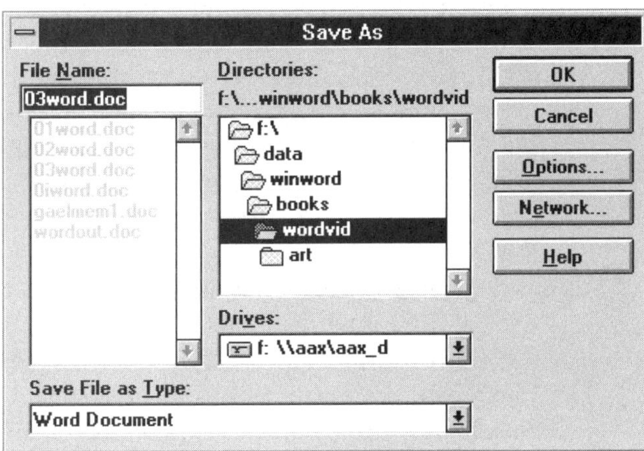

Using Templates

From the CD video's Create a Document screen, click on the Templates button.

Every Word document is based on a template, a set of basic formatting rules including the font that is used for body text and headings, the size of the text, page margins, text color, and all of the other features that go together to form a complete document. Most of these settings you never think about (most of the time), because Word takes care of them for you. But they're there all the same. Microsoft calls document templates blueprints for "text, graphics and formatting."

When you click on the New Document icon on the standard toolbar, for example, or when you just start typing in the default document that Word presents when the program loads, you are using the *Normal* document template. The Normal template provides basic formatting, including a set of heading styles, basic body text, a standard page layout, and so on. The Normal template is attached to the new document you create in this way, providing the background formatting and style for your work. But the features of the Normal template are available to all other documents as well. The Normal template is a *global* template.

If you modify the settings of the template attached to a particular document, however, the changes are available only to that document, not to the "global" world of the Normal template.

What's "Normal" from Word's standpoint? You can learn about the Normal template by starting a new document with the New Document icon on the standard toolbar, then examining the basic settings. Type a few characters and note the information on the format toolbar. You should see the Times New Roman font listed in the font window of this toolbar, for example. The font size is 10 points and the current style (at the far left of the format toolbar) is Normal. Text alignment is flush left and there are no special attributes such as boldface, italics, or underlining.

In addition, there are page layout settings that are part of the Normal template. To see what they are, select File and choose Page Setup... to display the Page Setup dialog, shown in Figure 3.2.

Figure 3.2 Page Setup Dialog

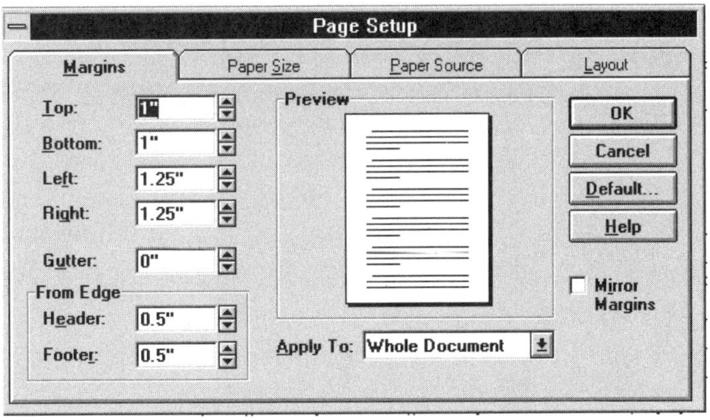

This is a tabbed dialog with different screens for Margins, Paper Size, Paper Source, and Layout. The Margins screen is displayed by default and, unless you changed something (or someone else has), you should see 1-inch top and bottom margins and 1.25-inch left and right margins. Click on the Paper Size tab and you should see an 8.5- x 11-inch paper size in Portrait format specified. The information on the Paper Source screen changes slightly depending on what printer you are using, but in general this tab shows where the paper for your printer will come from. On a laser printer, for example, Default Tray is frequently specified as the paper source.

Finally, click on the Layout tab. You should see specifications that sections start with a new page, vertical alignment is Top, and settings apply to the whole document.

Well, you get the idea. These are the basic settings that make up a new Word document and they are all stored in the global template named Normal. As the name implies, this template is designed to handle most normal document needs. You can use it to write letters, memos, articles, lists, or anything else you want to do with Word. If you base a document on the Normal template and want some special formatting to reflect some special feature of your creation, then you'll have to enter those formatting changes yourself.

Now, suppose you could choose another set of document settings more suited to the specific document type you want to design. A template with special settings for a memo might be useful, for example, and you could probably use another template for a fax cover sheet, and so on. As you might imagine, these features also are included in Word.

To base a document on a different template, simply choose the one you want from the Template dialog that is displayed when you use the File, New command sequence (see Figure 3.3).

NOTE: You don't see the Template dialog when you start a new document with the New icon on the standard toolbar. This tool assumes you want to use the Normal template.

You can see only a portion of the available templates in Figure 3.3. The complete list of templates available from this dialog is shown in Table 3.1. There also are some Wizards listed in this dialog. I tell you about these in the next section of this chapter.

Figure 3.3 Word Template Dialog

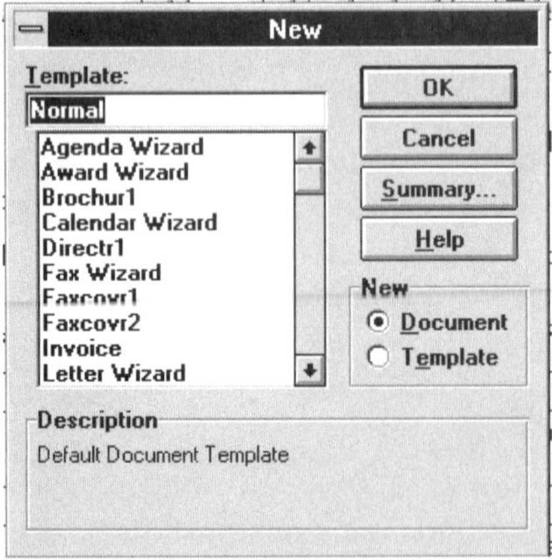

Table 3.1 Word Templates

Template	*Description*
Brochur1	Brochure. You can use this as a starting place for designing a trifold brochure for 8.5- x 11-inch paper.
Directr1	Directory template based on Normal.
Faxcovr1-2	Fax cover sheets. Two similar designs.
Invoice	One of the better Word templates. This helps you design professional invoices for products or services. Includes table math functions.
Letter1-3	Letter templates. These are basically the same, but each has a different default font and slightly different layout.
Manual1	Manual template; mostly Normal template settings.
Manuscr1,3	Manuscript templates. Manuscr1 is based on the Times New Roman font; Manuscr3 uses Courier.
Memo1-3	Three memo templates. They are similar, but each one is a little different.
Normal	This is the default template and the one on which most other templates are based.
Presrel1-3	Three press release templates.
Purchord	Purchase order. This template includes protected fields so users won't damage the basic form. Similar to the Invoice template. Very professional and functional.
Report1-3	General report formats. Report1 uses Times New Roman font, Report2 is based on Arial, and Report3 uses the Courier New font.
Resume1-2,4	Resume templates. Include section headings and formatting, each slightly different. Resume1 and 2 use the Arial font while 4 uses Times New Roman.
Thesis1	Thesis template. Basic formatting based on Normal.
Weektime	A weekly employee time sheet.

Each of the templates listed in Table 3.1 is slightly different. Some offer complex, preformatted objects while others provide only basic font and paragraph formatting. The manuscript formats, for example, present a blank screen with body text and other attributes set. The memo templates, on the other hand, include titles, lines, and the like to effect an overall design. The same is true of the Invoice and Purchase Order templates. Figure 3.4 shows a sample memo template; Figure 3.5 shows the Invoice template.

There are instructions for using these templates in the online help included with Word. A little experience and you can customize any of these templates to give your documents a personal touch. Notice that some templates, such as the Invoice and Purchase Order templates, include Word fields that are *protected*. That means you can't change them unless you use the Tools, Unprotect Document command to turn off protection. You'll want to turn off protection initially so you can enter your company name, address, telephone number, and other information; then you should turn protection back on. Leave the

Figure 3.4 Blank Memo Template

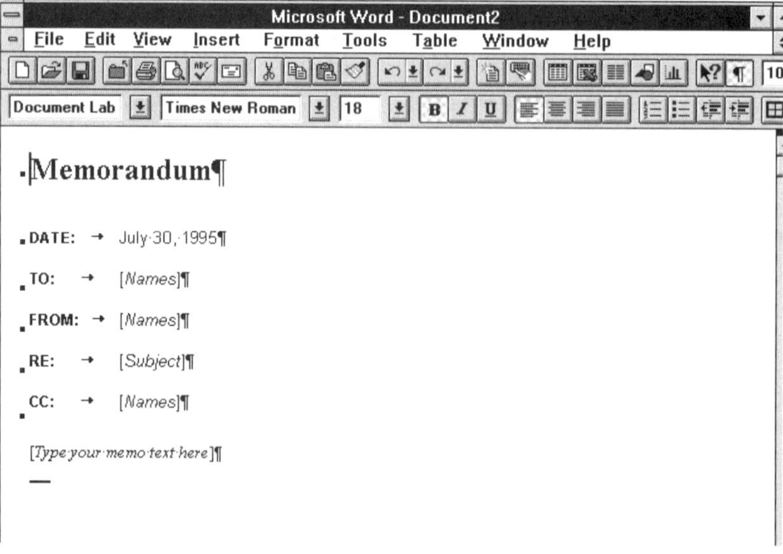

Figure 3.5 Blank Invoice Template

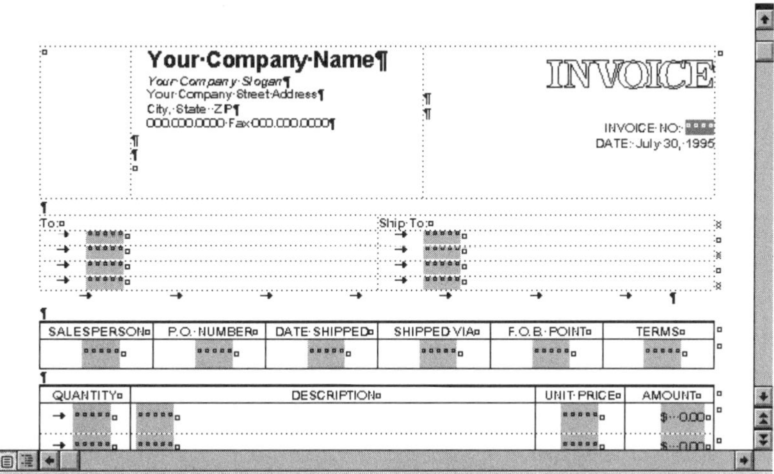

variable fields such as the To: and Ship To: fields blank. Then save the template as a document.

Now, fill out the variable information for this invoice or purchase order and save the document to another file. The next time you want to do an invoice or purchase order, don't start with File, New, use File, Open to load the blank version that has your company name and other data filled in.

The more basic templates that don't require you to enter custom data can remain as templates. Use a new template each time with the File, New command.

You can also create your own templates from standard Word documents. Start with a new document based on a template that is closest to what you ultimately want to achieve. Enter any changes to the basic formatting you want to include in your new template. This could include not only font and paragraph formatting, but static text, lines, graphic objects, or anything else that will appear on every document based on this template.

When the template is designed as you want it, use the File, Save As... command to display the Save As dialog. Pull down the file type list in the Save File as Type: field and choose Document

Template. Enter a name in the File Name: field and specify the Template directory as the destination. Don't add a file name extension. Let Word add the appropriate extension for templates.

Now when you use the File, New command to start a new document, the new template you just created will appear with the others in the Template dialog (refer to Figure 3.3).

You may never need to use templates other than the Normal one that is the Word default. However, if you regularly create documents that require special formatting or you want to ensure that certain documents are consistently designed throughout your company, then investigate templates. You'll probably find them useful.

Using Wizards

Click on Letter Wiz on the Create a Document screen. Also the Wizards button on the Word Features screen.

If you want to go beyond basic document formatting, you can create a new document with a Word Wizard. A Wizard is just a macro, or simple program, that prompts you for some of the steps required to create and format a document. You access a document creation Wizard from the Template dialog, which is displayed when you use the File, New command from the main Word menu.

Using a Wizard provides interactive guidance through creating certain kinds of documents. Table 3.2 lists the intrinsic Word Wizards that you can access through the Template dialog.

To use a Wizard just choose the one you need from the Template dialog and follow the instructions on the screen until all of the steps are complete. Most of the Wizards let you specify such features as page margins, personal or company information, and the like. For example, when you choose the Pleading Wizard, the first dialog asks for basic page layout information (see Figure 3.6).

As is typical with Microsoft Wizards, you click the Next button at the bottom of the dialog to move on to the next screen. You can return to a previous dialog by clicking the Back button.

Later dialogs ask for specific information about this document, as you can see from Figure 3.7.

Table 3.2 Word Wizards

Wizard	*Description*
Agenda	Creates an organized meeting agenda. Creative formatting and interactive operation help you design a professional and functional agenda.
Award	Creates a certificate with PowerPoint-like background, title, recipient, and official signature. Use as is, or use as a starting point for your own design.
Calendar	Creates a monthly calendar. Wizard lets you choose a calendar style, page layout, and more.
Fax	Choose from three fax cover sheet designs. Print in portrait or landscape modes. Interactive Wizard lets you input your company name, address, phone number, and so on.
Letter	Creates a personal or business letter. Wizard lets you use one of Word's prewritten business letters. Choose from three basic letter designs.
Memo	Create professional-looking memos in three styles with this interactive Wizard. Supports multi-page memos.
Newslttr	This Wizard won't automatically create every newsletter you might need, but it is a good starting point for an acceptable newsletter design. Choose from three basic designs. Supports multiple pages and custom elements.
Pleading	Interactive help for creating a legal pleading. On each dialog you can choose from among multiple alternatives for page layout and design.
Resume	Helps you create professional resume designs, including a prewritten cover letter that you can adapt for your situation. Choose from three types of resumes.
Table	Uses Word's Table AutoFormat feature to help you design a custom table with creative formatting.

When the Wizard is complete, Word closes the final Wizard dialog and displays the finished document on the screen so you can edit it if you wish, or save it to a disk file. Don't forget to save the finished document. The Wizard only creates the

Figure 3.6 Initial Legal Pleading Wizard Dialog

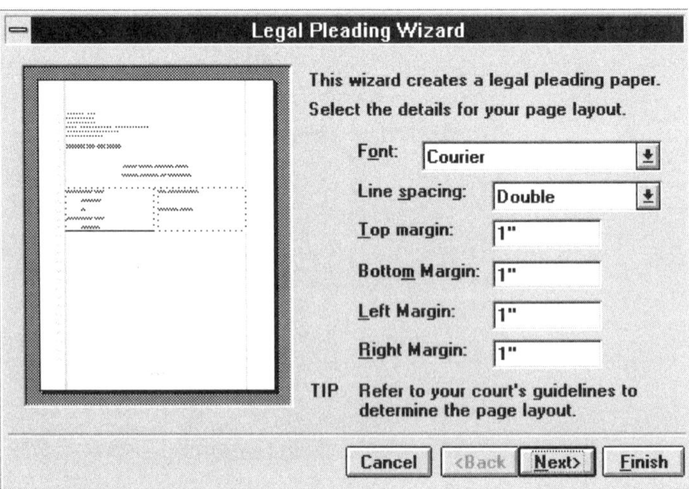

Figure 3.7 Pleading Name and Address Dialog

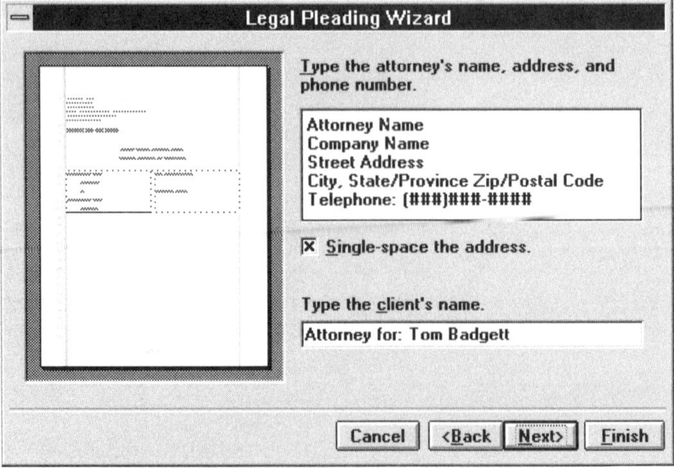

document and displays it in the Word editor. You have to be responsible for saving a copy of the document yourself.

Typing and Editing Basics

As with many features of Word, entering text is at once basic and potentially complex. In this section I'll discuss some general typing and editing considerations when creating a document in Word.

Type Text at the Insertion Point

Word is a *full-screen* or *page-oriented* editor. Early computer text-editing software was *line-oriented*, which meant you entered and edited text by the line. If you wanted to change information already entered, for example, you first displayed the line that contained the text you wanted to change, told the editor what old characters you wanted to change and what the new text should be. You couldn't simply move the cursor back and forth over the line of text to make changes. You typed old text, then new text, and the editor replaced the old text on the displayed line with the new text. Moreover, each line ended in a carriage return, so to add more than a few characters to an existing line meant you had to insert a new line. Changing and formatting text was rather a chore, as you might imagine.

With a page-oriented editor such as Word you don't press Enter (carriage return) except to start a new paragraph. Otherwise, Word automatically wraps the text from line to line as you type. When you add or remove text, Word doesn't really care whether you maintain line lengths because it automatically adjusts everything to fit. And, as a Windows product, Word lets you position the cursor—or insertion point—anywhere in a document to add new text or edit existing information. The whole process is visual, interactive, and intuitive.

Normally you will use the mouse to place the insertion point where you want to add or edit text. Use the scroll bars at the right of the Word screen to move up or down in the text to display the portion you want to change, then simply click in the line where you want to add or remove text and use the

Backspace or Del keys to remove text and type new text to add information.

Insert vs. Overtype

By default Word adds new text on a line by bumping existing text out of the way as you type. This is the *Insert mode* or setting. You can tell that Insert mode is enabled by observing the status bar at the bottom of the Word editing window. Close to the right side of the status bar is a tiled box labeled *OVR* (for overtype). In the default mode, this box is light gray, indicating this feature is not enabled.

If you prefer to type over existing text, erasing as you type, press the Ins key on your keyboard or use the mouse to double-click on the *OVR* button on the status bar. The button will light up, indicating that overtype (replace) editing mode has been enabled.

Which setting you use depends on your personal preference, and on the type of text you are editing. If you are changing data in a matched table, for example, you may prefer to set overtype so the new data replaces the old, maintaining the layout. However, for normal editing chores it is easier to have Word bump existing text to the right as you type anything new. If you then want to remove some of the old text, you can highlight it with your mouse or hold the Shift key and use the arrow movement keys to highlight what you want to remove. If you press the Del key with text highlighted, the selected text is removed. If you press Del without highlighting a block of text first, one character to the right of the insertion point is removed for each press of the Del key. Likewise, pressing Backspace removes one character to the left of the cursor.

NOTE: Pressing Del with text highlighted removes the text and does not copy it to the Clipboard. You may still be able to restore objects deleted in this way with the Undo button on the standard toolbar, but you may not. When in doubt about removing text, highlight it and use the Edit, Cut command or press Ctrl+X to remove the selected object from the Word editing window and place it on the Clipboard.

In addition to the Backspace and Del keys used alone, some key combinations help you edit text. Table 3.3 shows some of the key combinations.

Table 3.3 Keystroke Combinations for Deleting Text

Keys	*Results*
Del or Backspace	Removes highlighted text
Del	Removes one character to the right
Backspace	Removes one character to the left
Ctrl+Del	Removes one word to the right
Ctrl+Backspace	Removes one word to the left

Selecting Text

As I mentioned, removing more than a word or two is easier if you first highlight the text, then delete it. In fact, Word's general philosophy of operation is "Select, then do." That means, select the text or object you want to manipulate, then execute the command or operation to work on the text. You can use the mouse to "wipe" a highlight cursor over text by holding down the left mouse button as you move the cursor, or you can hold down the Shift key and use the cursor movement keys to mark a block of text. And, there are other methods for marking text.

For one thing, there is a section at the extreme left of the Word editing screen that helps you in marking text. Move the mouse cursor into this left margin and notice how it changes shape. When you move the mouse pointer over Word text, it is shaped like an I-beam, indicating a text insertion point. When the pointer moves into the left margin, however, it changes into a right-facing arrow. Move the arrow beside a line of text and click the left mouse button and Word selects all of the text on that line. Click twice and the entire paragraph is selected. See? It's a quick and easy way of selecting blocks of text that you want to delete, copy, or move.

Now try this. Move the I-beam cursor over a word and double-click the left mouse button. The entire word is selected. Triple-click a word, and the entire paragraph is selected. Table 3.4 summarizes some of the text-selecting techniques you can use with Word.

Table 3.4 Word Text-Selecting Techniques

Action	*Result*
Double-click a word	Select the word
Click a graphic object	Select the object
Ctrl+Click a word	Select sentence containing word
Triple-click a word	Select paragraph containing word
Click in selection bar at left margin	Select a line
Double-click in selection bar at left margin	Select paragraph
Triple-click in selection bar at left margin	Select whole document
Alt+Triple-click a word	Select square or rectangular block left of cursor to top of paragraph
Alt+hold left mouse button and move mouse	Paint a square or rectangular block starting at the insertion point

Using Heading Styles

Word includes a number of features for automatically formatting text and for helping you create such things as outlines or summaries. One such feature is a collection of heading styles. A style is simply a preformatted setting that you can apply within a document or across several documents. By using styles instead of creating custom formatting for each document, you can change formatting for a range of text by just changing the style.

Heading styles also are used to create numbered lists, multilevel outlines, and more. Use heading styles for the titles or subheadings within your documents. Use the Heading 1 style for the top-level title, Heading 2 for the second level, and so on.

Frankly, I think the heading formatting that comes with Word is not very pleasing or practical; too many italics, bold, and underlining. If you want to edit how various heading levels that use styles appear in your documents, edit the styles. To do that, place the insertion point within a heading that is formatted with a heading style you want to change. Use the Format, Style... command sequence to display the Style dialog shown in Figure 3.8.

The Styles: window at the left of this dialog lists all of the styles available in the current document. The style for the text under the insertion point when you brought up the Styles dialog will be highlighted. However, you can edit any of the styles listed, if you want.

Click on Modify to display the Modify dialog. From there you can choose the Format button to choose font, paragraph, or other formatting to change (see Figure 3.9).

Once you get to this level, the formatting is the same as if you had called up the Font or other Format dialogs directly from the main menu. The difference is you are changing the formatting associated with the selected style rather than for specific characters or paragraphs.

Just to see the effect of changing a style associated with a document, choose the Normal style from the first Style dialog, click on Modify, and pull down the Format list. Choose Font to display the Font dialog. Change the current font size to 14 points. Unless you have changed the style previously, this will

Figure 3.8 Style Dialog

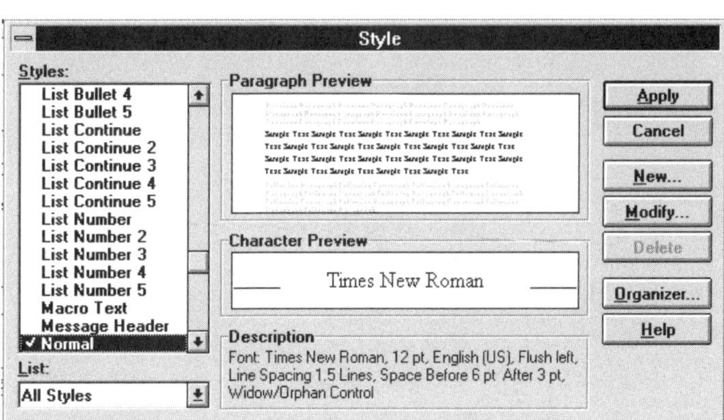

Figure 3.9 Modify Style Dialog with Format Pull-Down List Displayed

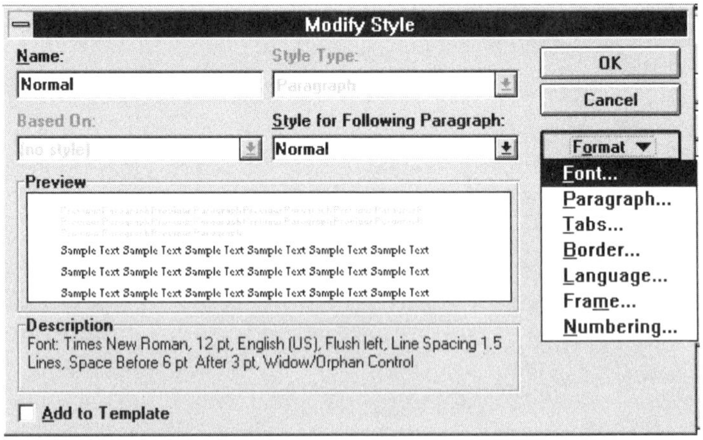

increase the size of all the text in your document based on the Normal style by four points. Click on OK to close the Font dialog, then close the Modify and Style dialogs. Notice how your document has changed. This simple technique lets you change formatting for all documents based on the Normal template (if you click the Add to Template check box in the Modify dialog). You can see how useful this would be if you were preparing a book, a series of reports, or other documents that need to have the same formatting.

Adding Date and Time

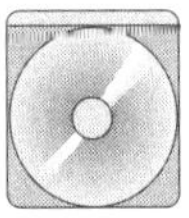

Click on the Date Codes button on the CD video's Create a Document screen.

Word includes some automatic data entry features as well. For example, you can insert codes that tell Word to place the current date and time at a specified location in your document. You can make this a static entry, or make it dynamic so that the date and time change each time you open the document.

To insert a dynamic date or time display:

1. Position the insertion point where you want the date or time to appear.

2. Click on Insert on the main menu and choose Date and Time... to display the Date and Time dialog shown in Figure 3.10.
3. Choose a date or time format from the list in the dialog.
4. Click on OK to insert a date or time field code in your document.

The date (and or time) stored in your computer will appear at the location of the insertion point.

To insert a static date or time value in your document, open the Date and Time dialog as before, but uncheck the box at the bottom that says Insert as Field. This tells Word to insert just the current date or time without the dynamic code that causes it to update when you load the document again later.

Using Paragraph Marks and Displaying Other Special Characters

Word presents a reasonably clean screen while you create or edit documents. However, there are a number of objects in the background, hidden from view, that help produce the formatting you see on the screen. You can turn on a special character display to view some of these objects, if you wish. For the most part, you will work with Word with these unprintable characters hidden

Figure 3.10 Date and Time Dialog

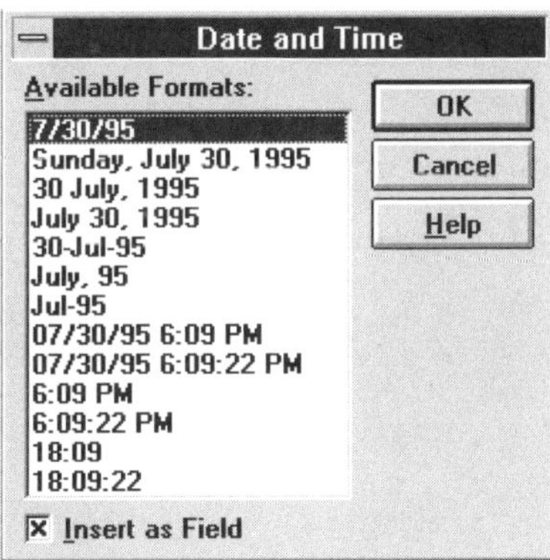

from view. Sometimes, though, you will want to show them to help you discover why a document is printing in a certain way, or why you can't get a document to look on the screen precisely the way you want it.

The simplest special character display is the paragraph mark. Paragraph marks are important in Word because these special symbols carry the formatting information for the preceding paragraph. To view paragraph marks and some other codes or formatting (such as table of contents codes), simply click on the paragraph icon on the standard toolbar.

You can display even more document information by selecting the Tool menu and choosing Options to display the Options dialog, shown in Figure 3.11. The View tab should be on top. If it is not, click on View to bring it to the front, as shown in Figure 3.11.

Look first at the group in the lower-left corner of this dialog, the Window group. This shows the default view settings for Word, with the bottom status bar and vertical and horizontal scroll bars displayed. If you want to free up more room on your

Figure 3.11 View Tab of the Options Dialog

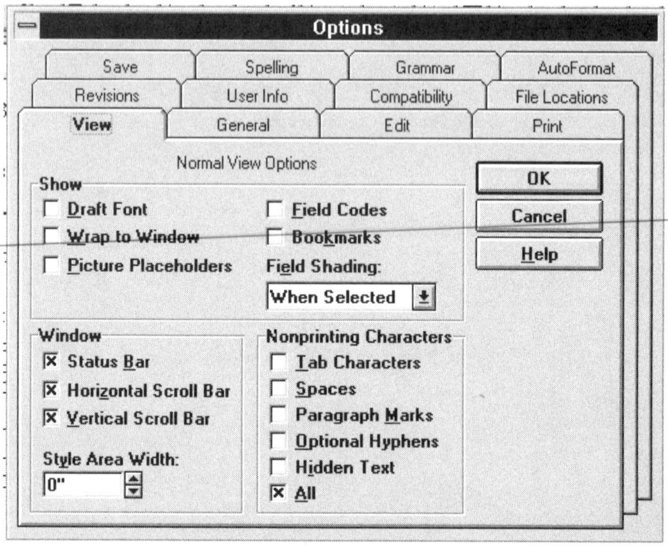

screen, making more room for the documents you create and less for the tools you can use in Word, remove some or all of these components.

NOTE: You can also press the right mouse button while pointing to any Word toolbar and uncheck the toolbar, format bar, or other features to present a cleaner screen display during document editing. The View, Full command also helps unclutter the screen.

Now, look at the lower right-hand group, Nonprinting Characters. This is the one that determines which hidden characters, if any, will be displayed. By default, Word displays none of these hidden characters. When you click on the paragraph mark on the standard toolbar, some of them are displayed. You can change the defaults so that Word always displays some or all of these by checking the ones you want to see all of the time.

The upper group, Show, lets you see field codes instead of the data they represent, as well as bookmarks and draft fonts. When you select Draft Font, true character formatting and graphic objects are not displayed. You will see underlined text to represent text with special formatting, and you will see only blank boxes for graphic objects. Particularly if you are using a slow PC or if you have 4 MB of memory or less, you may want to set Draft Font to speed up the display of your Word screen.

NOTE: There is an excellent help page associated with this dialog. Open the Options dialog and click on the Help button to display it.

Typing and Editing Do's and Don'ts

Normally as you create and edit documents in Word you type naturally, much as you would with a typewriter. If you know something about using a typewriter, you can type documents in Word. However, because Word is not a typewriter, there are a couple of differences you should be aware of.

Using the Spacebar

When you use a typewriter, it is fairly easy to use the Spacebar to move the typing head to the proper location for typing text. Because there is a ruler displayed on many typewriters, you can even use the Spacebar to line up columns of text.

This won't work with Word. Most of the fonts you are likely to use with Word are *proportional*, which means the spacing between letters and words varies with the letters. So a good general rule in Word is to use the Spacebar sparingly, only as space between words. When you want to line up text, use the Tab key or a table instead.

Also, most of us were taught to hit the Spacebar twice at the end of a sentence. Because Word and most document management programs today are intelligent enough to know what to do with words at the end of sentences, you should space only once at the end of a sentence. If you enter two spaces after a period, your document will probably print with really wide spaces after each period.

NOTE: Oops! Too late? You've already created a bunch of documents with double spaces after each sentence? That's OK. Load the document you want to change and use the Edit, Replace command (or type Ctrl+H) to display the Replace dialog. Enter a period and two spaces in the Find What: field and enter period and a single space in the Replace With: field. Now click on Replace All and Word will handle that little chore for you. Be sure to save the document after you have made the changes.

In general, you should also avoid hitting Enter twice at the end of a paragraph. Use Format, Paragraph to add spacing before and after a paragraph instead.

Don't Delete Paragraph Marks

Remember those special paragraph marks I discussed earlier? In general you don't want to remove those, either. They contain the formatting for the paragraph that precedes the mark. Remove the mark and you remove the formatting for that paragraph. If the formatting is complex, it might take you a while to recover from such a seemingly simple mistake.

Moving Around a Document

Click on the Navigation button on the CD video's Create a Document screen.

As you proof and edit a Word document, you'll need to move the insertion point to new locations for entering text, and you'll need to display specific portions of a document for proofing or editing.

Positioning the Insertion Point

If the portion of the document you want to edit is on the screen, you can move the mouse pointer to the location and click the left button. The insertion point is placed in the document so you can type new information or delete existing data.

Scrolling Through a Document

If you need to display other sections of the document, you can use the PgUp and PgDn keys on your keyboard to display the previous or next screen. The vertical scroll bars on the right of the screen let you move up and down in the document as well. To move a short distance, click on the up or down arrow keys on the scroll bar. To move longer distances within a document, grab the square position box on the scroll bar and drag it to the approximate location within the document.

Going to Previous Locations

As you edit a document you may want the ability to return to previous locations. Suppose you move to page 3 and make some changes, then you move to page 9 and edit the document, and move to page 20 for some more changes. To return to the previous locations, press Shift+F5. This jumps to the previous location. Press the key combination again, and you are taken to the second-to-last editing location. Press Shift+F5 again, and move to the page 3 location. This little feature keeps track of only the three most recent edits.

Go To Page

You can tell Word to jump directly to a particular page as well. Use the Edit, Go To (Ctrl+G) command sequence to display the Go To dialog, shown in Figure 3.12.

Type the page number in the Enter Page Number: field of this dialog. Notice that you can also choose what to go to. It need not be a page number: it can be a section, a bookmark, or one of the other Word features listed in the window on the left of this dialog.

Figure 3.12 Word Go To Dialog

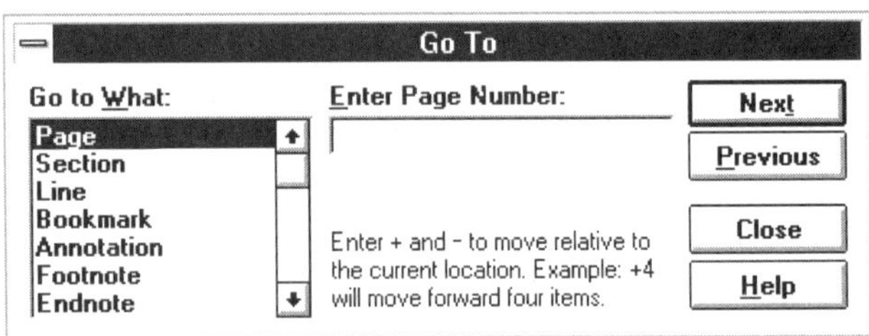

Copying and Moving Information

Click on the Selecting button on the Create a Document screen.

Copying and moving data are two editing tasks you certainly will want to do in Word. Because Word is a standard Windows product, these are simple tasks that use the standard Windows Clipboard.

To copy a block of text, for example, just mark the text you want to duplicate, click on Edit, and choose Copy (or press Ctrl+C). This places a copy of the selected text onto the Clipboard. Now position the cursor (insertion point) where you want the copy of the existing text to appear and use Edit, Paste (Shift+Ins) to copy the text from the Clipboard into your document.

NOTE: To copy the same text to multiple locations within a document, simply position the insertion point a second time, and copy it from the Clipboard. You can do this as often as you like, since the text stays on the Clipboard until you remove it.

The move process is similar, except you choose Cut from the Edit menu or press Ctrl+X, which removes the text from its original location during the process of copying it to the Clipboard. Now when you paste the Clipboard data into a new location, the text or other Word objects exist in only one place instead of two.

Word also supports drag and drop moving, as I mentioned in Chapter 2.

Choose Drag & Drop from the Editing Text screen.

You can mark a block of text with the mouse by using the Shift key and cursor keys. Then point to the marked block of text and press and hold the left mouse button. Now as you move the cursor a small document icon is attached to the pointer. Move the pointer where you want the text moved and release the mouse button. To copy text with drag and drop, press and hold the Ctrl key while you drag the text.

NOTE: If you have the Word status bar enabled, you will be prompted to drag and drop the text once it is marked, and Word will ask where you want to move or copy the text once you grab it with the mouse.

Another useful Word editing feature is the *Spike*, but in my experience not very many users even know about it.

I go to a very old-fashioned barber shop. After the barber is finished cutting your hair, you hand him $6.00 (Yep. Still only $6.00!) and he writes out a ticket to represent the work done. The ticket doesn't go to the customer. You can look in the mirror and remember you just had a haircut. Instead, the little transaction chit is shoved on a sharp metal spike that sits beside the cash register. At the end of the day he can remove the chits, count them, count his money, and thereby have a convenient cross-check.

The Spike in Word operates similarly, except it is designed to hold text or other objects so you can move them in a group to another location in the current document or to another document. Think about how the Cut and Paste process works: You mark text, remove it from the document, and copy it to the Clipboard. Then you change locations within the current document or open a new document, position the insertion point, and copy the contents of the Clipboard to the new location.

The only problem with this process is, each time you copy data to the Clipboard it erases what was there before. Suppose you want to capture several pieces of text or other screen objects and move them as a group to a new location or to another document? That's where the Spike comes in.

Mark the first object and press Ctrl+F3 to delete it in the present location and copy it to the Spike. This first block of text or other object now occupies position number 1 on the Spike.

Now, select the next object you want to place on the Spike and, again, press Ctrl+F3 to place it on the Spike in position number 2. Repeat the process for as many objects or blocks of text you want to move.

Position the insertion point within the document where you want the Spiked information to appear, and press Shift+Ctrl+F3. The Spike information will be copied into the current document in the same order as it was saved to the Spike. A carriage return will be placed between the objects. Note that this works as if you placed data on the old-fashioned barbershop spike, then turned the spike upside down to remove the information. This is what is called a *FIFO* buffer, a First In First Out buffer.

NOTE: When you move information off the Spike into a document, Word clears the Spike. But if you want to keep the data on the Spike, press Ctrl+Alt+V instead of Shift+Ctrl+F3.

The data on the Spike is really an entry in the AutoText area, so you can insert Spike data into a document by typing **spike** on a separate line and then choosing AutoText... from the Edit menu or by clicking on the AutoText icon on the standard toolbar.

Summary

We've covered a lot of ground in this chapter. With the information in this chapter and the additional instructions in the accompanying CD-ROM video, you should be able to create most any Word document you want and endow it with basic features and formatting.

In the next chapter I'll provide additional detail on document formatting, including character, paragraph, and page formatting, and I'll discuss some of the Word utilities such as spell checking.

Chapter 4

Formatting a Document

You learned in Chapter 3 how Word comes with a number of preconfigured formatting features. Basic document formatting such as page margins, the default font, line spacing, and other basic features are set automatically when you start a new document. For many documents, this basic, automatic formatting will work just fine. You can accept the defaults for much of what you do with Word.

On the other hand, the flexibility of Word's formatting features lets you design custom documents that look the way *you* want them to look. In this chapter I'll summarize some of the more common Word formatting features and give you some hints on designing your own documents. Use this chapter as a reference during your own document design. Information is organized from small object to large, from character formatting to page formatting, so you should be able to find the specific information you need easily.

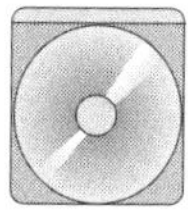

Choose Formatting Text or Page Formatting from the second screen of the CD directory for interactive help in formatting your documents.

Character Formatting

Character formatting is the most basic of Word's formatting features. It should be pretty obvious that you can't format an element any smaller than a single character. Most of the time you will set character formatting for a group of characters, but you can specify character formatting for a single letter, if you want. In this section I'll provide a brief summary of Word's basic character formatting features.

Font

A *font* is a collection of all of the available characters in a particular typeface in a specific style. Now that we have that straight. . .

What is a typeface? A *typeface* is a named shape or design of character, a distinctive shape and design of type that makes a collection of letters recognizable. Typefaces are generally identified by name, such as Times Roman, Helvetica, Palatino, and Century Schoolbook.

A font is a collection of all of the characters available for a particular typeface and style. Times Roman Italic, for example, is a font, as is Palatino Bold or Helvetica Bold Italic. Today the terms font and typeface frequently are used interchangeably. I'll follow that convention in this book, using the term *font* for a general collection of characters.

Style? That's how the characters within a typeface are presented. You can give a character in a typeface a bold style (or attribute), for example, or set it with italics or underline.

The characters you put on the screen are an important part of your message. Not only does the typeface you select help convey information, it also imparts a mood or style that is an integral part of the message. In Word you have a lot of control over the typeface and font you use.

You can tell what typeface is in use for the text where the insertion point rests or for any selected text by looking at the typeface (font) window on the format bar. The default font in Word is Times New Roman.

You can change the font for any characters you type by pulling down the list of available fonts from the format bar and choosing one. The characters you type after changing the font in this way will appear in the new font. Figure 4.1 shows a sample of available fonts in this pull-down list.

To see the effect of changing the font, type a line of characters in the default Word font. Press Enter to start a new line of text, then pull down the font list on the format bar. Use the scroll bar at the right of this list to locate the Impact font. Click on this font name to select it. Now type a second line of text—the same line as before or a different line—and note the difference. It should be significant, since the Impact typeface has a completely different style and weight from the default Times New Roman font.

NOTE: You can change the font of existing text by first selecting the text you want to change, then choosing the new font from the pull-down list on the format bar.

Other icons on the format bar let you specify font size (see the next section), and attributes such as boldface, italics, underline, and positioning.

You can also use the Font dialog from the Format menu to select fonts and specify attributes from a single screen. Select Format and choose Font to display the Font dialog shown in Figure 4.2.

Select a font from the Font window on the left of this dialog by using the scroll bars to move up and down the font list. Other windows in this dialog help you set other character attributes.

Figure 4.1 Available Word Fonts in the Format Bar Pull-Down List

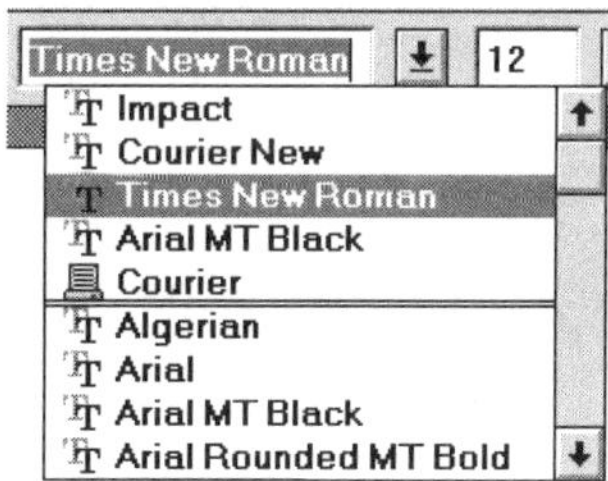

Figure 4.2 Font Dialog

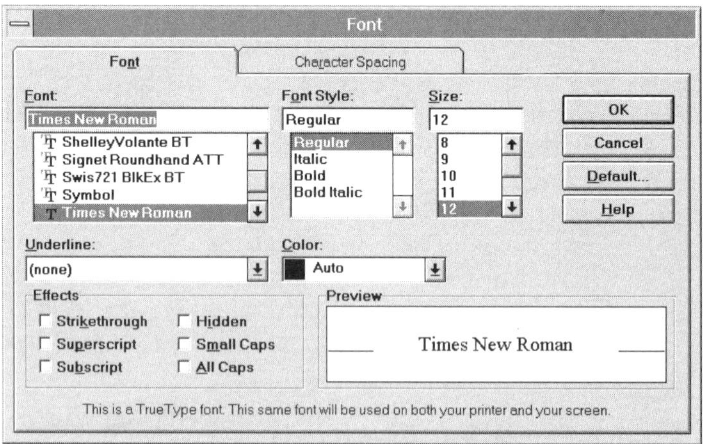

As you choose type for a document, also be aware of serif and sans serif designs. *Serif* type includes finishing strokes at the end of main strokes. Most typefaces use serifs, and serif type is usually easier to read than typefaces without serifs (*sans serif* type).

> Times is a serif type: Times
>
> Helvetica is a popular sans serif type: Helvetica

Word supports a wide range of text styles, sizes, and even colors. However, you should work with a limited number of fonts and styles within any given document. Accept Word's defaults or specify a font for heading text (Arial or another sans serif font is a good choice) and another for body text. Beyond that, you may need one or two more fonts for special formatting such as captions, but don't try to put too many fonts in a single document, even though you can.

The fonts within a document also should be somewhat related. Related type means type of the same general style. You *don't* want body copy of clean, modern Helvetica, for example, mixed with large titles drawn in florid Old English.

Point Size

In addition to the design of characters, you can also control the size of text. The size of the type you use is measured in *points*. One point is equal to 1/72nd of an inch, so 72-point type is about one inch tall. In most typefaces, 12-point type is standard for printed pages; for other typefaces a 10-point type is standard. In the final analysis, the precise point size you choose depends a lot on personal preference and on the application of the document you are writing.

You can also use the format bar to specify a new font size. Pull down the font size list and choose a different number to have any new characters you type appear in the new size. Select a block of text and choose a size from the pull-down list to change a group of characters at once.

For most standard documents you will use only two or three different font sizes. Like typefaces, different sized fonts can be distracting if you use too many in the same document. But Word also offers a great variety of font sizes. For cover pages, banners, posters, signs and the like, you can specify some really large fonts if you wish.

Bold

Set characters in boldface for emphasis. You can use the Bold icon on the toolbar to set selected characters or the next characters you type in bold. You can also press Ctrl+B to specify bold characters.

Word is intelligent about setting character attributes. If you select a word with the mouse or the cursor keys, then issue one of the bold commands, the word will take on the boldface attribute. However, to change the attribute of a single word, you need not mark it. Simply position the insertion point anywhere within the word and Word is smart enough to know you want to set the whole word in boldface when you use one of the boldface commands (this also applies to the italic and underline commands; see below).

If you want to change the attribute of a single character within a word, you must use the mouse or the cursor keys to select the character before using one of the boldface commands. This also applies to the italic and underline attributes; see below.

Italic and Underline

Italics and underline can be set in the same way as boldface. Set italics or underline one character at a time, by placing the insertion point inside a word before issuing an italics or underline command, or by selecting a block of text before issuing a command.

Using Format Painter

Word includes a specialty feature that makes it a lot easier to create and maintain consistent formatting throughout a document. The Format Painter, accessible from the standard toolbar, lets you "paint" the format of one block of text onto another block.

To use the Format Painter, position the insertion point anywhere within the block of text that carries the formatting you want to copy. Click on the Format Painter icon on the standard toolbar. The mouse cursor changes to a paintbrush. Use the paintbrush to select the block of text that is the destination for the new formatting. When you release the mouse button, the selected text takes on the attributes of the previous text.

Changing Font Defaults

Although Word installs with Times New Roman in 10-point size, you can change this default by editing the style specifications for the Normal template. Use File, Open from the main Word menu and specify Document Templates in the Files of Type field of this dialog. Choose Normal from the Templates directory within the Winword directory. Use Format, Style to display the Style dialog and click on the Modify button. Make any changes you want to the style by pulling down the Modify list on this dialog. When all of the changes are complete, close the Style dialog, then save the template file.

Now, the next time you start a new document based on the Normal template, the changes you made to styles in the template will show up in the new document.

Viewing Text Formatting (Reveal Codes)

I've shown you how to show paragraph marks by clicking on the paragraph symbol on the standard toolbar, and how to

Figure 4.3 Pop-Up Text Formatting (Reveal Codes)

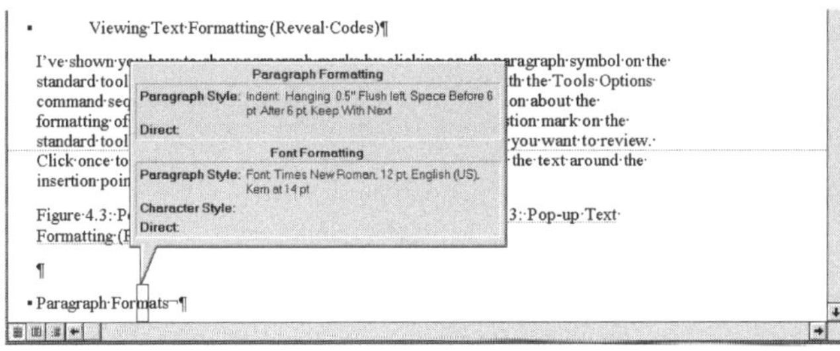

view some other document objects with the Tools, Options command sequence. But you can also get some additional information about the formatting of specific text in your document by clicking on the question mark on the standard toolbar, then moving the insertion point to the area of text you want to review. Click once to display a pop-up dialog that shows information about the text around the insertion point (see Figure 4.3).

Paragraph Formats

Beyond character formatting, you can set document formatting at the paragraph level. Whereas character formatting determines the typeface, font, and so on, paragraph formatting sets spacing between paragraphs, indents, and other broader characteristics. In this section, I'll give you a summary of paragraph formatting.

Types of Paragraph Formats

There are actually dozens of formatting characteristics associated with document paragraphs. Text alignment, for example, determines how the left and right margins of the current paragraph line up with the edge of the page. You can use indents to emphasize blocks of text, adjust line spacing for ease of editing or to help make the text fit on the page. You can add extra spacing before and after paragraphs for ease of reading and to make page layout easier if you import the Word document into a page layout program.

NOTE: The formatting characteristics discussed in this section are paragraph oriented. If you position the insertion point anywhere within a paragraph and change one of these formats, the format is changed for all of the text in the paragraph. On the other hand, you can use some of these formatting characteristics for blocks of text smaller than a paragraph by selecting a block of text prior to issuing the formatting command.

As you work with document formatting of any kind, just make sure that you don't delete the paragraph marks at the end of paragraphs. The formatting for the entire paragraph is stored in this paragraph mark.

Alignment

Word supports four basic types of alignment: left, center, right, and justified. By far the majority of your document work in Word will be left justified. This is standard typewriter formatting where the lines of text are flush on the left side of the screen but ragged on the right side (this basic formatting is sometimes called "flush left/ragged right").

You can set any of these paragraph alignments from the standard toolbar by clicking on the appropriate icon. The flush left icon is the one that shows text in a paragraph lined up on the left side, for example. The justified text icon shows text lined up on the left and right sides. You can also set paragraph formatting from the Paragraph dialog (Format, Paragraph from the main Word menu bar; see Figure 4.4).

NOTE: If you're having problems getting text to appear as it should on the screen, one of the first things to check is paragraph alignment. Position the insertion point within the problem paragraph and click on the left alignment icon on the standard toolbar.

You probably won't use center alignment for large blocks of text. Center alignment is usually reserved for titles, either in the body of a document or in a table, or for short lists. Centered text is ragged left and right and has lines of varying length. This type of formatting would be difficult to read in more than just short sections.

Figure 4.4 Paragraph Dialog

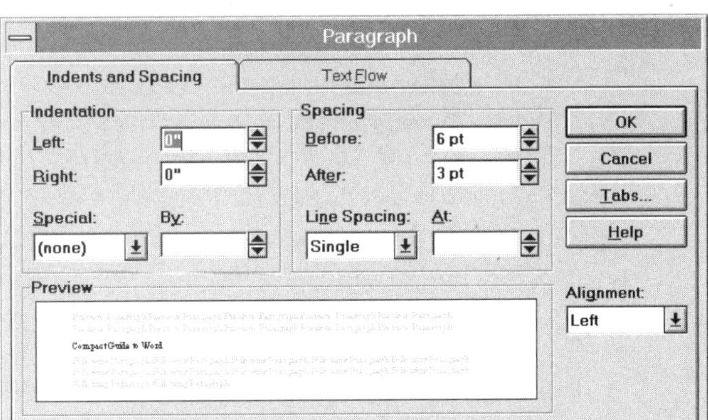

Likewise, right alignment (ragged left) is not practical for large blocks of text. It would be too unlike the text you are used to reading most of the time, and the transition from one to the other would be difficult. You can use ragged left text as part of titles, in name and address or other lists, or to place special emphasis on a small amount of text.

Finally, fully justified text (flush left/flush right) is used for formal manuscripts such as books, annual reports, and sometimes for business letters. Justified text gives a document a professional, somewhat formal appearance and can help you fit more text within a given space than an alignment with only one side or with no sides justified.

As you use fully justified text, study word spacing and alignment carefully before you make a final printout. Depending on the font you are using, full justification sometimes causes unusual spacing between words. If the word spacing isn't what you want, try changing the font. A proportionally spaced font will do better under full justification than a monospace or fixed-space font. You can tell which are proportional fonts by looking at the font list in the Format Font dialog. TrueType fonts are usually proportional and they are accompanied by a TT symbol. Other fonts may be proportional, but those with a printer symbol beside them probably aren't.

Indents

Using indents is another habit you should establish, doing away with the habit so many of us carry from the old typewriter days of using the Spacebar or Tab key to indent. Indenting is another paragraph-level code, so to set right- or left-side indents, simply place the insertion point anywhere within the paragraph you want to indent and use the Format, Paragraph command sequence to display the Paragraph dialog shown in Figure 4.5.

The Indents and Spacing tab, shown in Figure 4.5, should be on top of this dialog display. If it isn't, click on the tab to bring it to the front. Notice the Indentation group at the left of the dialog. You can use the up and down arrows beside the Left and Right fields to specify how much you want the text in the current paragraph to be offset. You can also type in the amount of indent in one or both of these fields. You can enter values up to 22 inches in these fields.

Use left and right indents to add emphasis to a block of text, for long quotes, or for anything else that requires some parts of a document to have different edge spacing from the main parts of the document. If you want to indent an entire document, use the Page Setup... dialog (File, Page Setup) to change how much

Figure 4.5 Paragraph Dialog

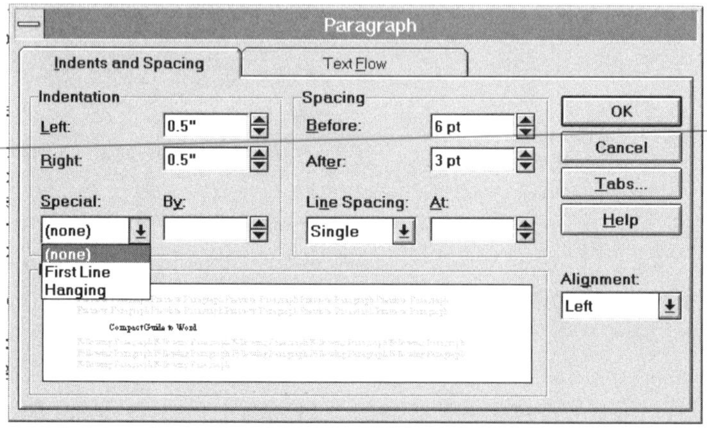

space Word leaves on the left and right sides of the page by changing the margin settings.

You can also specify special paragraph formatting with this dialog. As Figure 4.5 shows , you can pull down a list of special indents to create a hanging indent, for example, or to specify that the first line of each paragraph will be automatically indented.

Tab Stops

A tab is a way of indenting one line of text, frequently the first line of a paragraph. While you can use tabs to line up items in columns, you should resist the temptation to do it. A Word table is a much better choice for this application. It is easier to keep the alignment correct with a table than with a series of tabs.

Word installs with a number of predetermined tabs. Unless you have modified the Normal style, you will find default tabs at half-inch intervals. Starting from a new line, the first time you press the Tab key on your keyboard, the insertion point moves to a position that is .5 inch from the left margin. Press Tab again, and the insertion point is 1 inch from the left margin (one-half inch from the previous position). A third press of the Tab key, and the insertion point jumps to 1.5 inches from the left margin, and so on.

Word is quite flexible in handling tabs, however. You aren't stuck with this every-half-inch default setting. You can add or remove tabs and change tab alignment if you wish. There are two basic ways to change tab settings: by moving or placing tabs on the ruler or by using the Tab dialog available from the Format menu. Let's look at the Tab dialog first (Figure 4.6).

Click on Format and choose Tabs... to display the dialog in Figure 4.6. Using this dialog to add tabs to the basic Word configuration is really easy. The hard part is remembering that Word comes with tabs set every half inch, even though they don't show up on this dialog. You can tell this is so by referring to the Default Tab Stops field at the upper right of this dialog.

You can change the repetitive tab settings by changing this value. For example, if you want to reduce the tab spacing, use the down arrow at the right of this field to reduce the 0.5" setting to, say, 0.2". This setting applies to the whole document,

Figure 4.6 Tab Dialog from Format Menu

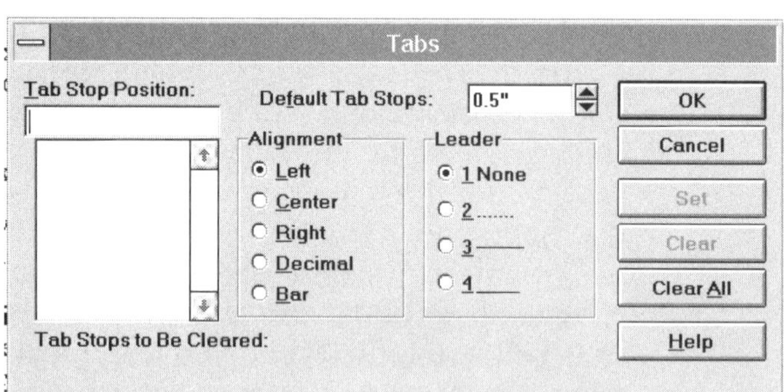

changing the default tab spacing to the new figure. Any tabs you have previously entered are not changed, however.

NOTE: Here's a good reason to use styles for paragraph formatting. If you create a style for indented paragraphs, for example, and one without indents, then you can change the amount of indent on the first line of all indented paragraphs in your document by editing the style.

Now notice the Tab Stop Position window on the left of this dialog. As you add new tab settings, the new settings are added to this window. Suppose you want to add two tab stops at specific locations for some special formatting. To place special tab stops at 3 inches and 7 inches, for example, do this:

- Select Format and choose Tabs... to display the Tab dialog.
- Select existing tabs in the Tab Stop Position window, if any, and click on Clear to remove them.
- Click in the Tab Stop Position field to place the insertion point and type **3**.
- Click on Set.
- Click in the Tab Stop Position field and type **7**.
- Click on Set.

NOTE: If you do not clear the existing tab settings, then the tab stops you add in this step will appear in addition to existing ones. You may want to leave a tab stop at 0.5" to keep the same initial tab setting you have used in other parts of the document, for example.

The tab stops you add by entering discrete values in the Tab Stop Position field apply only to the current paragraph and to subsequent paragraphs when you press Enter to open a new paragraph based on the current paragraph formatting. If you make a tab change in this way on the last line of the document, then any paragraphs you add after that point will contain the same tab stops because as you press Enter for a new paragraph, the current paragraph formatting is copied to the next one. On the other hand, if you move into the document—anywhere above the last line—and make such a change, then only the paragraphs you add between the change location and the next previously existing paragraph will contain the new formatting.

Notice that there are two other groups of settings on this dialog, one for tab alignment and one for tab leader. A *tab leader* is the character that appears in the spacing before the tab. If you have tab stops set every half inch, for example, and press the Tab key, the insertion point jumps ahead from the present position one-half inch. With no tab leader set, all you'll see between the current cursor position and the next tab stop is blank space. If you choose a dot leader, however, then Word inserts a series of dots to fill up the space to the next tab stop. Figure 4.7 shows a portion of a document with no tab leaders. Figure 4.8 shows the same document with dot leaders.

You can use this type of tab leader between a topic and a page number or to connect other items in a list. Setting a tab

Figure 4.7 Tab-Separated Document with No Leaders

Tab Setting Comparison

Accounting	Room 401
Astronomy	Room 406
Bible	Room 312
Botany	Room 408
Business	Room 402
Environment	Room 516
Music	Room D-12

Figure 4.8 Tab-Separated Document with Dot Leaders

Tab Setting Comparison

Accounting.....................Room 401
Astronomy......................Room 406
Bible...............................Room 312
Botany............................Room 408
Business ....Room 402
Environment...................Room 516
Music ....Room D-12

leader in conjunction with a custom tab stop, you can build such a list easily. Other choices for tab leader are dashed line and solid line.

Tab alignment is the final choice for settings in this dialog. By default, Word sets tab alignment to Left. With this dialog you can set alignment to Center, Right, Decimal, and Bar. Here's how the alignment works. With Left alignment, when you start typing after pressing the Tab key, characters start at the location of the tab and move to the right. Existing text that you tab to a left-aligned position jumps to the tab stop with the leftmost portion of the text lined up with the tab location. Left alignment is the normal text alignment for all Word tabs.

With Right alignment, when you start typing after pressing the Tab key, characters start at the tab location and move to the left. Figure 4.9 shows two pieces of text. The LLLLLLLLL text is lined up on a left-aligned tab set at 3 inches. The RRRRRRRRR text is lined up on a right-aligned tab set at 3 inches.

Similarly, you can align tabs at the Center, or you can choose Decimal alignment. Choose Decimal alignment if you want to line up a column of numbers at the decimal point. Finally, choose Bar alignment if you want Word to place a vertical Bar in your document at the tab position.

In addition to the Tab dialog, Word supports tab maintenance through the ruler. You can also use the ruler to review existing tab stop settings. The ruler doesn't show any document-wide settings, such as the built-in half-inch default tab.

Figure 4.9 Left- and Right-Aligned Tab Comparison

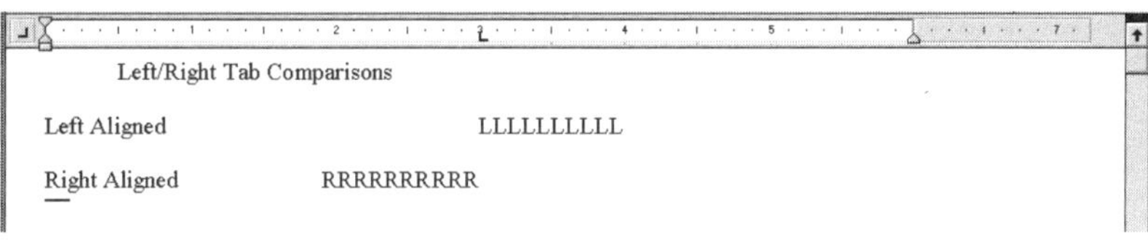

But you can see any tab stops you add. Not only does the ruler show tab positioning, but you can tell from the ruler how the tabs are aligned.

Consider the ruler in Figure 4.10. I've placed one tab of each possible type on the ruler and labeled them.

To use the ruler for tab stop maintenance, do this:

- If the ruler is not already displayed, click on View and choose Ruler from the main menu to turn it on. Unless you have added custom tabs to your document, you won't see any tab symbols on the ruler.
- Notice the "L" symbol at the far left of the ruler. This indicates that left-aligned tabs are the default.
- Use the mouse to point to the number 2 on the ruler and click the left mouse button. The small "L" symbol is inserted on the ruler over the number 2, indicating that a new, left-aligned tab has been placed at the 2-inch mark. This new tab is set for the current paragraph only.

Figure 4.10 Ruler with Tab Types Labeled

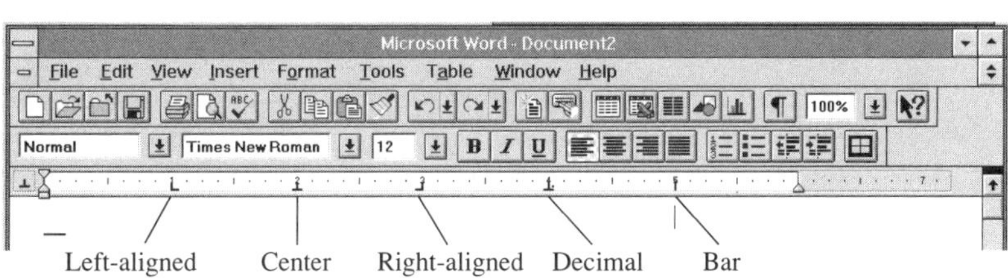

- You can remove any tab stop on the ruler by grabbing the symbol with the mouse and dragging it off the ruler. When you remove a tab symbol from the ruler, any tabs set in the current paragraph are removed and the text reverts to the non-tab position.
- Click on the "L" symbol at the far left of the ruler. The symbol changes to an upside down "T," indicating center alignment (as shown in Figure 4.10). If you click anywhere on the ruler now, you will place a center-aligned tab.
- Click on the symbol again and it changes to a backward "L," indicating a right-aligned tab. Another click produces a bar-tab symbol, and one more click returns to the left-aligned symbol.

Line Spacing

The default Word line spacing is Single, so that lines of text are positioned one under the other. You can change this setting easily. Click on Format and choose Paragraph to display the Paragraph dialog. Pull down the Line Spacing list to display the available line spacing options, shown in Figure 4.11.

Figure 4.11 Paragraph Dialog with Line Spacing Options

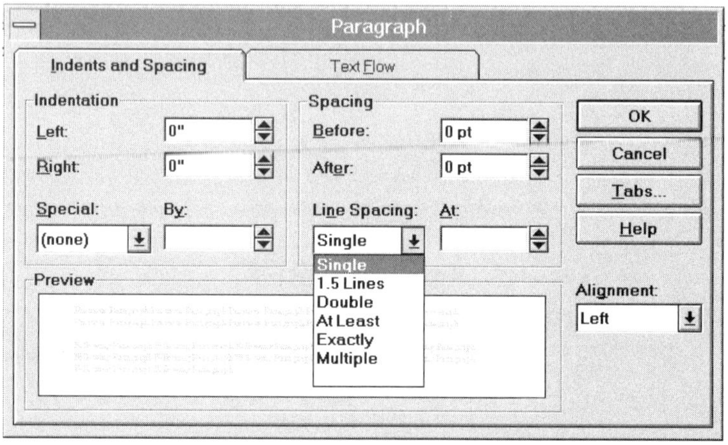

In addition to Single, you can choose 1.5 Lines and Double as standard line spacing. Then you can specify line spacing by points. Click on At Least, for example, and a number that corresponds to the point size of the current text appears in the field to the right of the pull-down list. If you are using 12-point text, then the number 12 appears in the field to the right. This is the same as single spacing, since it moves the next line of text 12 points below the current line. If you change the size of the font on the current line, line spacing will adjust to match.

You can experiment with line spacing by changing the number at the right of the pull-down list. Choose Exactly to have Word make the line spacing static, even if you change the size of the font on the current line. And, use Multiple if you want to specify more than double spacing. Three is the default for this setting, but you can specify up to 132 lines in this section.

Bullets

Use bullet lists (such as I have shown in this chapter) to present short lines of instructions or lists of items. Create a bullet list by starting each item in the list on a new line. End each line with a carriage return.

Then select all of the lines you want to include in the list and click on the Bullet List icon on the standard toolbar. You can also use the Format, Bullets and Numbering command sequence to display the Bullets and Numbering dialog, shown in Figure 4.12.

When you click on the Bullet List icon on the toolbar, Word chooses the default bullet for the current list. If you want to use another symbol for the bullets, then call up the Bullets and Numbering dialog. From this dialog you can choose one of the existing bullet styles, or use the Modify button to change the bullet symbol in one or more of the sample lists.

If you click on Modify, you will see the secondary dialog shown in Figure 4.13.

This dialog is straightforward. You can choose one of the existing bullets in this dialog to replace the one you selected from the previous screen. You can also set the bullet color, spacing from the text, and so on.

In addition, if you want to use another symbol for the bullet, click on the Bullet button to display the Symbol dialog shown in Figure 4.14.

Figure 4.12 Bullets and Numbering Dialog

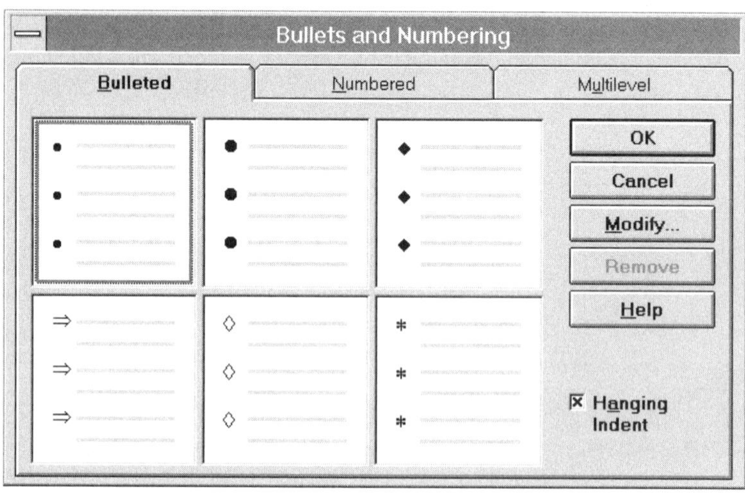

Figure 4.13 Modify Bulleted List Dialog

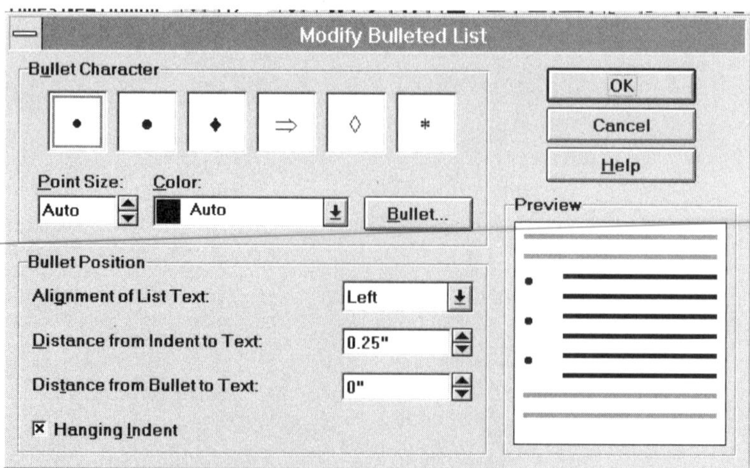

Figure 4.14 Bullet Symbol Dialog

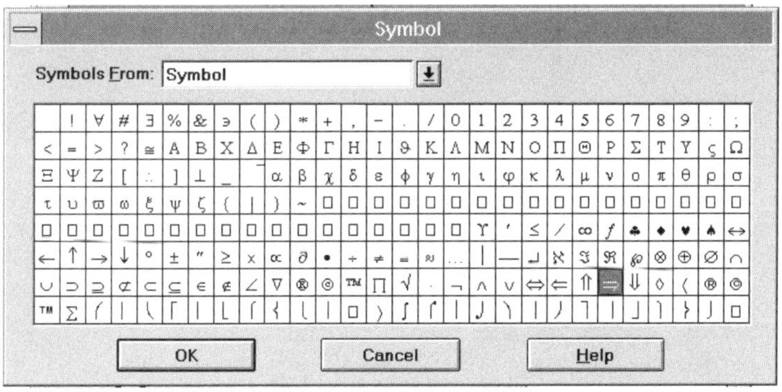

Click on a symbol in this dialog to review it. Word enlarges the symbol to make it easier to see. When you have located the symbol you want to use as a bullet, click on OK to close the Symbol dialog and place the selected bullet in the current bullet window. You can now choose this bullet to have it appear in the Bullets and Numbering dialog.

Numbers

You can create numbered lists in much the same way as bullet lists. Create a series of paragraphs with sentences, phrases, or words you want to number, select the list with the mouse, then click on the Number icon on the standard toolbar to have Word automatically number the items.

In addition, you can choose Bullets and Numbering... from the Format menu after you have selected the text in the list to display the Bullets and Numbering dialog (refer to Figure 4.12). This is a tabbed dialog with Bulleted in the front. Click on the Numbered tab to bring the numbered list information to the front of the dialog, as shown in Figure 4.15.

As with bullet lists, you can choose a numbering style from the main Numbered tab, or you can choose Modify to display the Modify Numbered List dialog shown in Figure 4.16.

Figure 4.15 Numbered Tab from Bullets and Numbering Dialog

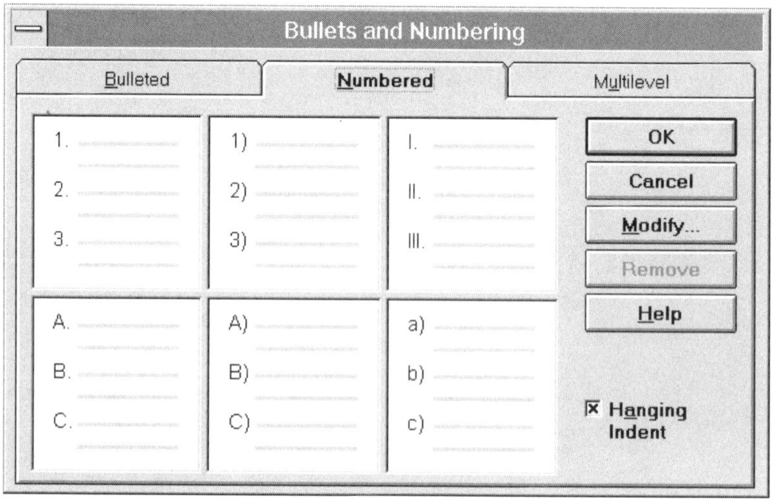

Figure 4.16 Modify Numbered List Dialog

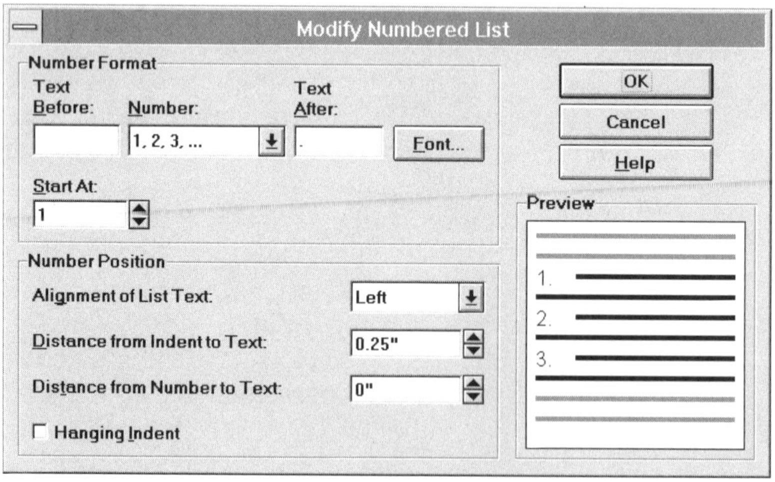

You can pull down a list of available numbering formats, including roman numerals, alphabetical, or number in words. In addition, you can specify text to appear before and after each number. This can be symbols, punctuation, or text. When you have finished the formatting you want in this dialog, click on OK to return to your document with the specified numbering style enabled.

Checking Spelling

Word includes a built-in dictionary with thousands of words. When you have finished typing your document, use the Tools, Spelling command sequence to start the Word spell checker. Word starts checking the spelling in your document at the location of the insertion point and runs to the end of the document. Once Word reaches the end of the document, the spell check starts at the top and continues to the starting point.

You won't see anything on the screen unless Word locates a word it thinks is misspelled. Then you'll see the dialog shown in Figure 4.17.

You have several choices for handling a word that may be misspelled. If the selected word is a specialty word or a name, then you want Word to ignore it this time and every other time

Figure 4.17 Misspelled Word Dialog

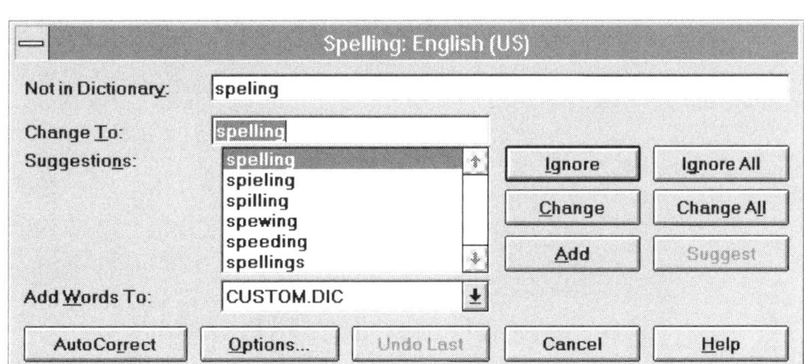

when it is found. Click on Ignore All and Word won't tell you about that word anywhere else in the document.

In the Suggestions window, Word displays a list of possible words to replace the marked word. If one of the suggested words is the right replacement, select the word and click on Change to have Word place the selected word in your document in place of the one marked as incorrect. If that word appears elsewhere in your document you can click on Change All to have Word correct every occurrence of the word in the current document.

NOTE: If Word seems to check your document too quickly and does not report any misspelled words, it probably means that the text in the document is set as No Proofing. Select all of the text in the document by triple-clicking in the left margin of the document, then use Tools, Language to specify English. Now you can run the spell check again.

On the other hand, if Word has marked a word as incorrect that is one you use regularly, click on Add and Word will add the word to your personal dictionary. When the word is encountered again, Word recognizes it as correct.

If you change your mind about the most recent change, click on Undo Last, and the Options button displays a dialog that lets you specify some configuration settings for the Word spell checker.

You can stop the spelling process at any time by clicking on Cancel. You can click outside the Spelling dialog to edit the document, then click on Resume to pick up the spell check where you left off.

Special Characters and Symbols

I showed under Bullets and Numbering how to use special characters for a bullet list. You can use this same dialog to insert special characters anywhere in your document. Use Insert, Symbol... to display the dialog in Figure 4.18.

This is a tabbed dialog that includes a tab for preformatted special characters such as copyright and trademark symbols. Click on the Special Characters tab to display a list of these characters.

Figure 4.18 Symbol Dialog

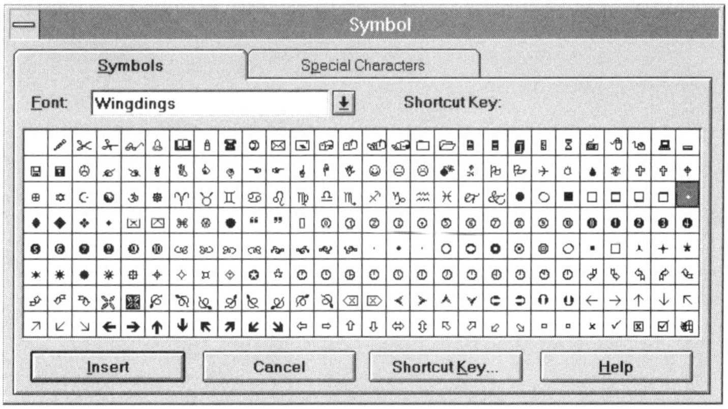

The Symbols tab, on the other hand, shows available symbols from a variety of font groups. You can select from a pull-down list of available fonts, then select a symbol to have Word enlarge it to make it easier to view. Click on Insert when you have located the symbol you want to insert at the location of the insertion point.

You can also use this dialog to create a shortcut key for a selected symbol. Simply select the symbol, one you will use regularly in the current document, and click on the Shortcut Key button on the Symbol dialog. You will see the standard Word Customize dialog (Figure 4.19). Press the keyboard combination you want to use as the shortcut key for the selected symbol and click on Assign.

Inserting Fields

A Word *field* is a variable storage location that lets you insert such objects as dates or page number information. I showed you earlier in this chapter how to insert a field for date and time data. Well, there are other Word fields you might want to use as well.

Figure 4.19 Word Customize Dialog

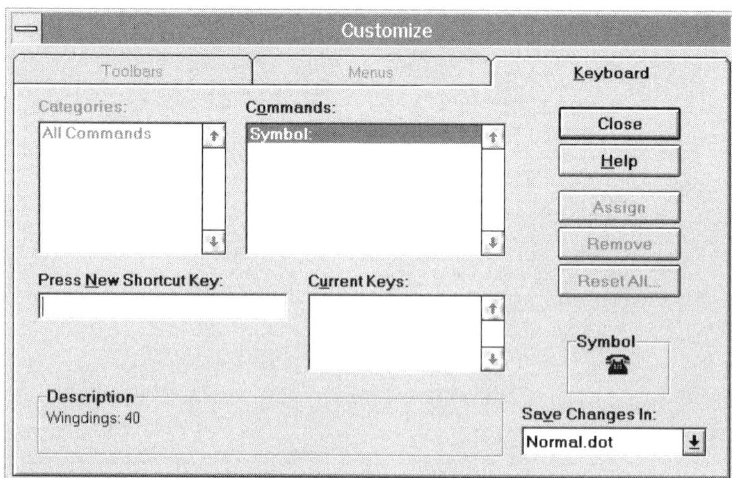

NOTE: If you try to remove a field code by pressing Backspace or Del, Word will beep and the field will not be removed. To delete a Word field code, use the mouse or Shift+Arrow to mark the field (select it), then press Del.

Page Number Field

You can insert a variable field in a Word document to report the current page number. In many cases you will want this field to appear in a header or footer, but you can place it anywhere in a Word document.

To insert a page number field into a document,

- Position the cursor where you want the page number to appear.
- Issue the Insert, Field... command to display the Field dialog, shown in Figure 4.20.
- Click on Numbering in the Categories list on the left side of the dialog to display the available number fields.

Figure 4.20 Field Dialog

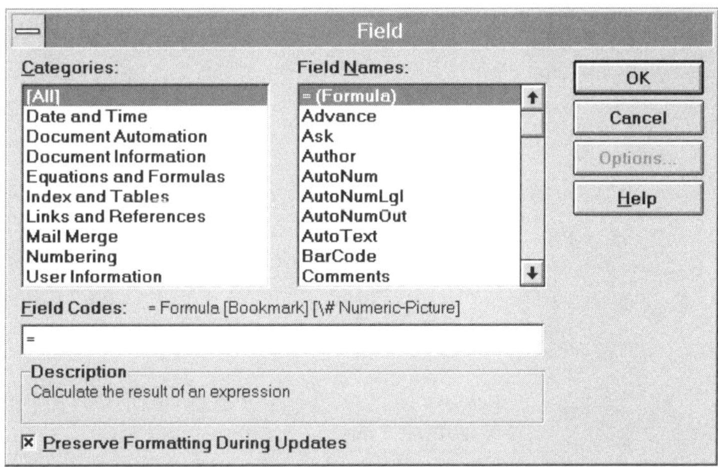

- Click on Page to insert a page number field. The current page number appears in your document at the location of the insertion point.

Unless you have changed the display defaults, fields in Word documents appear as the values they represent. A page number field displays the number of the current page, for example, or a date field displays the current system date, and so on.

If you move the cursor over the field, or point to it with the mouse, Word shows the field as a colored box.

*NOTE: You can turn on field displays by selecting Tools from the main Word menu and choosing Options. In the Options dialog, the View tab should be on top. Click on the Field Codes box on this tab to turn on Field Code view. Now date/time fields appear as {TIME @ "M/d/yy"}, and page numbers are shown as {PAGE *MERGEFORMAT}.*

Author Field

You can insert field data to report on the author of the current document as well. The process is the same: Position the cursor, use Insert, Field... and choose Document Information to display a list of document data you can insert, including the author code.

When you insert an author code, the name that appears is what you have stored as part of Word's profile data. You can insert data in this section to change what Word reports as the author and other information by selecting Tools and choosing Options... to display the Options dialog. Click on the User Info tab of this dialog to show the current profile information.

NOTE: As you can see by viewing the information on the Field dialog, there are many more fields in Word than I have discussed here. They work pretty much the same as these. Notice in particular the Filename field, which you can use in headers and footers to help you track the source of a printed document.

Page Formatting

You can change the way Word documents appear on the screen and how they print. And, although Word is fairly true to its WYSIWYG (what you see is what you get) design, there are times, with some combinations of fonts and other objects, as well as with certain printer drivers, that what you see varies slightly from what is printed. You can use Print Preview to correct the differences on the screen before you print.

Changing the Document View

When you first load Word it is configured for Normal view. This is the best view for typing text and to begin document formatting. Page Layout view, on the other hand, is used when inserting graphics and when you want to view the document on the screen the way it will appear when printed.

Normal View (General Text Editing) To select the Normal view, or any other view, select View and choose Normal from the pull-down menu. In Normal view, you will see fonts on-screen, but page breaks appear as a dotted line instead of a graphical page. And, graphic images and other objects don't appear in the proper position within your document.

The advantage of Normal view is the compact nature of the display, and the speed of the Word screen response. Obviously,

Figure 4.21 Document Fragment in Normal View

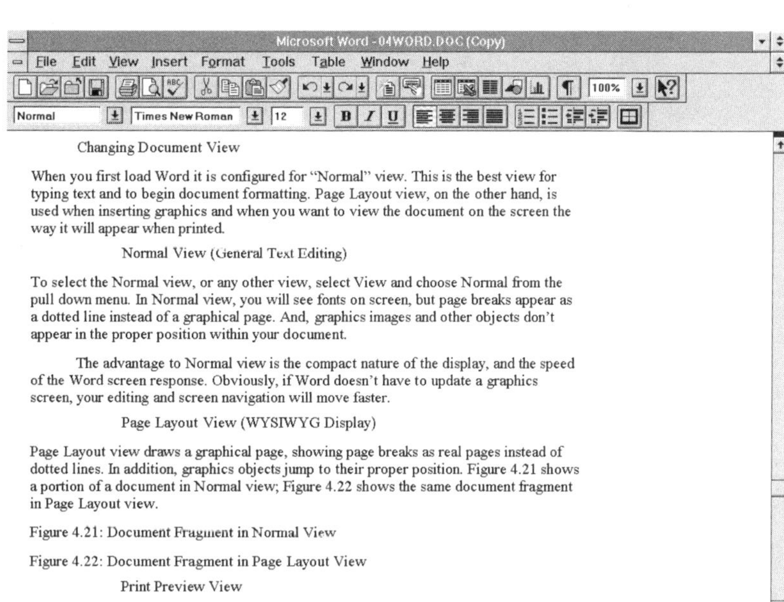

if Word doesn't have to update a graphics screen, your editing and screen navigation will move faster.

Page Layout View (WYSIWYG Display) Page Layout view draws a graphical page, showing page breaks as real pages instead of dotted lines. In addition, graphic objects jump to their proper position. Figure 4.21 shows a portion of a document in Normal view; Figure 4.22 shows the same document fragment in Page Layout view.

Print Preview View The Print Preview view is a modified Page Layout view. When you choose Print Preview from the File menu (or click on the Print Preview icon on the Word standard toolbar), Word opens the Print Preview screen and shrinks the display page so you can view a whole page on the screen at once (see Figure 4.23).

Figure 4.22 Document Fragment in Page Layout View

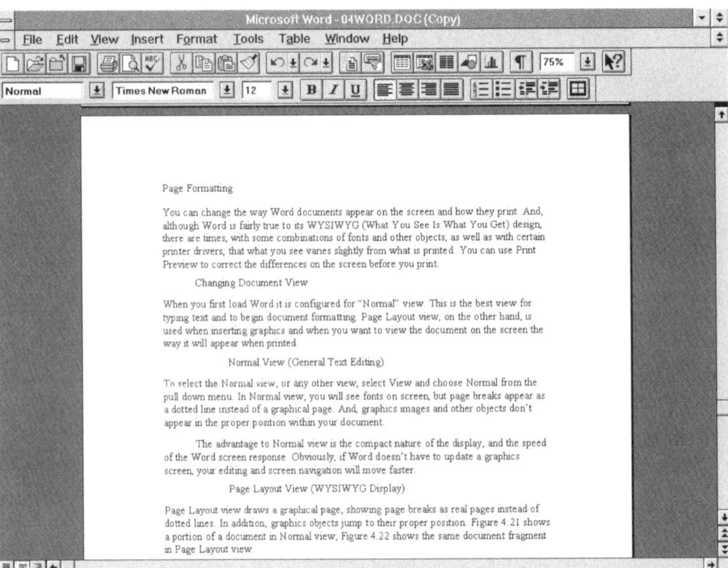

You can use Print Preview to see how your document pagination works as well as how a single page appears. To view more than a single page, click on the Multipage icon on the Print Preview toolbar. A six-page window pops up so you can choose how many pages you want to view at once. Click on the second page at the top of the pull-down, and Word displays two pages side by side (1 x 2). Click on the far right page on the bottom row, and Word displays six pages (3 x 3). Figure 4.24 shows a six-page Print Preview display.

The percentage field beside the Multipage icon shows the size of the displayed pages. If you move the cursor over one of the Print Preview pages, it changes to a magnifying glass. Click on the document and Word enlarges it to 100 percent so you can see the full page up close.

To close the Print Preview screen, click on Close and Word returns to the document in the view that was current when you switched to Print Preview.

Figure 4.23 Word Print Preview Screen

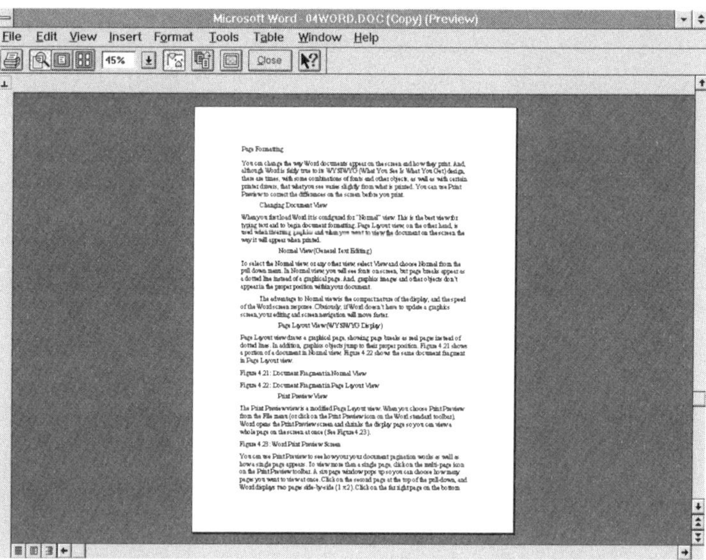

Outline View The Outline view lets you manipulate your Word document so you can view different parts of it. Although the name sounds like you would use this view only when creating outlines, that's not true. Outline view lets you shrink and expand document levels so you can view just major headings, subheadings, or the entire document.

For Outline view to be successful you need to use Word's standard heading styles for your document titles and subtitles. You don't have to accept Word's default formatting for these headings, but you do need to use heading styles for Outline view.

When you switch to Outline view with the View, Outline command sequence, Word inserts an additional toolbar under the format toolbar (see Figure 4.25).

The numbers on the Outline toolbar indicate what level you want to view. If you click on 1, you will see only lines formatted with Heading 1 formatting, the top-level divisions. Click

Figure 4.24 Word Six-Page Print Preview Display

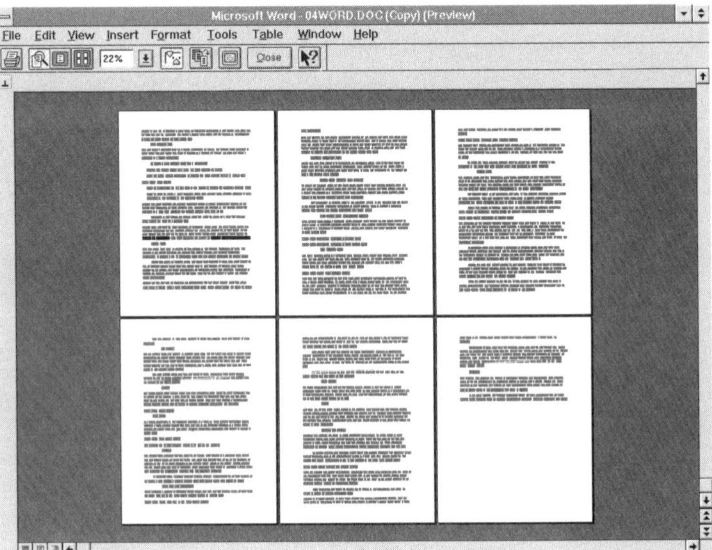

on 2 to see the first two levels, and so on. Try this with a fairly long document. By eliminating everything except the headings you get an excellent overview of your document. Click on 1 and you see only the main headings; step down one level to view the secondary subheads as well.

In addition, when you display a document in Outline view, you can edit large sections easily. Suppose you decide that an entire second-level section toward the end of the document should be moved up toward the top. You need only move the heading, and the text and subheads associated with the heading will move with it.

Notice the plus and minus buttons on the Outline toolbar. Use these to expand or compress a single outline section. Place the cursor on the heading you want to expand and click on the plus button. Word opens up only this section of the outline, revealing the levels beneath the line where the cursor resides.

Figure 4.25 Word Document in Outline View

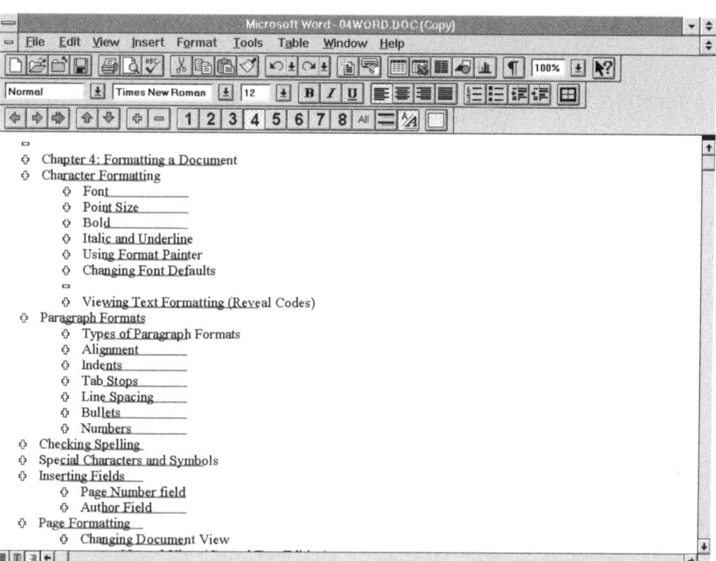

The arrow buttons at the far left of the toolbar let you change the level of outline components. The left/right arrows promote and demote outline elements. The up and down arrow keys move elements up or down in the outline.

Use File, Normal or File, Page Layout to close the Outline view and return to your document.

Full Screen View The Full Screen view will appeal to writers who long for the good old days of simple word processors, when screens were sparse and the word was the thing. Choose Full Screen from the View menu and Word removes the status bar, the menu bar, and other screen objects. All you see is your document and a small Full Screen icon that will let you return to the regular Word screen.

The Full Screen view lets you see more of your document and, some people believe, lets you be more creative without

Figure 4.26 Zoom Dialog

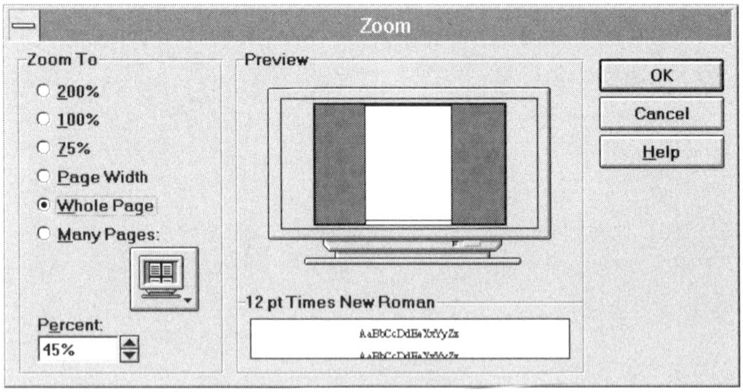

the distractions of the toolbars and menus that are normal on the Word screen.

Zoom The Zoom dialog (Figure 4.26) lets you determine how much of your document will be visible on the screen. If you click on Full Page, for example, you can see an entire page as you work, but the text will be pretty small. You can also specify a larger-than-normal display, which can be useful in editing graphics placement, for example.

Page Setup

In a sense, everything covered in this chapter so far is a form of page layout. However, Word includes a Page Layout dialog that you can use to set specific features of a Word page. Display the dialog with the File, Page Setup... command sequence. The dialog is shown in Figure 4.27. The Margins tab of this four-tab dialog is on top of the display.

Margins The default page margins are 1 inch on the top and bottom and 1.25 inches on the left and right. This results in a pleasing page layout that still leaves plenty of room for your text. You can change any or all of the margins by clicking on

Figure 4.27 Page Setup Dialog

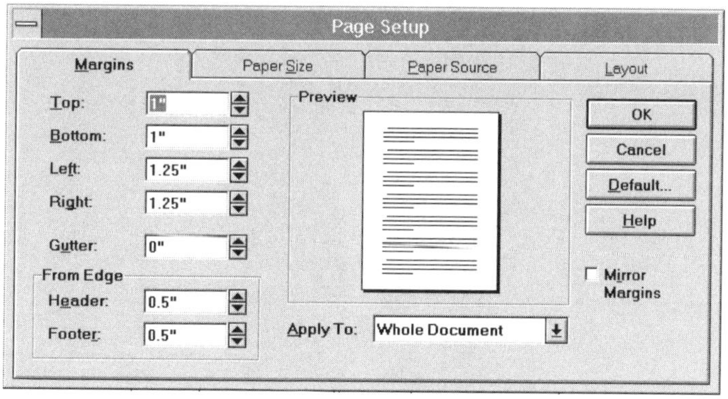

the up or down arrows in the margin value fields or by typing values directly into the fields. Just use care in changing page margins. You want to maintain a fairly close ratio between the top/bottom margins and the left/right margins.

In addition, most modern printers require around a three-tenths of an inch margin on all edges. If you specify a margin smaller than this, Word likely will report an error.

Paper Size and Orientation Word supports a variety of standard page sizes, and you can set custom sizes as well from the Paper Size tab of the Page Setup dialog, shown in Figure 4.28.

Click on the down-arrow to the right of the Paper Size field to pull down a list of standard paper sizes. Choose the paper you want to use for the current document from this list, or enter the paper height and width in the fields below.

This dialog also lets you specify the page orientation, portrait or landscape. *Portrait* orientation is for standard pages where the typing starts at the top of the long edge of the paper and moves down. When you have long lines or graphics to print, however, you may want to turn the page 90 degrees, to *landscape* orientation, so the left-to-right page is the widest part.

As you adjust values on this tab, the Preview window on the right side of this dialog shows you the result of any changes.

Figure 4.28 Paper Size Tab of the Page Setup Dialog

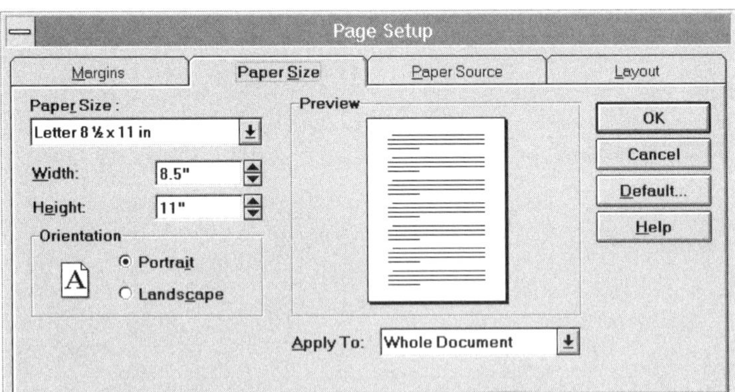

Paper Source For most documents you will let the printer decide where to get the paper it feeds. However, there may be times when you will want to load special paper in a secondary bin to feed letterhead, colored paper, and the like. Use the information on the Paper Source tab of the Page Setup dialog to do this.

Layout The final tab on the Page Setup dialog is for Layout. This dialog lets you specify where section breaks occur, how headers and footers will be handled (see the next section), and so on. For most of us, the main reason for using this dialog is to specify settings for the headers and footers. Experiment with this and other settings to see how they affect the layout of your document.

Headers and Footers Headers and footers are used to place repetitive information on every page of your document. Word sets aside special sections to make room for this data at the top and bottom of each page. Normally you will use headers and footers for page numbers, document or section titles, author information, dates, document versions, and the like.

To create headers and footers, select View and choose Headers and Footers. Word places document text in the background, turning it a light gray, and places boxes for the header and footer information at the top and bottom of the page (see Figure 4.29).

With the header and footer information displayed, you can't type anything into the body of the document. You can only enter data inside one of the header or footer boxes. Move between header and footer by using the scroll bars at the right of the Word screen, by pressing Alt+Up Arrow or Alt+Down Arrow, or by using the icons on the Header and Footer toolbar.

Type whatever you want to appear on all pages of the document, and click on Close to return to the document view.

NOTE: It is good practice to keep your header and footer information smaller than the body copy. A difference in size of about four points is usually a pretty good ratio. If your body copy is 12 points, then make header and footer information 8-point type, for example. You can use the same character formatting features in the header and footer area as you use with the rest of the document.

Regardless of what page you are viewing when you call up the header and footer screen, the information you place into the header and footer areas will appear on all pages. You can make

Figure 4.29 Word Header and Footer Screen

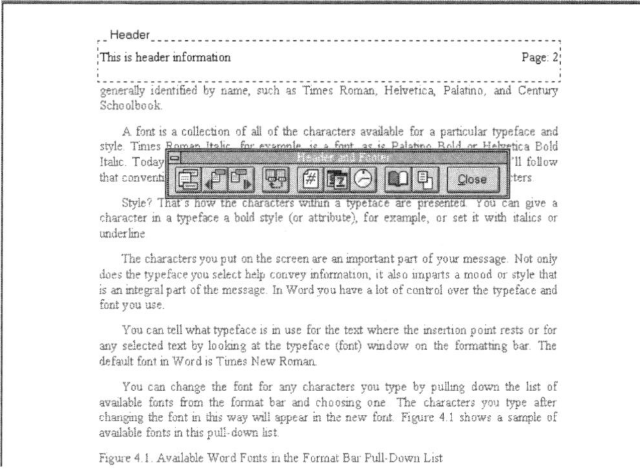

the first page have a separate header and footer, however, by clicking on Different First Page on the Page Setup Layout tab. Word also supports different header and footer information on odd and even pages. Just click that box on the Page Setup Layout dialog.

Summary

This chapter has covered the basics of document creation and formatting. This doesn't cover all of the possibilities of document design in Word, but if you master the major sections of this chapter, you should be very comfortable with Word and you should be able to create most of the documents you need.

In the next chapter I'll provide additional detail on page formatting and on using special Word features such as snaking (newspaper) columns, matched columns, and more.

Chapter 5

Page Layout

I discussed page layout a little in Chapter 4. Remember that Word helps you design a basic document page automatically. The intrinsic formatting and layout that are provided as defaults within the Normal template take care of basic layout. However, as your document needs change, you'll probably want to experiment with more variety in your designs. I'll touch on a few issues in this chapter that will carry you to the next level with Microsoft Word.

Using Newspaper Columns

Think about how you read a newspaper or newsletter. Each page consists of relatively narrow columns. You read the left-most column top to bottom, then you start at the top of the next column and read down. Of course, sometimes a story is continued on another page, but basically, so-called *newspaper* or *snaking columns* are made up of text in narrow columns that read top to bottom in sequential columns.

In earlier word processing software, designing columns could be a lengthy and sometimes difficult process. Word, on the other hand, supports this type of page layout rather well, making the chore easy to learn and to do. Newspaper columns can take multiple forms: columns of equal width, columns of unequal width, multiple column styles within a single document. In Word, however, when you want to use columns for lists of data where information in the left column must match up with information in the right column, you use a table instead of straight columns.

I'll discuss each of these column options in the following sections.

Columns of Equal Width

The simplest column format in Word is newspaper columns of equal width. You can set up columns when you start a new document, or you can enter the text for a document and format it in columns later. Either way, you simply place the insertion point where you want columns to begin, select Format from the main Word menu and choose Columns. The Columns dialog shown in Figure 5.1 is presented.

Figure 5.1 Columns Dialog

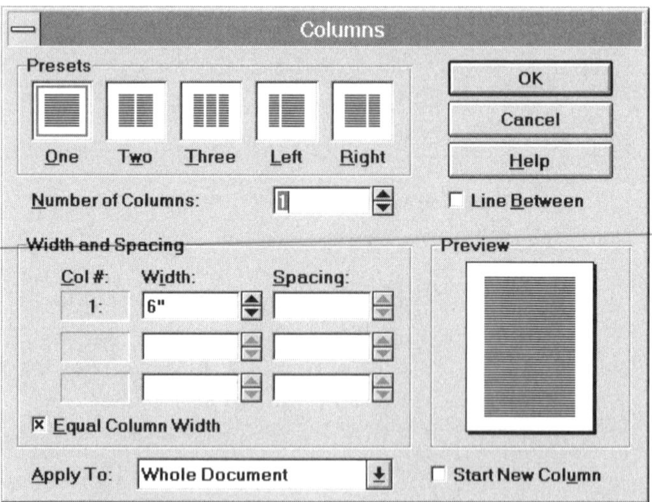

As you can see from Figure 5.1, Word sets up some column configurations automatically. Notice the sample page at the far left on the top row of this dialog. This is the Word document default, a single-column page. If you're starting with a document that contains text, you can experiment with different column configurations by clicking on the different choices.

Click on the second window, which represents a two-column page layout. Word shows the column configuration in the lower part of the dialog. When you choose a two-column layout, for example, Word selects a 2.75-inch column width with half an inch between them. Because the Equal Column Width button is checked, you know that both columns will be 2.75 inches wide. You can see how the pages will appear in the Preview window at the lower right corner of this dialog. When you click on OK in this dialog, Word formats your document with dual columns (see Figure 5.2).

The Apply To: field at the bottom of the Columns dialog specifies how much of the document will receive the new column formatting. The default is Whole Document. If you want to start dual columns from the current cursor position (as you might if you want to have an opening page or section that uses the entire page width), then pull down the list and choose This Point Forward.

NOTE: As you work with columns, think about the overall page design. Two columns of 2.75 inches accounts for 5.5 inches of a standard page. The half inch between columns makes the total width 6 inches. When you add the standard Word 1.25-inch left and right margins, you've used up the full 8.5-inch page.

Another optional setting in this dialog is Line Between. With this button checked, Word inserts a rule (thin line) in the space between the columns.

Choosing three columns is as easy as choosing two. Simply click on the sample window at the top of the dialog that has three columns in it. The data at the bottom of the screen that shows column width changes to reflect how Word will format your document when you click on OK to close this dialog.

I'll show you a little later how to customize Word column formatting, but the easiest way to use newspaper columns is to select two or three columns, click on OK, and start typing.

Figure 5.2 Sample Document with Two Columns

inches wide. You can also see how the pages will appear in the Preview window at the lower right corner of this dialog. When you click on OK on this dialog Word formats your document with dual columns (See Page 5.2)

Figure 5.2: Sample Document With Two Columns

The Apply to: field at the bottom of this dialog specifies how much of the document will receive the new column formatting. The default is Whole Document. If you want to start dual columns from the current cursor position (as you might if you want to have an opening page or section that uses the entire page width) then pull down the list and choose "This Point Forward."

NOTE: As you work with columns, think about the overall page design. Two columns of 2.75 accounts for 5.5 inches of a standard page. The half inch between columns makes the total width 6 inches. Then when you add the standard Word 1.25-inch left and right margins, you've used up the full 8.5-inch page.

Another optional setting on this dialog is "Line Between." With this button checked, Word inserts a rule (thin line) in the space between the columns.

Choosing three columns is as easy as two. Simply click on the sample window at the top of the dialog that has three columns in it. The data at the bottom of the screen that shows column width changes to reflect how Word will format your document when you click on OK to close this dialog.

I'll show you a little later how to customize Word column formatting but the easiest way to use newspaper columns is to select two or three columns, click on OK, and start typing.

NOTE: If you are viewing your document in Normal mode, columns will be stacked or in a single, long column. You won't see the columns across the page. To work with column formatting as it will appear when printed, switch to Page Layout formatting by selecting View and choosing Page Layout.

Again, this type of column formatting is designed for newspaper or snaking columns. A two-column page, for

NOTE: If you are viewing your document in Normal mode, columns will be displayed stacked or in a single, long column. You won't see the columns across the page. To work with column formatting as it will appear when printed, switch to Page Layout formatting by selecting View and choosing Page Layout.

Again, this type of column formatting is designed for newspaper or snaking columns. A two-column page, for example, splits the page in two and places the information that once stretched across 7 inches or so into two 2.75-inch columns. The flow of text is from the top of the leftmost column, down the page to the end of this column, then to the top of the rightmost column and down the page.

The text on the next page starts at the top of the leftmost column, moves to the top of the second column, and on and on.

A similar arrangement exists for pages with more than two columns. The page is split as I described above, but three columns are used instead of two, or four columns, and so on.

Using Tables for Matched Columns

There is another kind of column layout that you may find useful. Matched columns are used when you want information in the left column to match up with an explanation in the right column. In Word, this kind of column layout is accomplished with a two-column table.

Suppose you have a list of products or services that you want to describe in a two-column page layout. Position the cursor where you want the two-column layout to begin and click on the table icon on the standard toolbar to pull down a grid of table cells. Pull down a two-column table with as many rows as you think you will need for the list. If you guess wrong, don't worry. You can insert additional rows if you need to, and you can remove any rows you have left over.

NOTE: Word's table feature places dotted lines along table cell borders to help you enter data, but these lines don't print when you send your document to the printer. If you want to insert lines around your data, use the border toolbar by clicking on the border symbol on the format bar. Use Table, Select Table to highlight all cells in the table, then click on outline or full cell borders to create the line pattern you want to use.

You can use this same technique for more than two columns that need to be aligned across a page. You might want to create a price list that shows part number, description, and price, for example, in a three-column page layout. When you create a table in Word, the software automatically adjusts cell width to fit the page.

Using Sections for Multiple-Column Layouts within the Same Document

Normally when you create a column layout with the Format, Columns... command, whatever layout you choose—two columns, three columns, and so on—will apply to the entire document. Whether you create the columns before entering data, or turn on column display after you have entered the text for your document, Word will turn on multiple column displays for the entire document.

There may be times, however, when you want a full-page layout in part of your document and multiple columns elsewhere. You may want a full page for the title page of a newsletter, for example, with multicolumn pages for the rest of the publication. You can do this by creating different sections within your document for the different layouts.

In fact, the Word Column dialog will handle this type of setup for you. On the Column dialog, there is a pull-down list that lets you choose how much of the current document will be formatted with the specified column layout. The default choice is Whole Document, but also on the list is This Point Forward. If you choose this option from the Apply To: pull-down list, Word creates a new section to hold the column formatting. Pages ahead of the current cursor position will retain their original formatting.

Now, suppose you want to stop column layout later in the document and return to a full-page layout. You just need to create a new section after the multiple-column pages. The Columns dialog will do that for you, too. Here's how:

- Position the cursor where you want to start the new page formatting, whether it is a return to a single column (full-page layout), or to increase the number of columns.
- Use Format, Columns... to display the Columns dialog.
- Pull down the Apply To: list at the bottom of the dialog. Notice that now the two choices are This Section and This Point Forward.
- Choose This Point Forward and select the type of column formatting you want to start.
- Click on OK to close the Columns dialog and begin the new formatting.

Word inserts a new section break at the cursor and starts the new column formatting.

CREATING COLUMNS OF UNEQUAL WIDTH

So far I've described a multiple-column layout that uses columns of equal length. Word also supports page layouts with columns of unequal width. You can choose the basic layouts from the Columns dialog: one has a small column on the left and a wider column on the right, while a second layout has a wide column on the left and a narrow column on the right. Figure 5.3 shows the Columns dialog after the Left unequal column layout has been chosen.

Notice the settings in the Width and Spacing area of this dialog. The left and smallest column is 1.65 inches wide while the right and widest column is 3.79 inches wide. The standard half-inch spacing between columns is specified.

You can reverse this layout by choosing Right from the Columns dialog. That creates a left column that is 3.79 inches wide

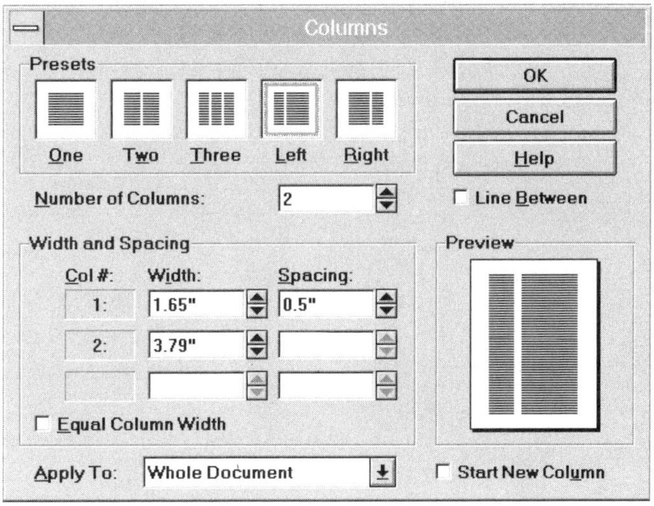

Figure 5.3 Columns Dialog with Left Unequal Columns Layout Selected

and a right column that is 1.65 inches wide. Notice these changes in the Width and Spacing area of the dialog.

You can also create custom columns of your own. You're not limited to just two unequal columns. By specifying the column width you want in the Width and Spacing fields, you can create just about any multicolumn layout you wish.

NOTE: Use care when designing page layouts. The sum of all column widths, between-column spacings, and left and right margins should not add up to more than the width of the page.

Changing Column Width

Of course you aren't stuck with the column settings Word picks for you or that you specified yourself. Simply place the cursor within the column you want to change and bring up the Columns dialog again. Change the settings in the Width and Spacing area of this dialog to produce the column layout you want.

NOTE: You can also display the ruler (View, Ruler) and drag the column markers to adjust column width.

Basic Page Setup

Designing multicolumn pages is just one aspect of page setup and design. There are more basic page design considerations that you have to deal with at some level. Word automatically sets basic page formatting, but you can change things around if you want.

Margins

Whatever size page or paper you are using, you need to allow some room on either side and at the top and bottom. The Normal template specifies a 1-inch margin at the top and bottom of each page, and a 1.25-inch left and right margin. This produces a pleasing overall page layout, but you may have several reasons to adjust this default.

Suppose you have a document that almost fits on one page, but not quite. You can reduce the size of the font slightly, and you can reduce the page margins. If you reduce the left/right margin from 1.25 inches to 1 inch, you have increased the effective width of your page by half an inch.

Choose Page Formatting and click on Margins for interactive instruction on setting page margins.

Setting Exact Margins

For me, the easiest way to set page margins is with the Page Setup dialog, shown in Figure 5.4. Call up this dialog from the File menu (File, Page Setup...).

The Margins tab of this dialog is on top by default. You can change any of the page margins by just typing the new margin information in the proper field, or by using the up and down arrow keys at the right of the field you want to change. Click on OK to close this dialog and effect the margin changes.

Setting Margins with the Ruler

If you prefer a visual way to change margins, use the Word ruler:

- If the ruler isn't already displayed, use the View, Ruler commands to turn it on.
- If Page Layout view is not set, turn it on with the View, Page Layout command sequence.

Figure 5.4 Page Setup Dialog

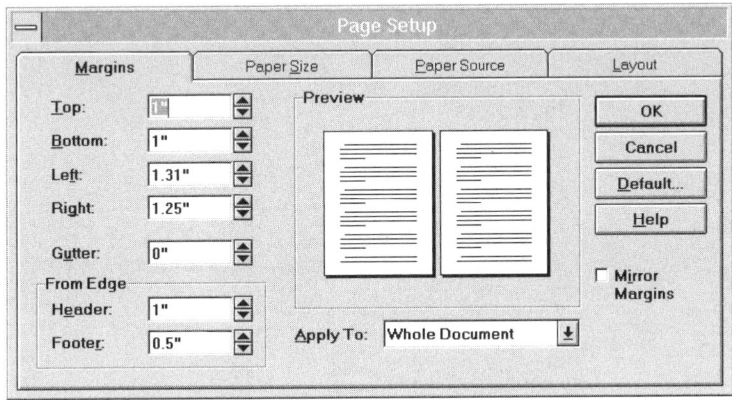

- Move the mouse pointer into the ruler and toward the left or right margin.
- When the pointer turns into a double-ended arrow, press the left mouse button and drag the margin to the new location.
- Release the mouse button.

HEADERS AND FOOTERS

Headers and footers provide a way for placing repetitive information at the top or bottom of your document pages. I introduced the concept of headers and footers in Chapter 4. I'd like to provide a little more detail in this section.

Choose Page Formatting from the CD Directory, then click on the Headers button for interactive help on using headers and footers.

Adding a Header or Footer

I usually like to finish my document, or get it nearly completed, before I add the header and footer. I don't really know why this is, except that to me the header and footer step in document design is like tying a ribbon on the package, finishing the last step. As I think about it, there is no real technical reason to wait to the end to create a header and footer, but that's the way I do it.

Anyway, whether you add the header and footer at the beginning or the end, use the View, Header and Footer... command sequence to display the Header and Footer dialog. This is one dialog in Word that is really different from the rest. For one thing, it is more a toolbar than a dialog, but by default it appears in the middle of your Word screen instead of attaching itself to the toolbars at the top of the screen.

For another thing, when the Header and Footer dialog, or toolbar, appears, the text on your Word screen is dimmed, making the toolbar and the header/footer areas prominent. Notice from the labels in Figure 5.5 that this toolbar provides access to several Word features.

If you haven't already done it, one of the first things you should do when you display the Header and Footer toolbar is

Figure 5.5 Header and Footer Toolbar with Components Labeled

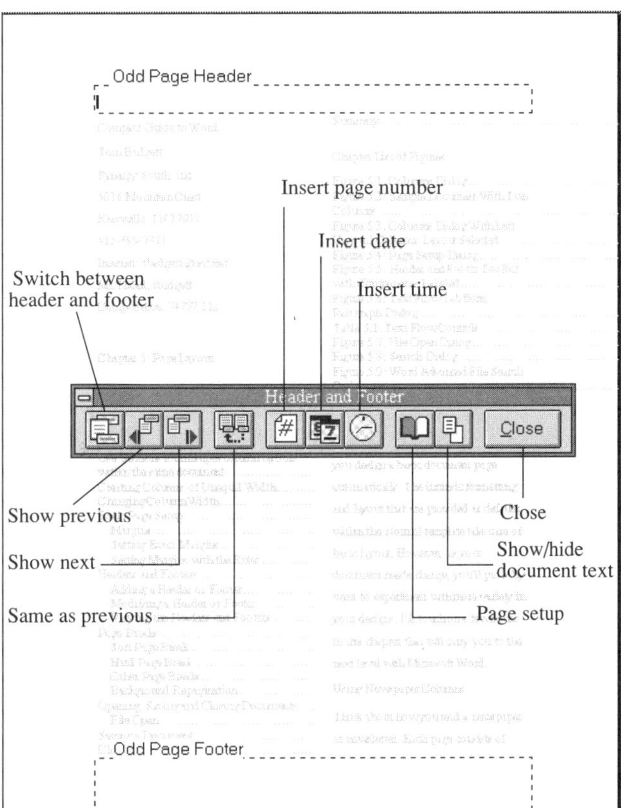

to bring up the Page Setup dialog. Do this by clicking on the Page Setup icon on the Header and Footer toolbar. On the Page Setup dialog click on the Layout tab and click in the box beside Different First Page. This tells Word to separate the first page of your document from the rest as far as the headers and footers are concerned.

After all, you've probably put the document title and other information on the first page anyway. You don't need whatever information you will put in the header or footer on the first page in addition. Even page numbers, dates, and other data common in headers and footers typically don't need to appear on the first page. Click on OK to close the Page Setup dialog and return to your document with the Header and Footer toolbar floating atop the grayed-out text.

NOTE: If you are producing a document that will be printed on both sides of the paper (duplex printing) then you may want to have a different header and footer for the odd and even pages. There is a check box for that on the Layout tab of the Page Setup dialog as well. Choosing a different header and footer for the odd and even pages lets you offset information so that it appears at the outside of the pages, for example. Or you may want chapter or section information on the left pages and document titles on the right.

If you have specified different information for the first page, or for odd and even pages, then you'll need to type separate data in the header and footer areas of these pages. To create a header or footer, display the Header and Footer toolbar, then press the down arrow or up arrow on the keyboard to jump from the header area to the footer and back up again, or use the appropriate icon on the Header and Footer toolbar to switch from header to footer (see Figure 5.5).

With the insertion point within the proper area, you can simply type as if you were typing in the body of the document, and you can use the usual Word formatting features to make the text appear the way you want it. You could even insert graphic images or other objects into the header or footer area if you wish, but use this capability sparingly. The header and footer data in your document should guide the reader, providing information about the type of data being read and its location within a document, not become a major part of the information being conveyed. Remember, this is repetitive data that will appear on more than one page.

Notice again the buttons available on the toolbar (see Figure 5.5). You can insert variable information such as the current page number by clicking on the appropriate icon after placing the insertion point inside the header or footer area where you want this data to appear. The number symbol inserts a page number field when you click on it.

NOTE: When inserting page numbers within a header or footer, you can add other information in front of the number or after it, if you wish. For example, to note that the reader is in section 5 of the current

document, you could type the static data, ***Page 5.*** *and then click the number symbol on the Header and Footer toolbar to insert the variable information for the current page number. This makes the header or footer on page 10 appear as* ***Page 5.10****.*

Beside the page number icon there are two others that let you insert variable data. Immediately to the right of the page number icon is one for the current date and to the right of that is a time icon. Again, these are basically toolbar assignments to the field commands that insert this same information.

In addition, the Header and Footer toolbar includes icons to help you navigate around your document while in Header and Footer view. At the far left of the toolbar is a button for switching between the header and footer areas of the document. If the insertion point is in the header area, for example, and you click this button, the insertion point is placed immediately into the footer area.

To the right of this button are two more navigational buttons. The first jumps to the previous header or footer entry while the second one to the right of the Switch button jumps to the following entry. Notice that this is not to the previous or next page. Rather, this button jumps to the previous header, assuming you have one that is different from the one currently displayed. This is for times when you have a different first page header, for example, or when you have specified different headers for odd and even pages.

The next button, Same as Previous, tells Word to copy the previous header or footer into the current location. Suppose you specify different odd and even page headers and footers, for example, and you have already typed the even page section on page 2 of the document. You jump to page 3, an odd page, and there is no data in the header area. You can copy the previous data by clicking on this button. That lets you make some of the information from odd to even pages the same, and some different, if you want. You might want to copy the odd page header that contains the chapter title and page number, for example, then add more data for the even pages.

Finally, the button just to the left of the Close button lets you hide the grayed-out body copy of the underlying document, if you wish. I personally don't use this button at all, but I could see where it might be useful if the text becomes distracting while you are trying to enter header and footer information.

When you have completed all of the data entry you want for the header and footer sections, just click on Close and you are returned to your Word document so you can once again enter text, if you wish. Notice, however, that the header and footer information you just created isn't visible unless you are in Page Layout view, in which case the header and footer text is shown in the background, grayed out. You can also see how the header and footer appear by switching to Print Preview mode.

Modifying a Header or Footer

Editing the header or footer information is the same as editing any other text within a Word document. All you need to do is choose View, Header and Footer and make any changes you wish. As you type within the header and footer boxes, Word automatically expands the boxes to accommodate the text you enter. However, you should avoid lengthy headers and footers. Again, this data is a guide for the reader and should not carry primary information.

NOTE: If you are printing a double-spaced document, as you generally do for draft manuscripts, then you'll probably want to modify the formatting of the header and footer text to specify single spacing. Select the text and use the Format, Paragraph command to display the Paragraph dialog. From there you can set the line spacing you want to use. Also, consider boldface, lighter toned, or smaller type for the header and footer to help set them off from the rest of the document.

Varying the Headers and Footers

I mentioned at the beginning of this section how you can have different header and footer information for odd and even pages, or for the first page. If you are building a larger document by creating individual elements from different files (as you would in storing individual chapters in separate files, for example), then this is sufficient.

However, if you want to create a long document such as a book or annual report and store it in a single file, you may need a way of varying the header and footer data according to the chapter or section. This is easily done, because you can use the same technique that Word uses when you tell the software to create a different header and footer for the first page:

- Create separate sections for the parts of the document you want to have individual headers or footers. This is typically a division by chapter or document section, by topic, etc.

- Display the Header and Footer toolbar.
- Position the insertion point on the page where you want the new header or footer to appear. You can use the scroll bars on the right of your screen or the arrow keys to navigate to the desired area of the document.
- Click on the Same as Previous icon on the Header and Footer toolbar.
- Type the header or footer information for the current section.
- Click on Close to close the Header and Footer toolbar.

PAGE BREAKS

As you type a Word document the software automatically handles positioning the text on the page and spilling text over from the current page to the next. This *soft page break* shows you where the end of the printed page will be, yet remains flexible, moving as the amount and type of data you enter into your document varies. This is normally desirable. In fact, you don't want to become involved in worrying about precise text placement, most of the time. When you do, you can cause overall document formatting to get out of control.

Soft Page Breaks

In Normal view you can see a soft page break as a thin, dotted line. In Page Layout view you see these soft page breaks as an end-of-page drawing.

In general , you can't do much to or about these soft page breaks. Word puts them in according to page layout settings such as margin widths, font size, page size, and the like. But you can insert forced page breaks and you can tell Word to keep certain data together so it won't break in the wrong place.

Hard Page Breaks

Choose Page Formatting from the CD Directory, then click on the Hard Page button for additional information.

There are times when you may want to force some information to skip to the next page instead of appearing at the very bottom of the current page. Suppose you have a graphic image you want to place in a particular position, but because of the way the page breaks fall, the text appears on one page and Word forces the graphic image to move to the next page.

One way to handle this undesirable formatting is to insert a *hard page break* just before the text you want to keep with the graphic. Word closes off data entry on the current page and forces everything to move down one page.

This is easy to do:

- Position the cursor (insertion point) where you want to force a page break.
- Press and hold the Ctrl key and press Enter (Return).

If the document is in Normal view, you will see a thin, dotted line appear in your document where the cursor was positioned. In the middle of this line is the label Page Break. In Page Layout view, Word inserts another graphical page.

NOTE: Hard page breaks don't adjust as you add or remove text. Wait to add hard page breaks until all text entry is complete.

You can select, move, and delete these hard page breaks like any other Word object.

Other Page Breaks

Somewhere between the "Word does it all" soft page break and the "you do it all" hard page break are a couple of additional page break choices that can help you keep the right data together. You can get a look at some of these possibilities by selecting Format from the main Word menu and choosing Paragraph. From the Paragraph dialog, click on the Text Flow tab to bring forward the dialog shown in Figure 5.6.

This dialog has a number of check boxes that affect how Word document text flows across page boundaries. I've summarized these controls in Table 5.1.

Background Repagination

As you enter new text into a Word document, the software automatically computes page breaks and inserts a soft break at the proper location. However, you may want to turn off this setting, especially when you are working with a large document on a computer with low memory. This can speed up data entry and navigation around a document.

Figure 5.6 Text Flow Tab of the Paragraph Dialog

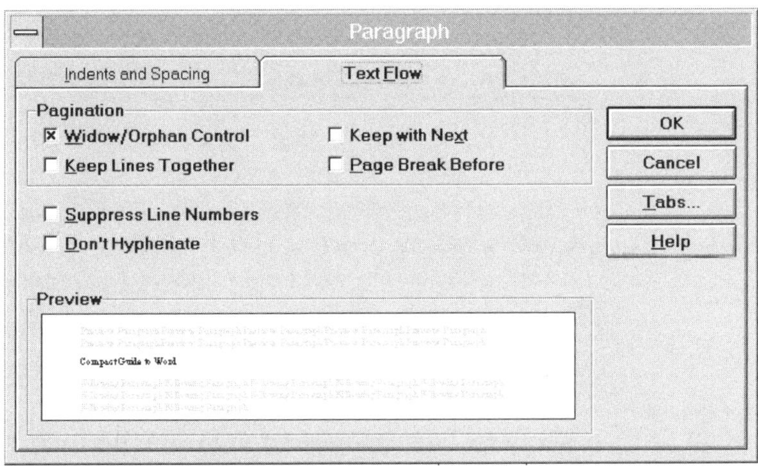

Table 5.1 Text Flow Controls

Control	*Action*
Widow/ Orphan Control	A default setting, this prevents Word from inserting a page break where only one or two lines from a paragraph will appear on a page by themselves.
Keep Lines Together	Whereas Word's Widow/Orphan control keeps a predetermined number of lines together at the bottom or top of the page, this setting lets you select a block of text and tell Word to keep them together on a page. Instead of placing an automatic page break where the number of lines on a page would dictate, Word places a break before or after the selected text.
Keep with Next	A modification of the previous setting, this control tells Word to keep selected text with the next line.
Page Break Before	This control tells Word to place a page break before the current paragraph. This sounds like a hard (manual) page break, and it is, but with a difference. Choosing this control lets you add text ahead of this block, inserting soft (automatic) page breaks when necessary. However, a page break will be placed ahead of the specified block, regardless of where a break would normally occur. This allows the forced page break to 'float' as text is added and removed from the document.

Turn off background repagination by selecting Tools and choosing Options to display the Options dialog. Click on the Background Repagination button to disable this default feature.

Opening, Saving, and Closing Documents

This final section in this chapter is pretty basic stuff, but as I summarize the document load and save process, I know there will be a couple of things you'll be glad you read. Most of us don't make the most use of the load and save tools Word provides. And, even after reading this you probably won't either. But sometimes you will and here are the tips you need to do it.

File, Open

After you have previously created a file in Word, you may want to call it back up to make changes or to print it. Click on File and choose Open to display the Open dialog shown in Figure 5.7.

There are several basic parts to this dialog. In the middle is the Directories list box, which shows a list of available directories on the current drive. You can use the scroll bars at the right

Figure 5.7 File, Open Dialog

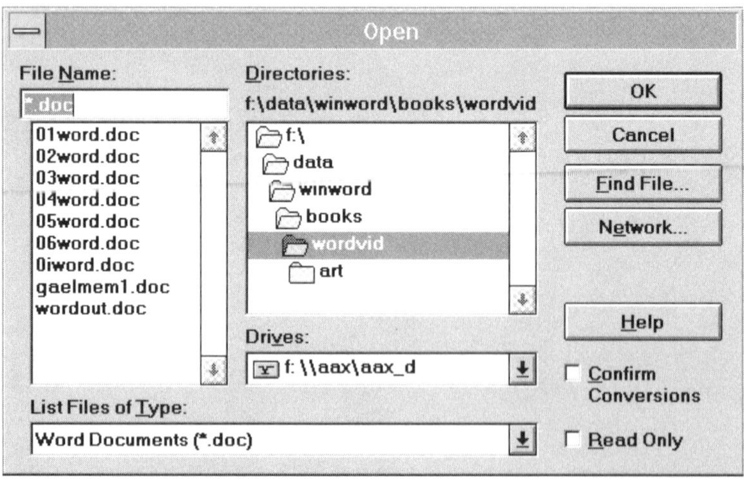

of this window to move up and down in the directories list to locate the one you want to search.

Below the Directories: window is a Drives: list box that you can use to select another disk drive to search. Depending on the configuration of your system, there may be only the A: and B: floppy drives in this list, or there may be many hard drives that are part of your local machine or that reside on a network.

At the very bottom of the dialog is another pull-down list that lets you specify the type of file you want to load. The default is Word document files (*.doc extension), but you can also display other file types, including Word templates (*.dot), rich text format files (*.rtf), and text files (*.txt). Of course, you also can choose to view all files (*.*).

NOTE: The asterisk in these file specifications is a wildcard character that stands for any group of characters. Use a question mark to stand for any single character.

Finally, in the File Name list box of this dialog you will see a list of all of the files within the specified directory that match the file search criteria specified in the File Type list box.

Once you find the file you want to edit, double-click on the file name or select the name and click on OK or press Enter.

That's the easy way. You remember the name of the file and know, or can find, the proper directory where it resides. But what if you can't remember all this? What if you have only a notion of the file you hope to find?

Word can help you with that, too. Instead of stepping through the directory and file list, click on the Find File... button in the Open dialog to display the Search dialog shown in Figure 5.8.

Enter the name of the file, or part of the file name and one or more wildcard characters in the File Name: field. To find files that begin with "Book" and end with anything else, for example, type **book*.*** in the File Name: field. To find all of the figure files for chapter 5 of a larger document, enter **fig05??.tif**, or whatever defines the more specific file name.

Specify the starting directory for the search in the Location: field and, if you want Word to search beyond the starting directory into its subdirectories, click on the Include Subdirectories check box at the right of the dialog.

You can also click on Advanced Search to display the Advanced Search dialog shown in Figure 5.9.

Figure 5.8 Search Dialog

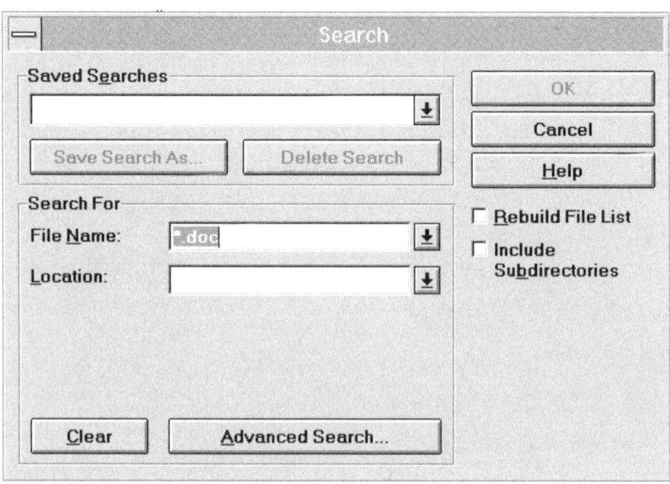

Figure 5.9 Word Advanced File Search Dialog

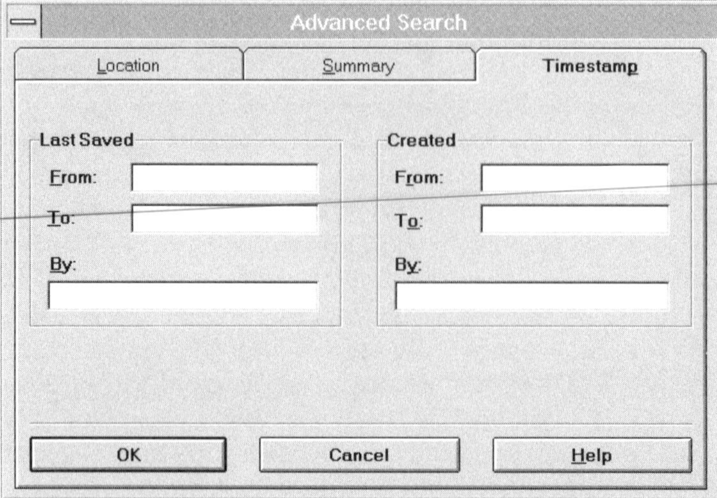

Use this dialog to add directories to the search area, to build and store searches, and to add other data to the search criteria, including file creation dates or information from the file's summary data.

There's another way to open a document. After you have edited a document in Word, the name of the file appears at the bottom of the File menu. You can double-click on the file name and have Word load it without having to worry about what directory the file is in or even the file type.

Saving a Document

Whatever kind of documents you create with Word, it is important that you save your information regularly. By default Word saves open documents automatically to a special recovery file. If something happens to cause the computer to shut down before you have a chance to save open files yourself, you can recover everything up to the last automatic save by simply reloading Word and noticing the recovered files Word loads automatically.

In addition to this automatic save, however, you should get in the habit of storing your documents regularly yourself. You'll likely develop your own file-saving habits, but here's what I use. When I start a new document I type a title on the first line. This may not necessarily be the final or formal name for the file, but it is a place to start. Then I usually add another line with the date the file was started and what it is for.

Once I've entered this basic information, I save the file. Use File, Save As... to display the Save As dialog. You can specify the disk drive, directory, file type, and file name, much as you do when loading a file.

Now you have saved the file once, and Word knows its name and location. As you work with your document you can save the file regularly by clicking on the Save button on the standard toolbar, or by pressing and holding the Ctrl key and touching the s key (Ctrl+s).

Of course you can use the File, Save command sequence to save the current file as well, but I like Ctrl+s. You don't have to take your hands off the keyboard, and Word saves the document more quickly so you can get on with editing or typing.

Whatever method you use, get in the habit of saving the files you're working on regularly. Roughly every 10 minutes or so is a pretty good average, but I usually save my work every paragraph or so, regardless of how long I've been working on the file.

Closing a Document

When you're finished editing a Word document, you can exit Word without closing the document separately if you have not changed the file since you saved it to disk. If you try to exit Word with a changed and unsaved file in memory, you will be asked if you want to save the changed file.

If you want to leave Word open while you work on another document, just use the File, Close command sequence to close the current file but leave Word open for additional editing. You could leave the completed file in memory, but it is best to get into a habit of closing files you don't need right now. This frees memory and potentially speeds up Word.

Summary

Use the information in this chapter as a reference for your formatting work with Word documents. You won't necessarily find a use for such techniques as inserting date and time fields, or conducting an advanced file search. But when you need to go beyond basic Word use, the information in this chapter can help.

In the next chapter I'll provide some additional details on printing Word documents and offer some tips on specialty printing such as printing on envelopes and labels.

Chapter 6

Printing Documents or Envelopes

For most of us, sending a Word document to the printer is the ultimate goal of creating the document in the first place. And, the good news is, for the most part printing Word documents is a relatively easy, straightforward process. In this chapter I'll give you some hints on getting the most out of Word's printing capabilities.

Choose Printing from the CD Directory for help in printing Word documents.

Before You Print

Before you can print successfully from within Microsoft Word, you must first install a printer. A full description on how to install all the possible printer combinations with Word is beyond the scope of this book. However, if you are just getting started with Microsoft Windows in general and Word in particular, there are a couple of things you should consider as you get ready to send the fruits of your Word labor to the printer.

Connecting the Printer

In general, you connect a printer to your computer in one of three ways: via a parallel port connection (LPT1, usually), through your serial port (COM1 or COM2, usually), or over a network connection. A parallel printer is the most common of these, with a network connection in second place. In general, even if you have a network connection for your printer, the port definition will be LPT1. The network software takes output from software such as Microsoft Word destined for LPT1 and reroutes it to the appropriate networked printer.

If you are using a local printer it should be fairly easy to determine whether your printer is attached properly to your computer. For a networked printer, on the other hand, it is up to your system administrator to maintain the hardware. And, it is up to you to understand what port to use for a networked printer and which printer definition to use with each printer. The good news about using Word on a network is there likely are multiple printers available for your documents, perhaps even a color printer so you can enhance documents or document covers with color objects or type. The bad news with using a networked printer is that the printer may not be close to your working location and, more importantly, it may sometimes be difficult to determine which printer you are using.

However, if your network system people have done their job, and Microsoft Windows and Word are installed properly, using a networked or local printer with Word should be fairly easy, as soon as you understand how printer definitions in Word operate.

Selecting the Printer in Word

You can find out what printers are available to your system by selecting File from the main menu, clicking on Print... and then choosing Printer... from the Print dialog. The dialog shown in Figure 6.1 is displayed.

In the Printers window of this dialog is a list of installed printers. Depending on your configuration, there may be only one or two printers in this list, or there may be ten or more. Even if you don't have more than two or so printers available on your system or over the network, you may have several printer definitions in your system.

Figure 6.1 Word Print Setup Dialog

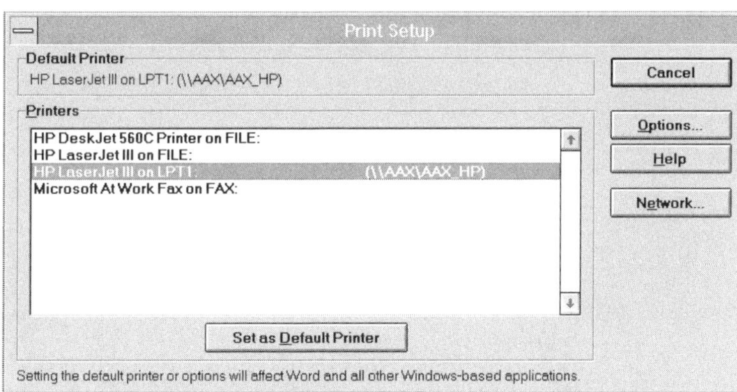

Why? For one thing some printers are capable of acting like more than one printer. You may want different definitions in Word or in Windows to get the most out of each printer. I have one Hewlett-Packard printer, for example, that uses HP's own PCL5 page definition language or can support PostScript with the addition of a language cartridge. I use a standard Hewlett-Packard printer definition for PCL5 and an Apple LaserWriter (a PostScript printer) definition for times when I plug in the PostScript cartridge.

I keep a couple of other definitions for printing PostScript and PCL5 to a disk file, as well. I usually have a printer definition for plain text so I can send text without special formatting to a print file.

Before you send a Word document to a printer, make sure you have specified the correct printer driver in Word. Otherwise you might get strange output from your printer. The default printer is shown at the top of the Print Setup dialog. The default printer is the one Word will use when you send a document to be printed. You can change the default by highlighting the name of the printer driver you want to use and then clicking on the Set as Default Printer button at the bottom of the Print Setup dialog.

You can also control some aspects of printer operation by choosing the Options... button on the Print Setup dialog to

Figure 6.2 HP DeskJet 560C Options Dialog

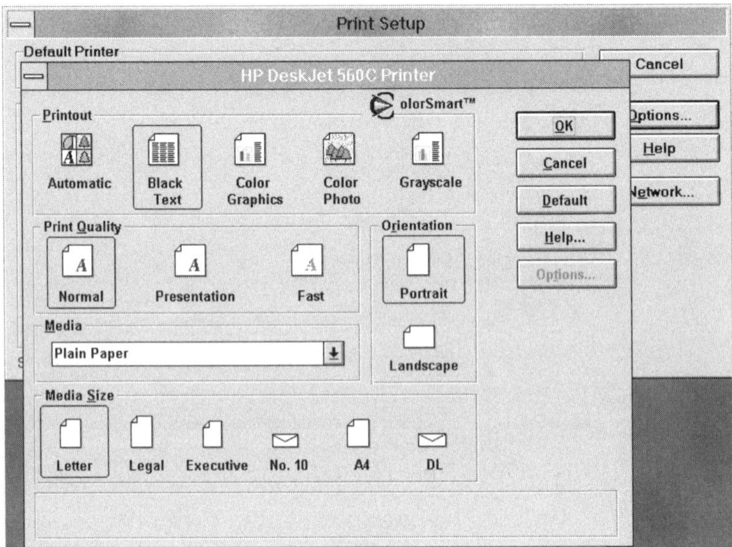

display the Options dialog. This is a dynamic selection that changes with the printer driver you have selected in the Printers window. Figure 6.2 shows a printer Options dialog for a Hewlett-Packard DeskJet 560C. If you're using another kind of printer, the Options dialog will be different.

Among the options you are likely to find on the Options dialog are type of paper, relative darkness of the text, page orientation (portrait or landscape), and so on.

When you are satisfied with the settings on the Options dialog, click on OK to return to Print Setup and click on OK again to close the dialog and set the printer definitions you have specified.

Previewing the Document

I discussed Print Preview in Chapter 4. This is a feature you can access from the standard toolbar or from the File menu.

The Print Preview screen will show you pretty accurately how your document will appear when you print it.

However, Print Preview may work differently with different printer definitions. So, before you accept a given page layout by studying Print Preview, make sure you have selected the correct printer. Of course, you can use Print Preview to show how your document will look with different printer definitions, if you wish.

Printing a Document

Once you have completed document entry, installed the proper printer hardware and drivers, and previewed your document, you are ready to actually send it to the printer.

Use File, Print (or Print Icon from Toolbar)

If you want to print the entire document to the default printer, the quickest and easiest way to print is to click on the printer icon on the standard toolbar. This launches a routine that sends the current document directly to the default printer. Word doesn't ask for confirmation, nor do you have a chance to select a portion of the document to print or change printers.

If you want to specify a different printer, change page orientation, or select only a portion of the document to print, use the Print dialog by entering the File, Print... command sequence. The Print dialog, shown in Figure 6.3, is displayed.

Fill Out the Print Dialog

At the simplest level, you'll use the Print dialog to verify which printer you'll be using. If you are using only a standalone PC, this doesn't seem like a viable reason for checking the Print dialog. Those of us who spend the day working with a networked machine, however, understand the frustration of quickly printing a document you want right now, only to discover (after standing in front of the printer for several minutes) that the job went to the printer in the next office or even on the next floor.

Figure 6.3 Print Dialog

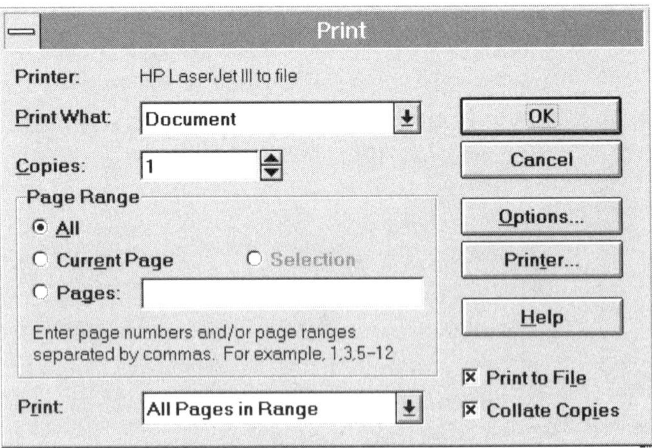

The default printer and printer path are shown at the top of this dialog. If this is the printer you want to use, simply click on OK and the job will be sent out. If this is the wrong printer, click on the Printer button to display the Print Setup dialog you saw in Figure 6.1. Choose the printer you want to use from the list, then proceed with the print job.

In addition to choosing the printer as you print a document, you can click on the Options button to set whatever printer options are available for this particular printer. See the earlier parts of this chapter for more details on these selections.

The rest of this dialog lets you set what you want to print, the number of copies, which pages to print, and whether you want to send the document to a file. In addition, you can tell Word to print just the even pages or just the odd pages within the range of pages you have specified in the Page Range section of this dialog.

Duplex Printing Why would you want to print just the odd numbered pages, or just the even numbered pages? You wouldn't, unless you're building a booklet from the current document, printing on both sides of the paper. If you are using a printer that supports duplex printing (printing on both sides), then you'll print the whole document at once and get two-sided output. To get double-sided printing with a simplex printer, you have two choices: run the paper through the printer twice, or use a copy machine. Either way, you'll want to print the odd and even pages separately.

If you want to run the paper through your printer twice, print either the odd or even pages, then reinsert the paper into your printer and tell Word to print the other side of the paper. Now it may not be as simple as I just made it sound. Different printers move the paper through the print process differently. With some printers you place the page printed-side up with the top of the page toward the printer; with others you place the printed paper face down with the top edge toward the outside.

Your printer manual may tell you how to send a page back through the printer. If not, here's a simple test you can run before you try to print the second side of the paper:

- Remove one sheet of paper from the default paper tray.
- Type **TOP** somewhere near the middle of the page.
- Draw an arrow from the word TOP toward the narrow edge of the paper.
- Replace the paper in the paper tray with the word TOP visible and the arrow facing the printer body.
- Print a sample page.

Now you can inspect the printed results to find out how the page is sent through the printer. If the page you printed is oriented so that the word TOP appears under the printed material and the arrow points to the top of the printed material, then to print a second page you would turn the printed side down with the top toward the printer body.

If the printed side is opposite the one with the word TOP on it and the top of the printed page is opposite the edge pointed to by the arrow, then to print on the other side of a printed page, place the page in the printer with the printed side up and the top away from the body of the printer.

Well, you get the idea. It may take a couple of trials to fully understand how your printer works. However, once you see the picture, printing both sides of the paper is a quick and easy process that saves paper and helps you prepare professional-looking documents.

NOTE: Although the majority of today's laser printers will print on both sides by running the paper through the printer a second time, some older printers and a few of the newer ones just won't let you do it. Check your printer manual before you try this. If the documentation says you can't print on both sides, use a copy machine. If you try running a couple of pages through twice and the printer hangs or the quality suffers, use the copy machine.

If you can't use your printer to produce double-sided print-outs, you can do it with a copy machine. Print separate odd and even pages, just to make it easy to separate the pages. Next, place the even or odd pages in the copier's paper tray and the other pages in the document feeder (or place the pages one at a time on the copy glass). Run the copies, placing copies of one set of pages on the back of the other.

Of course, you must understand how your copier feeds paper just as you must learn about your printer. You can use the same kind of test I described above to learn about your copier before you try to feed printed paper through the machine.

Printing to a File Another choice on the Print dialog is Print to File. If you click on this box, then click on OK, Word displays a file manager dialog so you can specify the name and path for the print destination file. Once you have specified the file name and click on OK, Word sends the current document to the specified file.

There are various reasons for printing to a file instead of to paper. Perhaps the most common reason is to create a file you can reproduce on a printer at a distant site. Suppose you want to format a document for a particular printer to make use of fonts or other formatting your printer doesn't support. You may be able to see the formatting on the screen, but your printer won't reproduce it.

In this case, send the output to a file, copy the file to a floppy, carry the diskette to a computer that has the proper printer, and use the DOS copy command to copy the printer file to the printer:

```
COPY a:printfil.prn lpt1
```

This should reproduce the document as if you had printed it directly from your computer.

NOTE: If you have difficulty getting the file to print on the distant printer, try modifying the command by adding **/b** *at the end of the command line. This tells DOS that you are copying a binary file, not a text file. This will usually correct the printer output problem.*

Notice from this description that printing to a file in this way creates a printer image file that contains whatever special codes are required to reproduce the current document, including fonts, character attributes, colors, or graphic objects. If your goal is to produce a text file (one without special codes or formatting) that you can import into another program, you can't simply click on Print to File on the Print dialog.

To produce a text file with the Print to File option, you first need to create a printer definition that produces plain text (or ASCII files). When you do this, you lose special text formatting and probably other objects such as graphic images. However, a text-only printer will give you text output you can use elsewhere. Of course, you can use the Word File, Save As... command sequence, and choose Text Only from the file type pull-down list to do the same thing, and do it a little easier.

Specifying What to Print Whether you realize it or not, there are many parts to a Word document. The most visible part is the text you type into Word's editor. And, for most of us, that's exactly what you want to print. However, you may also want to print the background parts of a document as well.

If you click in the Print What field of the Print dialog, you'll see the list displayed in Figure 6.4.

As you can see, there are several choices besides printing the document body. The Summary Info choice, for example, lets you print the information *about* the current document instead of the document itself. Figure 6.5 shows a typical document summary of the type you might print with this choice.

Figure 6.4 Print What Pull-Down List in the Print Dialog

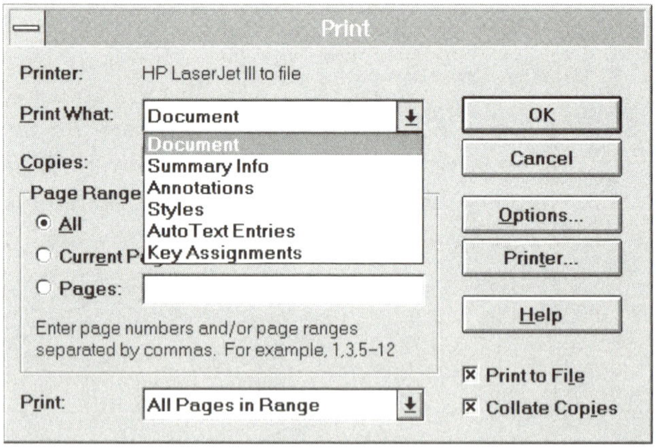

Figure 6.5 Typical Document Summary

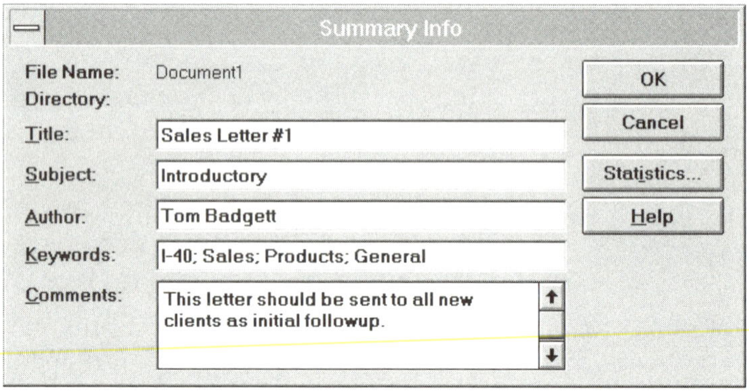

Or, choose Annotations to print any document notes separate from the body of the document itself, or click on Styles to get a printed list of the styles used in your document, and so on.

Specifying Number of Copies By default Word prints one copy of the current document. You can click in the Copies field and enter the number of copies you want to print. Or, you can use the up and down arrows at the right of the field to click to the number of copies you want.

Specifying Print Range Particularly if you are working with documents of only a few pages, you probably will just print the entire document most of the time, However, if yours is a large document or if you have configured a new printer, you may want to print one or two pages from the main document as a test. Or, if you print a whole document and during editing you find a mistake on one or two pages, you may want to make corrections and print only the corrected pages.

The All button in the Page Range group is the Word default. If you choose the Current Page button before clicking on OK, Word will print only the page where the cursor resides. Click on Selection and Word will print only text you selected before calling up the Print dialog. And, if you choose Pages, then you can enter a range of pages for Word to print.

You can enter page ranges in a couple of ways. To print pages 10 through 15 inclusive, for example, type **10-15** in the Pages field of this dialog. You can also print more than one section: **2-5, 10, 15-18**.

Printing Envelopes and Labels

Now that you know how to handle basic printing chores, let's look at a couple of specialty print jobs you might want to tackle: envelopes and labels. Word has made this process relatively easy, and it is about time. For years we had capable word processing software that ran on computers that cost thousands of dollars, yet many of us kept typewriters on our desks just to address envelopes or type labels. Not any more! Even beginning Word users can print envelopes and labels successfully.

Printing a Letter with Mailing Address

If you're working on a letter or other document that has a mailing address near the top of the first page, Word can, in most cases, ferret out this address and place it on the envelope form when you choose Envelopes and Labels... from the Tools menu (see Figure 6.6).

Figure 6.6 Envelope Form with Mailing Address

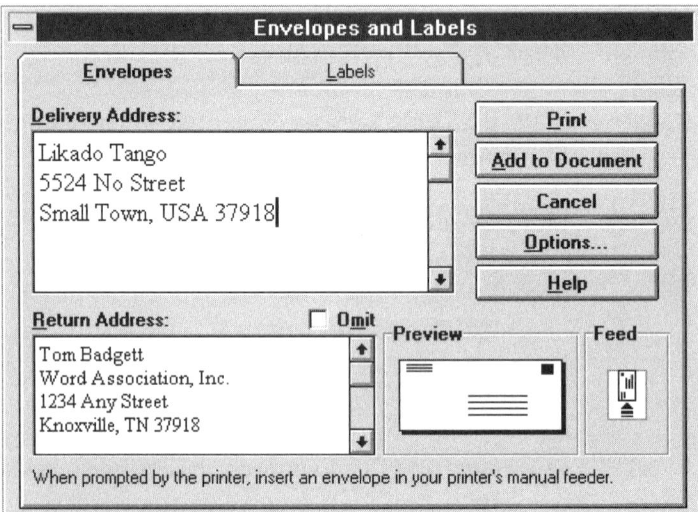

If this address isn't quite right, you can click in the Delivery Address area of this dialog and edit it so that it is correct. Notice that the icon in the lower right corner of this dialog shows you how to feed the envelope into your printer. The orientation of this icon changes with different printer definitions. This little helper isn't always 100 percent accurate, but it is pretty good.

If the return address that Word automatically places on the envelope form isn't correct, you can edit it as well. You can also click on the Omit button to tell Word not to use the return address at all. You'll want to do this if you are printing a letterhead envelope that has the return address printed on it.

NOTE: If you change the return address Word will ask if you want to make this the permanent return address. If you say yes, then this information is stored in the Tools, Options, User Info area of Word.

Whether or not you choose to print the envelope immediately, you may want to store the formatted envelope inside your document as a reference so you can print it again later without having to redo the formatting. You may also want to save the envelope information to a document to give you more freedom in formatting the addresses.

Click on the Add to Document button to have Word copy this information into the current document. Now you can add any formatting you wish before using the File, Print... dialog to print just the page that contains the envelope address and formatting information.

Click on the Options button of this dialog to display the Options dialog shown in Figure 6.7.

Use this dialog to add bar codes to the envelope, to change the envelope size, or to change the Return or Delivery address formatting. As I said, you can format the addresses by copying the envelope information into a document. But you can also do it from this dialog.

Click on Font in the Delivery Address or Return Address groups to display the standard Word Font dialog. The typeface and size you choose in this dialog applies to the entire address you selected. Again, for more control in formatting addresses, copy the envelope information into the document.

Figure 6.7 Envelope Options Dialog

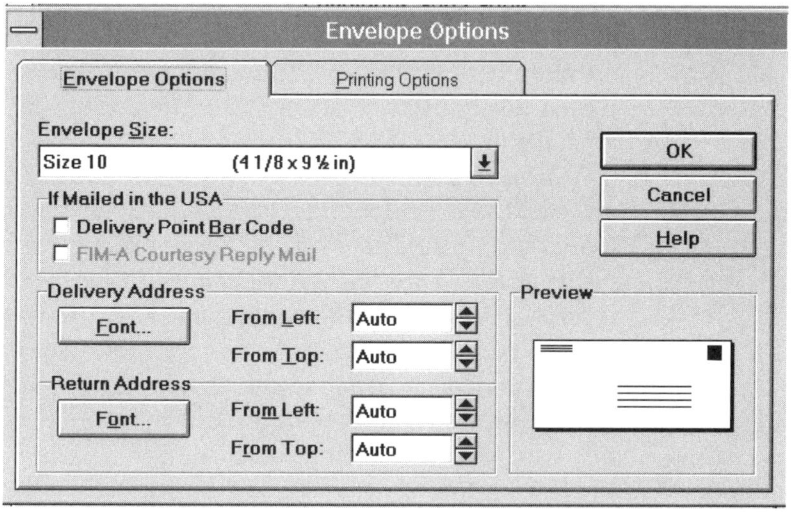

Printing Labels

For one or two letters, printing directly to an envelope is the way to go. However, if you need a stack of return address labels, or you want to send a letter or promotion to a larger list, you might want to print labels instead.

Luckily, Word helps you with label printing, making it as easy as printing to an envelope. Included with Word is a relatively large list of label definitions that you can choose by number. Avery is a large label company that produces a wide range of label sizes and types. By choosing the proper Avery label number, Word can format a document automatically to handle text printed to this label type.

For example, if you want to print a series of mailing labels on Avery 5161 labels (1-inch × 4-inch labels), click on the Label tab of the Envelopes and Labels dialog and choose Options. From the list on the lower left of the dialog, choose Avery 5161 and click on OK.

Now you have two options, printing a full page of the same label or printing one label. You might want to print a full page of the same label to print return address labels or equipment labels. The single label choice lets you print one address. Notice that below this choice are numbers. The defaults are 1 and 1. That means you want to print in the first row of the label stock and you want to print label 1. That way, if you have printed a few labels, you can tell Word which label to use. This means multiple passes of the label stock through your printer, which probably works for a few passes, but might get unreliable after several runs.

You have another option that might not be as obvious. Click on New Document to have Word open a new document and format it with a full page of the chosen label. Now you can type individual address information in each label. Simply place the insertion point in the first label and type the data. Press Tab to move to the next label, type that data, and so on. You can save this document to disk so you can use the same form for additional labels. In fact, you can maintain an ongoing mailing list in this way. Just keep typing labels and tell Word to print only the page with the new labels. Then at any time you can print all pages or selected pages to get a page of the new labels you need for follow-up, or to create file cards or Rolodex entries.

SUMMARY

Printing is the ultimate goal of working with Word. You put data into a word processor so you can get it out in the proper form. If you study this chapter and practice some of the techniques I suggest here, you should be quite comfortable conducting any of Word's common print operations.

In the next chapter I'll give you a short tutorial on searching for data within a Word document and for specific Word files.

Chapter 7

Searching for Data

Among the useful and convenient features of a product such as Microsoft Word is the ability to search for specific data within a document or to change one word or phrase or symbol to another automatically. The basic process is really simple and Word handles it rather well. There are a few hints that might help you with your own documents, however. I'll discuss them in this chapter.

Click on Searching Data on the Directory screen for interactive information on searching.

TEXT

The classic application for searching for text in Word is document editing. When I finished this chapter, for example, it was read by a couple of editors, who suggested changes for clarity or accuracy. The change suggestions might read something like, "In Chapter 6, paragraph beginning 'To modify text...' change 'sarch' to 'search' and add sentence with more detail." Rather than try to scroll through the text to find the area under discussion, you can use Edit, Find... (or Ctrl+F) to display the Find dialog, shown in Figure 7.1.

Figure 7.1 Word Find Dialog

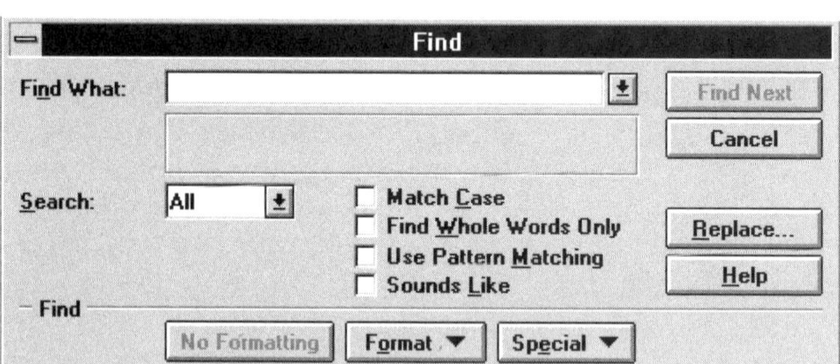

You type a word, a phrase, or even a part of a word that you want to find in the Find What: field of this dialog. In this example, an easy word to find is the misspelled "sarch." Simply enter the word in the Find What: field and click on Find Next. Word scans the current document, beginning at the location of the insertion point, for the word you specify. If Word reaches the end of the document without finding the word, the scan resumes at the beginning of the document.

When the search string is located, Word highlights the specified text and pauses for your next action. The Find dialog remains on the screen. If the found text is the wrong one, you can click on Find Next (or press the f key or Alt+F combination) to tell Word to resume the scan to find the next occurrence of the specified text.

If the located text is the proper one, you can press Esc to remove the Find dialog from the screen so you can edit the document. Now you can edit the found text, or add new information at this location in your document. You can conduct another search, for the same text or new text, beginning at the current document location by pressing Ctrl+F. The Find dialog pops up again with the last specified text in the Find What: field of the dialog.

If you want to search for the same text as before, press Alt+F. Otherwise, type the new search text and Word replaces the highlighted previous text with what you type.

Match Case Search

Notice that this dialog includes some switches (check boxes) that change the way a basic search is conducted. If you click on Match Case, for example, Word searches for the characters exactly as you type them in the Find What: field. Unless you check this box, Word considers uppercase and lowercase characters to be the same. Suppose, however, you want to find any occurrence of the phrase "microsoft word" that is not capitalized. If you check this box and enter **microsoft word** in the Find What: field, Word will ignore Microsoft Word, but show you any noncapitalized entries.

Whole Word Search

Likewise, you may want to search only for whole words and not just a string of characters. For example, if you tell Word to search for the characters **word**, the Find routine will locate *word, foreword, Wordsworth, wordsmith,* and so on. To tell Word to look only for a whole word, click on the Find Whole Words Only box in this dialog.

Pattern Matching Search

If you check the Use Pattern Matching box, you turn on some really sophisticated and useful search extensions. Without this box checked, Word simply looks for whatever characters you type in the Find What: field of the Find dialog. With pattern matching enabled you have classic wildcard, AND, OR, and other searching features at your disposal.

To use pattern matching, you enter some special characters with the words you are looking for in the Find What: field. Some of these probably are familiar to you if you've done any work in DOS or with databases. Others are kind of special to Word.

For example, to find any single character that is part of a group of characters, enter a question mark in the location of the character. Suppose you want to find any three-letter word that ends in *ip*. Enter **?ip** in the Find What: field, check Use Pattern Matching, and Word will locate *tip, dip, sip* or other combinations of characters that end in *ip*. You can use this single-character wildcard within longer words, or you can use it more than once within a single search string. Type **?right** in the Find What: field and Word locates *fright* or *bright*; **b?te** finds *bite* or *byte*; **??ght** finds *fright* or *blight*, and so on.

To find a broader range of characters, use a more general wildcard. The asterisk is a general wildcard that finds any combination of characters. Enter **foot*** in the Find What: field and Word finds *footstool*, *football*, *footloose*, and so on.

NOTE: When you check Use Pattern Matching, it is as if you also checked Match Case. Searches using pattern matching are also case sensitive.

The pattern matching features of Word include some additional tools that let you find just about any combination of characters you can imagine. Look at the list in Table 7.1. This shows you the range of search codes you can enter in the Find What: field and the search results.

Sounds Like Search

One more useful and powerful search tool in Word is the approximate or Sounds Like search. Sometimes you may know approximately what you want to find, as when you may have misspelled a word or when you want to find a word you don't know how to spell correctly (this happens to me more often than I'd like to admit).

When you click on the Sounds Like box in the Word Find dialog, you can enter **week** in the Find What: field and Word will locate not only *week*, but also *weak*. Similarly, enter **seen** and also find *scene*; **rode** also finds *road*; **to** also finds *too*; but, interestingly enough, it won't find *two*. So the Sounds Like feature isn't foolproof, but it is pretty good. You'll probably be surprised at how much Word seems to know about the way words sound.

You can also control the search with the choices in the Search list in this dialog. If you click on the down arrow beside the Search field you'll see three choices: All, Up, and Down. All is the default, which tells Word to begin searching the document at the location of the insertion point down to the end of the document, then move to the top and search down to the insertion point.

Table 7.1 Pattern Matching Search Tools

Operator	*Description*	*Example*
?	Any single character	**?and** finds *sand, band*
*	Any combination of characters	***ide** finds *tide, pride, side*
[ ]	Any one of the characters contained in the brackets	**t[io]ck** finds *tick* or *tock*
[-]	Any single character within a range of characters	**[r-t]ight** finds *right, sight, tight*
[!]	Any single character except those within the brackets	**[!ts]ock** finds *dock, rock,* or *lock* but NOT *tock* and *sock*
[!x-y]	Any single character except those within the range represented by *x-y*	**[!d-j]ock** finds *rock, lock, sock,* or *tock,* but NOT *dock, hock,* or *jock*
{n}	Exactly *n* occurrences of the previous character	**e{2}** finds *feed, feet, fleet*
{n,m}	Find *n* to *m* occurrences of the previous character	**o{1,2}** finds *bottle, book, boot, toot, tot*
@	One or more occurrences of the previous character	**10@** finds *10, 100, 1000, 10000*
<	Find characters at the beginning of a word	**<(in)** finds *into, interesting, information* but NOT *bin*
>	Find characters at the end of a word	**(in)>** finds *bin, win, within* but NOT *into, interesting*

By choosing Up, you tell Word to start at the location of the insertion point and search backward (toward the top) until the beginning of the document is reached, at which point the search is halted. Choose Down and the opposite is true. Word begins the search at the location of the insertion point and continues down to the bottom and stops.

In general, you can use one of these search methods to find anything you type in: letters, numbers, punctuation. However, Word documents also include other features, such as character attributes, fonts, and symbols you can't type directly from the keyboard. You can find them too, but the process is slightly different. I'll show you how to do that in the next section.

Formatting Codes and Special Characters

When you want to search a Word document for special characters or formatting codes, you start with the same procedure. Use Edit, Find to display the Find dialog shown in Figure 7.1. Now, instead of just typing in the characters you want to find in the Find What: field of this dialog, click on the Format or Special buttons. If you click on Format, you'll see the pop-up menu shown in Figure 7.2.

Format Searches

The choices from this menu—Font, Paragraph, Language, and Style—call up the same dialogs you have used for text formatting before, but now you are specifying what formatting you want Word to look for. For example, if you choose Font from this pop-up menu, you'll see the dialog shown in Figure 7.3.

Figure 7.2 Format Pop-Up Menu on the Find Dialog

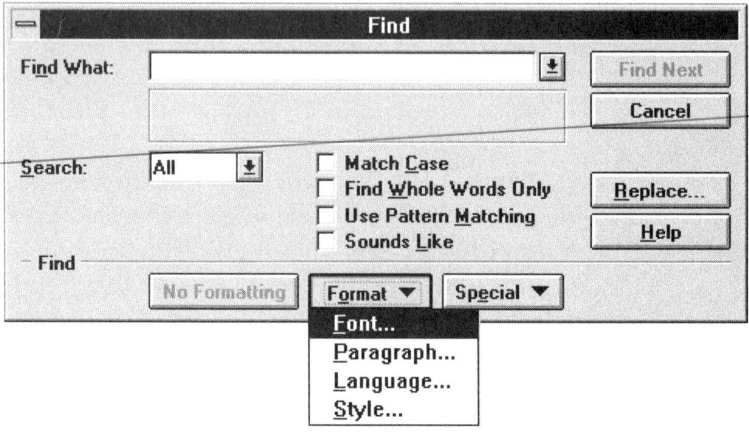

Figure 7.3 Find Font Dialog

Find Font
Font | Character Spacing
Font: | Font Style: | Size:
Roman, Script, ShelleyVolante BT, Swis721 BlkEx BT, Symbol
Regular, Italic, Bold, Bold Italic, Not Bold
8, 9, 10, 11, 12
OK | Cancel | Default... | Help
Underline: | Color:
Effects: Strikethrough, Hidden, Superscript, Small Caps, Subscript, All Caps
Preview

This is the same Font dialog you use to specify what font you want to use, but the title says Find Font.

Make whatever specifications you want in this dialog. The process is the same as if you were choosing character attributes. So, if you want to search for 12-point, Times New Roman text, for example, you would simply make these choices in this dialog.

Likewise, if you want to look for text that is underlined, text of a particular color, or special text such as superscript or subscript text, you can do it by making the proper settings in this dialog. Notice that when you make a selection from the Find Font format dialog, the button labeled No Formatting on the Find dialog becomes active. Prior to making a Format selection, this button is grayed out so you cannot select it. When you want to search for plain text or when you want to tell Word to disregard any text formatting as part of the search, click on the No Formatting button.

NOTE: Many search errors can be traced to leaving formatting enabled from a previous search. If you have problems completing a successful

search for text you are reasonably sure exists, make sure the No Formatting button is clicked. This could solve your searching problems.

The same technique works for other attributes. Pop up the Format menu and choose Paragraph, for example, and you'll see the familiar Paragraph formatting dialog but with a Find Paragraph title (Figure 7.4).

From this dialog you can specify text alignment (find all centered text, for example, or all text that is set to full justification), indents, line spacing (find all double-spaced text), and so on. Just as you can create a custom paragraph format from this dialog, you can tell Word to search for any of this formatting from this Find version of the same dialog.

To search for language settings, choose Language from the pop-up Format menu on the Find dialog to display the Find Language dialog shown in Figure 7.5. This is a straightforward search for any text that is formatted with the language type you specify from this dialog.

Finally, you can search for style information by choosing Style... from the Format pop-up to display the Find Style dialog shown in Figure 7.6.

Figure 7.4 Find Paragraph Dialog

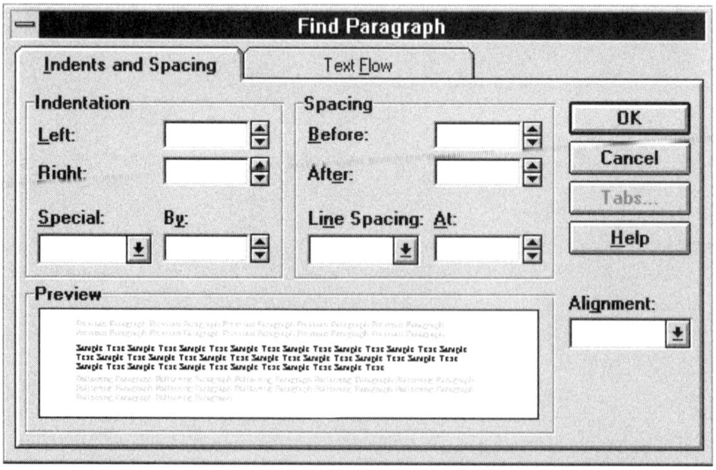

Figure 7.5 Find Language Dialog

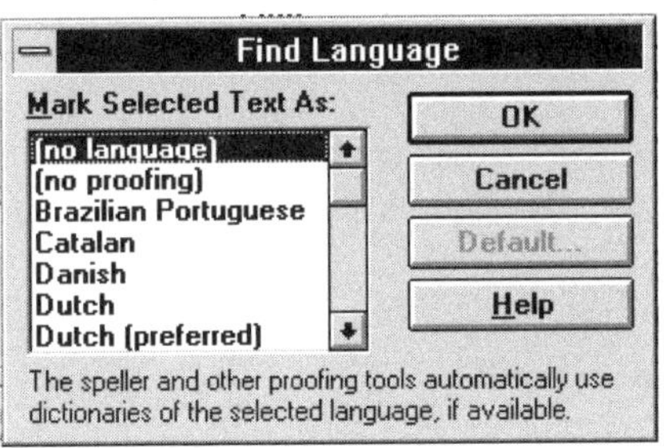

The Find Style dialog is simpler than Word's Style dialog. The Style setup dialog is among Word's more complex dialogs, simply because it has several levels. However, this Find Style dialog merely lets you specify the name of a style that resides in the current document. You could search for all of the Heading 1 styles, for example, or all of the text formatted with one of your custom styles.

My primary use for the style search routine is to locate areas of the document that have been misformatted. Sometimes when you are working on a lengthy document, you set up styles as headings that will serve as automatic table of contents

Figure 7.6 Find Style Dialog

Find Style
Find What Style:
(no style)
Body
body - no indent
Caption
Default Paragraph Font
Heading 1
OK
Cancel
Help
Description

entries. Occasionally, whole paragraphs of text appear as a title. That just means that a block of text has mistakenly been formatted with a heading style. This style search routine will find it for you.

Special Searches

Just as you may want to find character or paragraph formatting, you may want to search for special characters. Click on the Special box on the Find dialog and you'll see the pop-up list in Figure 7.7.

Double-click on one of the entries in this pop-up and Word places a special character to represent this selection in the Find What: field of the Find dialog. For example, click on Paragraph Mark and the ^p symbol appears in the Find What: field. If you choose Field from this list, the ^d symbol is placed in the search field, and so on.

This type of extended searching is extremely useful when you want to find special character formatting. The paragraph mark search is particularly useful. I use online services such as the Internet extensively. When I download a text document from the Internet, it usually is formatted so that it can be read on the simplest of dumb terminals or imported into any word processor for further editing. However, each line ends in a car-

Figure 7.7 Special Find Pop-Up List

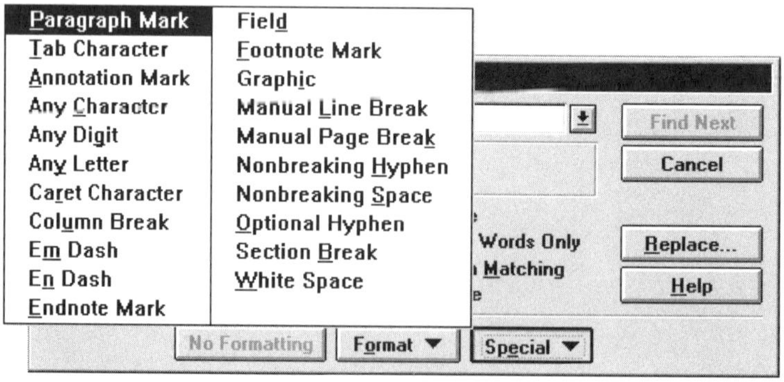

riage return/line feed combination. This makes it difficult to let Word automatically format the file into a Word document. To make Word formatting easier, you want to remove the hard returns at the end of each line and the double carriage returns that are almost certainly placed between paragraphs.

It is true that the Word AutoFormat utility can handle a lot of this conversion for you, but this utility is also prone to change text formatting by adding heading styles to anything it thinks might be a heading. You can try AutoFormat, and if the results are not satisfactory, you can use Word's ability to search for a paragraph mark and replace it (see the next section) to enable Word's automatic formatting of text.

Notice that the Special pop-up list has some choices that go beyond simply finding preset features such as paragraph marks. You can search for any number (any digit) for example. This is useful when you know you have a table or list of numbers that you'd like to edit. Most Word documents consist mainly of letters, so if you search for any digit you can find your numbers easily. The Any Digit search inserts the ^# code in the Find What: field of the Find dialog.

Notice also that you can search for any graphic object. If you want to step through the graphic objects you have created for the current document, you can use Graphic from the Special pop-up to insert a ^g code. When you click on Find Next, Word locates the next graphic object in your document.

Finding and Replacing Data

I don't need to say too much about finding and replacing data, because the search techniques are the same as described in the Find section of this chapter. And you can use the same character input tools to specify what you want to change the found text to.

When you choose Replace... from the Edit menu, you will see the dialog shown in Figure 7.8.

At the top of this dialog is the familiar Find What: field from the Find dialog. At the bottom is the Replace With: field. Enter the text or other information you want to substitute for the specification in the Find What: field and Word will automatically

Figure 7.8 Replace Dialog

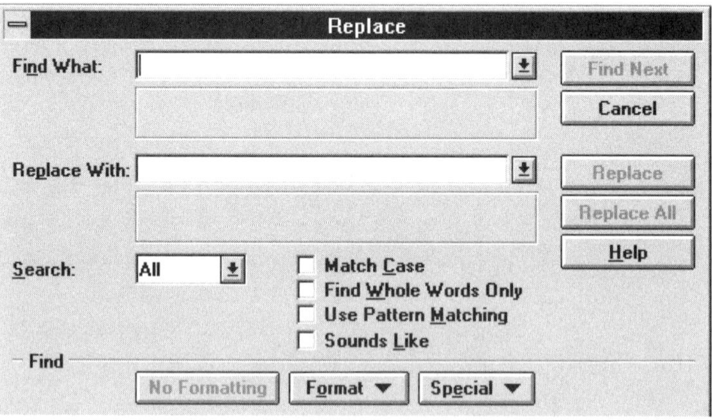

find the data and replace it with what you place in the Replace With: field.

This combination of Find and Replace uses the same techniques as a plain Find. You can specify special characters or formatting, and you can use pattern matching, sounds like, and the other search criteria as well.

In addition, you can pull down the Search list to specify whether to search all of the document or just from the location of the cursor up to the top or down to the bottom.

After you have specified the text to find and what you want to change it to, you have three choices for the next step. You can click on Find Next, which is the same as the Find Next button on the Find dialog, and Word searches the document until the Find What: text is located and stops. You can then click on Replace to replace the found text with the text specified in the Replace With: field. Word then finds the next instance of the search text and pauses. If you click on Find Next, no change is made but the next instance of the specified text is located.

I usually do a manual search of this type for a couple of times, then when I am sure the search and replace specifications are correct, I click on Replace All to tell Word to find and replace all occurrences of the specified text without asking for confirmation.

NOTE: Make sure you have saved your document before conducting a replace operation. That way if you make a mistake in the specifications, and data you didn't mean to change is altered, you can load the original version and try again.

SUMMARY

Finding and replacing data in Word is pretty basic stuff, but also pretty important. It is the basis of significant document editing and gives you the ability to make global changes to a document or to several documents relatively easily. As you can see from the material we have covered in this chapter, document searching goes well beyond the simple text searches most of us are familiar with. By using the special switches on the Word Find dialog, you can customize a search to help you locate just about any combination of text, numbers, and formatting you are likely to include in your documents.

In the next chapter I'll provide more details on using Word tables. I have discussed the use of tables in previous chapters, but in Chapter 8 I'll show you how to use tables like spreadsheets and how to add creative formatting, if you wish.

Chapter 8

Using Tables

I've already talked about how to use tables in conjunction with columns or instead of columns to format a document. Remember that you can use tables to format matched columns in a document. But Word tables are much more flexible than that and are excellent tools for organizing lists and even conducting basic mathematical operations on numbers in table cells. That's what we'll look at in this chapter.

Creating a Table

You can create a Word table easily "on the fly" as you come across data that lends itself to table organization. Tables can substitute for simple spreadsheets for numerical data, for matched lists (for columnar data), and for combination data such as product price lists with text and numbers.

You can create a table and then enter data into it, or, you can decide later to convert existing text to table format. However, it is easier to create the table first and add information to the table structure, rather than the other way around.

There are three basic ways to create a table in Word: with the Table menu, by using the toolbar table icon, and by using the

Table Wizard. Whatever table creation method you use, the basic process is the same and the results are similar.

For example, you need to know at least the general structure of your table before starting to create it. And you should understand well the data that will be put into the table. This helps you format the table and to arrange the data for the most effective presentation.

First, I'll describe basic table creation, then I'll show you how to format and edit table information.

Using the Table Menu

To create a Word table from the menu:

- Position the insertion point where you want the table to appear in your document.
- Select Table from the main Word menu and choose Insert Table... to display the Insert Table dialog shown in Figure 8.1.
- Specify the number of columns (top-to-bottom cells) you want in this table. Either type a number in this field, or use the up and down arrow keys at the right of this cell to set the number of columns.
- Specify the number of rows (left-to-right cells) you want in this table. Either type a number in this field, or

Figure 8.1 Insert Table Dialog

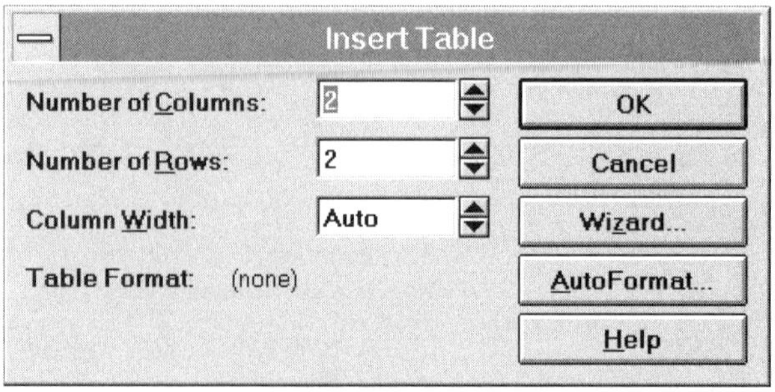

use the up and down arrow keys at the right of this cell to set the number of rows.

- Click on OK to close the Insert Table dialog. Word inserts a table with the specified number of cells into your document at the location of the insertion point.

Word shows the table structure as horizontal and vertical dotted lines that define a group of cells. For example, if you specify a table with three columns and five rows, Word inserts into your document the dotted structure shown in Figure 8.2.

Use the mouse to position the insertion point in any cell and you can type data—numbers or text—of about any length. Word automatically adjusts the height of the cells to hold the data you enter.

I'll discuss additional data entry and formatting topics later in this chapter.

Using the Toolbar

Creating a table with the toolbar table icon is even easier:

- Position the insertion point where you want the table to appear in your document.
- Click on the toolbar table icon to pull down a sample table (see Figure 8.3).
- Click in the first cell (upper lefthand corner) and hold down the left mouse button.

Figure 8.2 Word Table with 3 Columns and 5 Rows

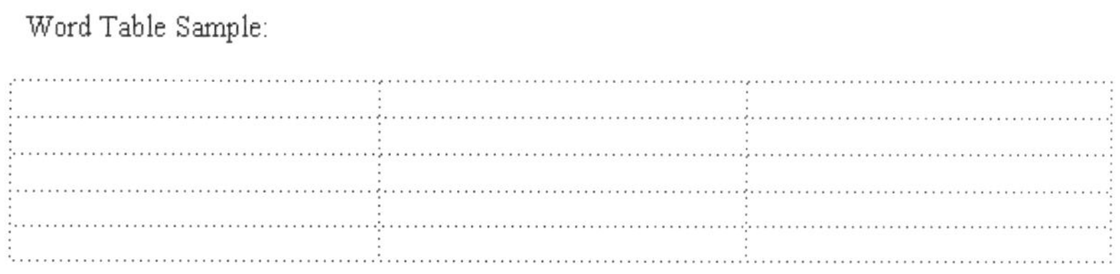

Word Table Sample:

- Drag the highlight to select the number of rows and columns to include in your table.
- Release the mouse button to insert the specified table structure.

Word paints the cells that will be included in the table and also shows at the bottom of the sample table the number of rows and columns for the table. When you release the mouse button, Word inserts horizontal and vertical dotted lines in your document to define the table you have specified. Enter data in the table by clicking in any cell and typing the information you want to include in the table.

Using the Table Wizard

Creating tables from the Insert Table dialog or by using the pull-down icon from the toolbar produces basic table structures without special formatting. Word also includes a Table Wizard to step you through the process of creating a table and of adding some additional formatting.

To create a table using the Table Wizard:

- Select Table from the main Word menu and choose Insert Table... to display the Insert Table dialog.
- Click on the Wizard... button to start the table creation program and display the initial Table Wizard dialog shown in Figure 8.4.

Figure 8.3 Toolbar Table Pull-Down

Figure 8.4 Initial Word Table Wizard Dialog

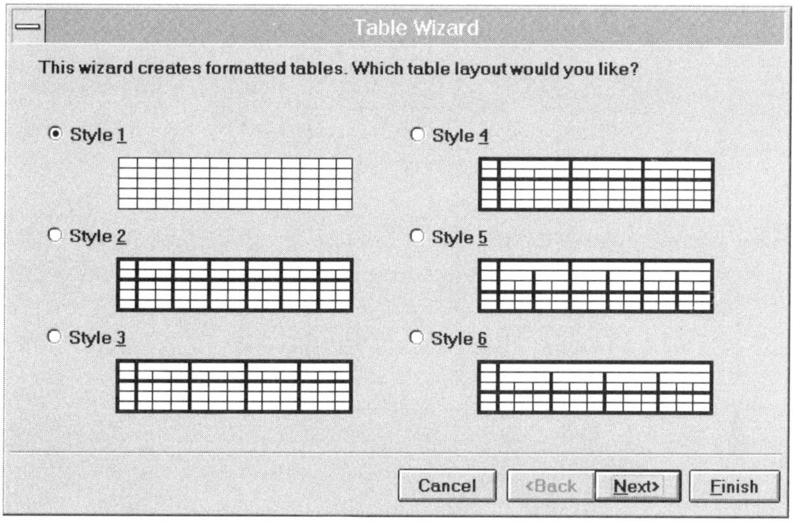

Table Wizard

This wizard creates formatted tables. Which table layout would you like?

Style 1 | Style 4

Style 2 | Style 5

Style 3 | Style 6

Cancel | <Back | Next> | Finish

- Choose the table style you want from this dialog and click on Next to display the columns dialog, shown in Figure 8.5.

  Notice that the default style is the standard Word table without special formatting, but you have five other choices for line styles that help you emphasize different parts of the table data.
- Choose the column style and contents you want from the column dialog.

  You can either enter a specific number of blank columns, or tell Word to fill the top row with the months of the year, quarters, days of the week, numbers, or years. What you choose on this dialog sets the number of columns. If you select months of the year, for example, the table will have 12 columns.
- Click on Next to display the row dialog, shown in Figure 8.6.

Figure 8.5 Table Wizard Column Dialog

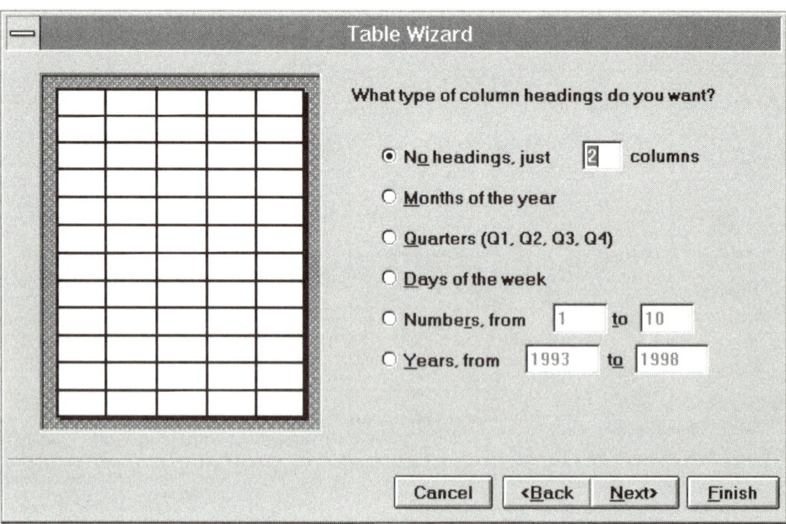

Figure 8.6 Table Wizard Row Dialog

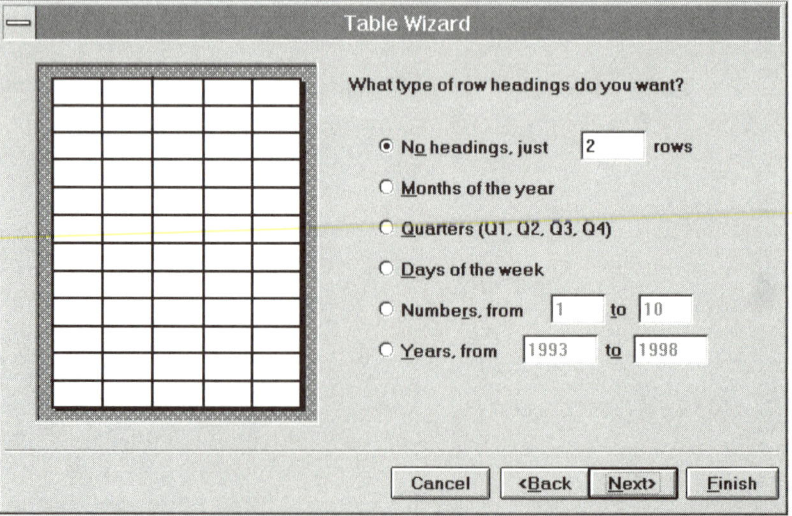

Figure 8.7 Table Wizard Cell Formatting Dialog

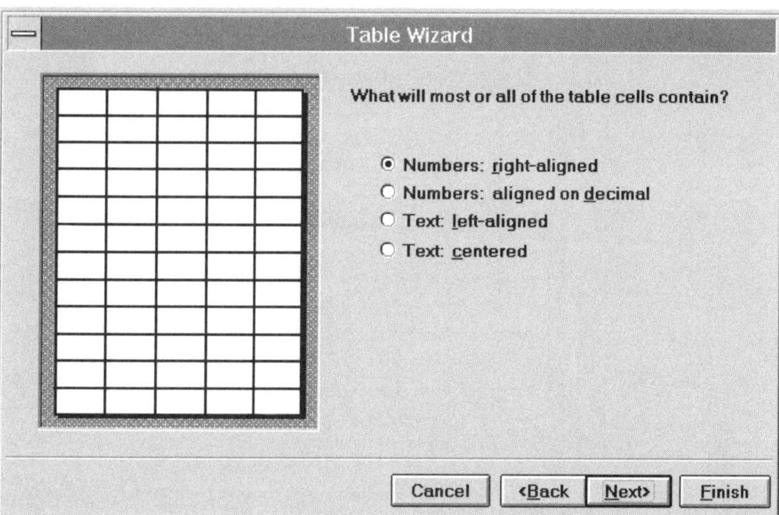

As with the column specifications, you can have Word insert a specific number of rows, or you can have Word fill in basic row data.

- Click on Next to display the cell formatting dialog shown in Figure 8.7.

  You can tell Word to align numbers to the right of each cell or on the decimal point, and you can select left-aligned or centered text. These are just two choices. Others are available and you can use them after the wizard is complete, if you wish.

- Click on Next to display the page layout dialog shown in Figure 8.8.

  The default layout is Portrait, where the table is oriented with the top of the table across the narrow side of the paper. Choose Landscape formatting to turn the paper on its side so that the table is oriented with the top of the table along the wide edge of the paper. Which orientation you select depends on the structure of your table. Obviously, if the table is wider than it is

Figure 8.8 Table Wizard Page Orientation Dialog

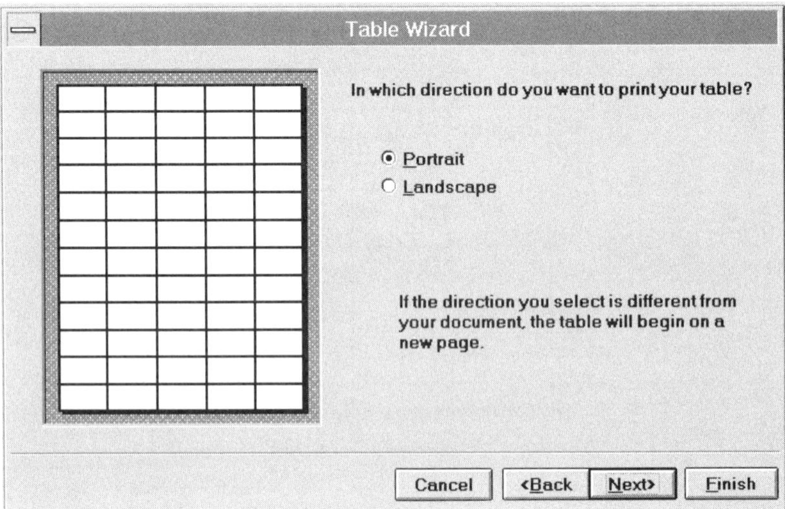

tall, turn the paper on its side by choosing Landscape formatting. On the other hand, if the table has more cells up and down than side to side, Portrait formatting is the correct choice.

- Click on Finish to display the final Table Wizard dialog (see Figure 8.9).

  There are two final choices on this dialog. The default is to just finish the wizard and insert the table. The second choice is to have Word pop up continuous help as you enter information into the table and format it.

- Click on Finish to close the Wizard.

  Word ends the Table Wizard program and displays the AutoFormat dialog to help you format the table you just designed. You can step through the AutoFormat choices to add special formatting to the table, or choose Cancel to use basic table formatting. (See the

Figure 8.9 Final Table Wizard Dialog

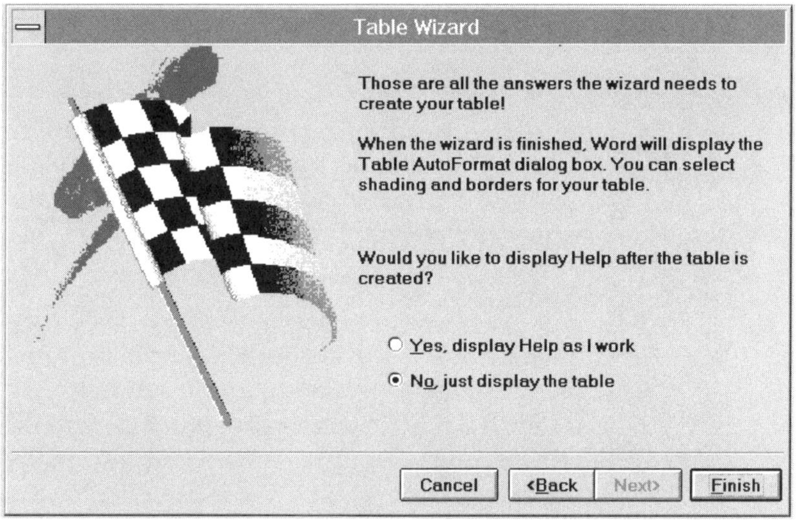

Table Wizard

Those are all the answers the wizard needs to create your table!

When the wizard is finished, Word will display the Table AutoFormat dialog box. You can select shading and borders for your table.

Would you like to display Help after the table is created?

○ Yes, display Help as I work

◉ No, just display the table

Cancel | <Back | Next> | Finish

section below for more details on using the AutoFormat feature.)

Entering Table Data

Once you have created the basic table form you can enter information into individual cells by just typing what you want. Use the mouse pointer to select the first cell you want to fill with data and type the information. Initially, don't be too concerned with how the information appears. Get the basic text and numbers in the proper cells. You can format the table or move data around later, if you wish.

Move to the next cell to the right of the current cell by pressing the Tab key or the right arrow key. Return to a previous cell with the left arrow key and move down to the next row with the down arrow key. Note that once a cell contains data, the right and left arrow keys move the cursor across the text already in the cell. The cursor jumps to the next or previous cell only when you are at the end or beginning of the line of text within the current cell. If the cursor is within a row of text, press Tab to move to the next cell and Shift+Tab to move to the previous cell.

NOTE: When you use Tab and Shift+Tab to move to a different Word table cell, the entire contents of the destination cell are selected. If you start typing immediately, you will replace everything already in the current cell with what you type. If you only want to edit existing data, press the right or left arrow key or use the mouse to click where you want to start editing.

You can also enter data into table cells by copying it from the Clipboard. Select text in another part of the current document or within a different document and use Edit, Copy or Edit, Cut to place the data on the Clipboard. Now, click in the cell within the table where you want the Clipboard information to appear to select that cell. Press Shift+Ins or use Edit, Paste to copy the data into the current cell. You can move text, numbers, or graphic images into a Word table using the edit/paste technique.

EDITING TABLE DATA

Basic table editing is the same as editing plain text anywhere else in a Word document. Click in a cell you want to edit, then use the Backspace or Del keys to remove text, or type new information to add to what is already in a cell.

In addition to this basic editing, you can do some other things to change information or add new information to a Word table.

Adding Rows and Columns

Suppose you have created a table and entered the basic information, only to discover that you need another row or several more rows to hold all of the data you want to place in the table.

Easy!

Place the cursor within a row below where you want a new row, select Table from the main Word menu and choose Insert Rows. Word inserts a new table row above the current row and selects the row. To insert another row, issue the same command again. You can insert as many rows as you like in this way.

NOTE: To insert a row as the last row in your table, place the insertion point in the last row and issue the Table, Insert Rows command sequence. Word inserts a row above the final row. Move the mouse pointer to the left of the last row and click to select the entire row (or click anywhere in the last row and use Table, Select Row to select it). Use Edit, Cut to cut the entire contents of the column to the Clipboard and remove the last row of the table. Click in the leftmost cell in the new last row and use Edit, Paste Rows to insert a new row above the last row of the table.

A similar technique works to insert new columns. Use the mouse to select the whole column to the left of where you want to insert a new column. Do this by moving the mouse pointer up to the top line of the table until it changes to a down-facing arrow. Click the left mouse button and Word highlights the whole column.

Now click on Table on the main Word menu to pull down the Table menu. Notice that this menu has now changed. The first item on the list is now Insert Columns, whereas it was Insert Rows before you selected a table column.

When you click on the Insert Columns menu item, Word adds a column down the length of the table. The new column is inserted to the right of the column you just selected.

NOTE: To insert a column to the right of the last column of the table, click just to the right of the top right cell of the table. Word places a thin, vertical cursor in this location. Use Table, Select Column to select the vertical area just outside the table boundaries. Now use Table, Insert Columns (the Table menu changes after you use the Select Column command) to add a new column at the far right of the table.

There are other editing techniques you can use with an existing Word table as well.

Deleting Cells

You can use the Table menu to select a row or column, then call up the Table menu again to choose Delete. Word removes the entire selected row or column.

NOTE: If you remove a column or row by mistake, select the Edit menu and choose Undelete Rows or Undelete Columns to reverse the deletion.

To delete individual cells, position the cursor within the cell you want to delete, select Table and choose Delete Cells to display the Delete Cells dialog, shown in Figure 8.10.

Choose one of the options from this dialog to tell Word how to rearrange the remaining cells. The default is Shift Cells Left. With this option selected, when you delete an individual cell, the remaining cells in that column will move left to fill in the blank left by the removed cell. This leaves a blank space at the far right of the current row.

If you choose Shift Cells Up, Word moves cells beneath the current cell up one row, but the rows beneath the current row are not deleted. The other two choices on this dialog delete an entire row (the row that contains the cursor), or an entire column.

Merging Cells

You can adjust table contents by merging two or more cells within a single row into one cell. Do this by selecting the cells you want to merge by clicking in the first cell and dragging the highlight across the cells you want to select. Now use the Table, Merge Cells command to collect all of the data within the selected cells into a single cell. The data is collected into the leftmost cell of the row within the selected range.

Figure 8.10 Delete Cells Dialog

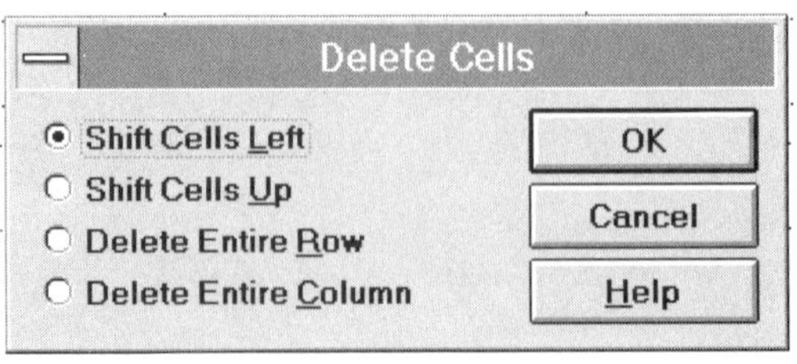

This technique modifies the basic table format by removing the cell definitions for the selected cells. This may result in an asymmetrical table design, one that contains more cells in some rows than in others.

Splitting Cells

Just as you may want to merge information from two or more cells, you may want to split information within a single cell into two cells. Word includes a command to help you do this as well.

Suppose you have a table that looks like the one in Figure 8.11. Multiple lines of information within a single cell could result from merging cells, from importing data from the Clipboard, or by just typing in too much information. You also may want to use this procedure to split data in a table so that it fits under a single column title.

To split this data into two columns, use the mouse to select the information in the cell, then issue the Table, Split Cells... command to display the dialog shown in Figure 8.12.

Specify the number of columns for the split data by typing in a number or by using the up and down arrow keys to the right of the columns field. Click on OK to tell Word to split the selected data across that number of columns. The result is shown in Figure 8.13.

The final format of the data in your table may differ from that in Figure 8.13, depending on the starting format and on the type of data you are reformatting.

Figure 8.11 Sample Table with Multiple Lines in a Single Cell

Word Table Sample

Monday	Tuesday	Wednesday	Thursday	Friday
Item 1	Item 2 Item A			

Figure 8.12 Split Cells Dialog

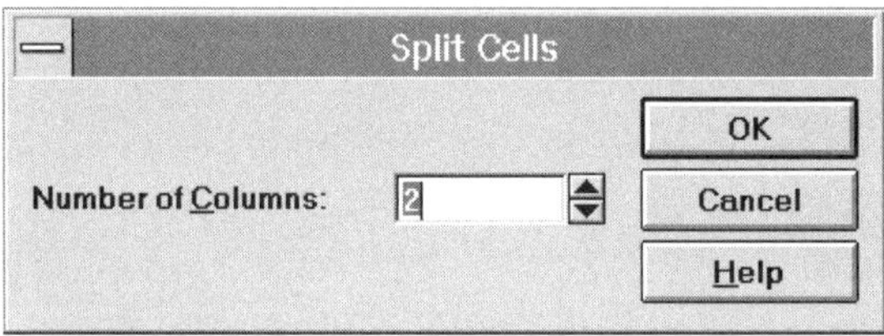

Figure 8.13 Sample Split-Cell Table

Word Table Sample

Monday	Tuesday		Wednesday	Thursday	Friday
Item 1	Item 2	Item A			

Formatting a Table

So far we have looked at basic Word tables. Word inserts the dotted-line cell boundaries into your document so you can enter data in the proper location. However, when you print the table, no lines appear with the data. If you want lines around cell data or if you want other table formatting such as shading, you have to add it to your table.

Adding Printable Borders

One of the simplest formatting additions you can make to your Word tables is printable lines and borders. Here's how:

- Place the insertion point within the table.
- Use the Table, Select Table command sequence to select the entire table.

- Click on the borders icon on the standard toolbar to display the Borders toolbar.
- Click on the outline icon (second from the right) to place a box around the outside of the table.
- Click on the cell icon (third from the right) to place a border around each cell in the table.

Now when you print the table the borders will appear with the data. Notice also that you can selectively border cells in a table. Just select the cells to which you want to add borders and issue the Borders command. The icons on the left of the toolbar also let you place a line along any single edge of a cell: right, left, top, and bottom.

Adding Graphics

I've mentioned that you can use graphic images in a Word table. You might want to do this as a way of designing creative headings or to help illustrate an idea. Particularly if the table appears within a document cover or as a section title, you might want to use symbols as column headings, for example. Suppose you wanted to create a table that showed sales summaries for various products. You could place drawings or scanned images of the products at the head of each column for individual products.

To do this:

- Position the insertion point within the cell you want to hold a graphic image.
- Use the Insert, Picture... command sequence to display the Insert Picture dialog.
- Choose the directory and file for the image you want to insert.
- Click on OK.

Word inserts the selected image into the current table cell. Depending on the original format for the graphic, the image may be too large for your table. Simply select the image by clicking on it, then use the mouse to resize it. Move the mouse over the edge of the graphic until the pointer changes to a double-ended arrow. Press and hold the left mouse button and drag the edge of the image to the size you need.

Changing Column Width and Row Height

Word creates tables with default cell widths that will handle much of your data entry needs. Remember, too, that as you enter information into table cells, Word adjusts row height to hold information that wraps to the second line. Word does not increase the column width. Rather, it moves information that is too wide to fit within the cell to the next line within the current cell.

If you want to change the width of any cells within the table, simply move the mouse pointer to the column you want to change and over a column boundary. The mouse pointer changes to a double vertical line with a double-ended arrow. Press and hold the left mouse button and drag the column border to its new location. When you release the mouse button Word changes the column width to the new value, wrapping or expanding text within the column accordingly. You can use this technique to increase or decrease the width of individual columns.

You can also use the Cell Height and Width dialog from the Table menu (see Figure 8.14).

This is a tabbed dialog that lets you specify settings for columns and rows separately. The row settings are on top by

Figure 8.14 Cell Height and Width Dialog

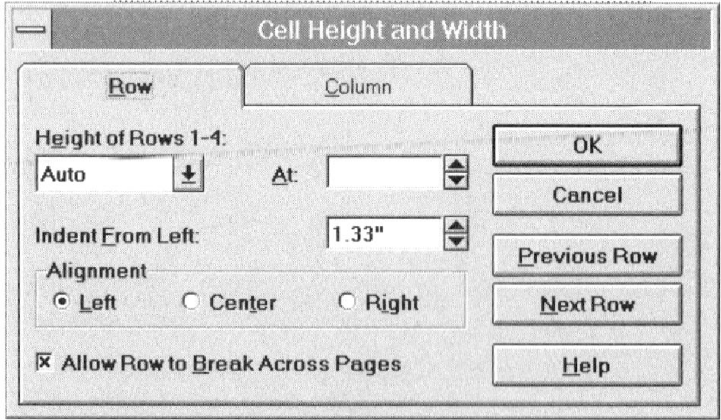

default. Row height is set to Auto and will match the font you are using within the table. If you specify a 12-point font, for example, then the row height is set to 12 points.

Pull down the list to the right of the Height of Rows field to select from At Least and Exactly. Choose either of these options and a number appears in the At: field of this dialog. The height of the current font appears in this field by default. You can enlarge or reduce the figure if you wish. Just be cautious in reducing the number too far or the data will be difficult to read.

Use the Previous Row/Next Row buttons to move among rows on the table. And, you can adjust the way text appears in the cells by changing the Indent From Left value or by clicking on one of the Alignment buttons.

Click on the Column tab in this dialog to display the choices shown in Figure 8.15.

The settings in this dialog let you set the width of table columns in inches. Either type a number in the Width of Column field, or use the up and down arrows to the right of the field to select a number.

Also use this dialog to select the previous or next column, and to adjust the spacing between columns.

Figure 8.15 Column Tab of the Cell Height and Width Dialog

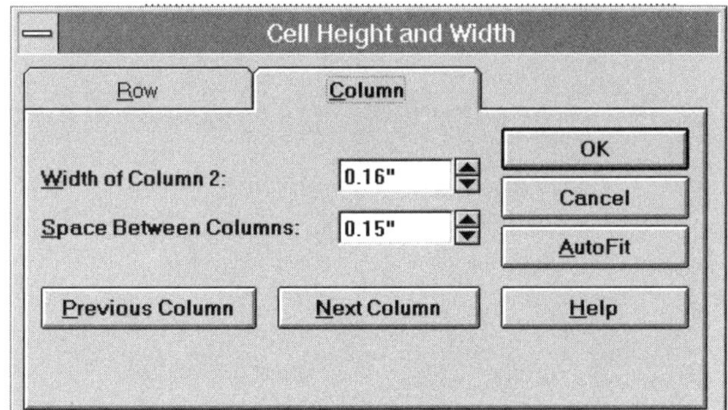

Using Table AutoFormat

I have shown you several techniques for changing the basic format of your Word tables. Word includes a sophisticated software routine to help you adjust table formats creatively.

To display the AutoFormat dialog, click anywhere inside the table you want to format, then use the Table, AutoFormat... command sequence. The dialog shown in Figure 8.16 will appear.

This dialog provides 34 separate, preformatted table designs that you can use. Simple 1 is the default design and the one shown in the Preview window of Figure 8.16. Others offer more shading and color, different sets of lines, and so on.

Most of this formatting uses fairly standard Word paragraph formatting features, including borders, shading, and colors. Which format you choose depends on the type of data your table contains and the intended audience for your document that contains the table. If you are including the table as part of a larger document that will be printed, a relatively simple format

Figure 8.16 Word AutoFormat Table Dialog

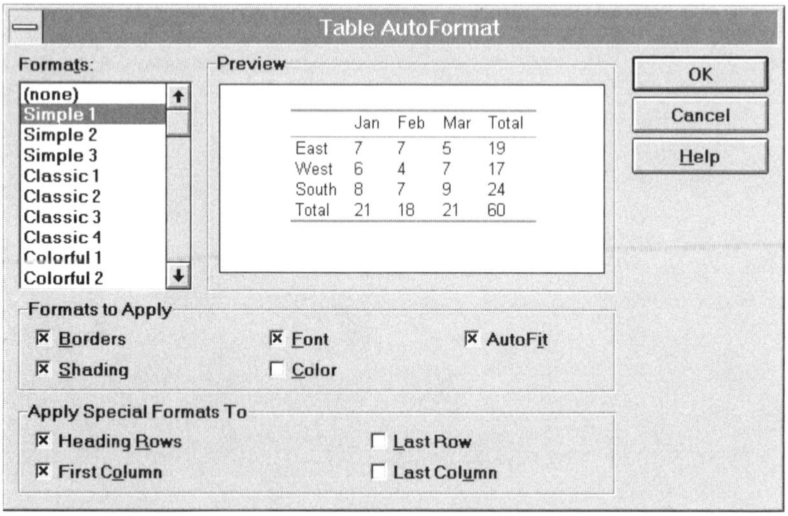

is probably the best choice. If you are designing an overhead slide, or an illustration that is a standalone figure within a document, then a more complex design is acceptable.

Notice that in addition to the defaults, the AutoFormat feature includes check boxes to help you adjust the basic formats included with this routine. And, of course, when you have specified the preformatted design you can further adjust the settings by changing border, shading, and color settings with standard Word command sequences.

Summary

Word tables offer a powerful and useful tool for organizing and presenting data. Word tables are used for price lists, performance or sales data, reference lists, and more. Word tables help you create document illustrations or slides for overhead projection. They can be simple or complex, but Word utilities help make using tables easy.

One of the keys to successful table applications is simply to remember to use them. Frequently we tend to create in-document lists with data separated by tabs or spaces. However, this type of data presentation is difficult to edit and maintain and isn't always consistent in its presentation. Anytime you need to present comparative data, lists, and other reference or illustration material, consider using a Word table.

In the next chapter I'll show you additional information on using Word styles. I introduced styles earlier in this book. In Chapter 9 I'll give you more details on using styles for creative document design.

Chapter 9

Using and Creating Styles

Styles are an important part of Microsoft Word. Whenever you create a new document in Word you are using styles because Word establishes styles as part of the templates on which all documents are based.

You need to know something about Word styles, if for no other reason than that Word uses styles automatically and you should know a little about how this works to make your documents work for you.

Beyond that basic need, however, you should know about styles because when you have control of Word styles you have control of your document. Styles work for you in individual documents, but they become even more important when you use Word in a workgroup where several users work with the same or a series of documents.

I introduced styles in Chapter 3. In this chapter I'll reiterate some of that information, but I'll also show you how to use styles you design yourself in Word documents. And I'll introduce some style management and creation procedures you'll probably find useful.

Choose Formatting Text from the main CD Directory, then click on the Styles button for interactive help with Word styles.

What Is a Style?

Until you've consciously used styles, understanding just what a style is can be difficult. I'd like to define styles in two ways: I'll try a standard, dictionary-type definition, and I'll also describe styles in terms of what they do in your document.

A Word style is a specification for typeface and character attributes as well as other document appearance characteristics. The document specification may include paragraph formats, page margins, and the like.

Now for some more detail.

Why use a style instead of just setting the typeface and attribute for a word or line of text? After all, you can use the Format, Font dialog to set a wide range of text specifications. Suppose you have designed a lengthy company report and you used Times New Roman type set in 14-point bold for main headings. In a long document there may be 20 or 30 of these. At some point you decide that headings at the highest level should use 12-point Helvetica bold.

If you have formatted individual heading lines with the Font dialog, then you have 20 or 30 changes to make. If you used a heading style—and you've used it consistently—then you have only one change to make. With Word styles you can play "what if" with your document design, sort of like plugging in different numbers on a spreadsheet.

To continue the heading change example, suppose you change all of the headings from Times New Roman to Helvetica, only to discover that this is the wrong font for your document. Want to make another 20 or 30 changes?

Well, you get the idea.

Styles let you define character, paragraph, and other document features once, then apply them in one document or many documents, in one area or many areas. Once you become aware of the default Word styles and learn how to use them and modify them, you can achieve a great deal of consistency across a range of documents.

Want to specify how all periodic departmental reports will appear? Just design a series of styles to specify character and other characteristics, and distribute the styles to everyone involved in creating the reports.

NOTE: For this type of document consistency you also can consider the use of a custom template. A template can carry the styles you want your departmental writers to use and can include any preformatted document features that can apply to all documents.

Types of Styles

There are two basic types of Word styles: character and paragraph. As you would expect from the name, a *character style* applies to one or more characters that you select prior to invoking the style. A *paragraph style* includes character and paragraph formats and applies to an entire paragraph.

By far the majority of Word styles are paragraph styles, styles that apply to an entire paragraph. To apply a paragraph style:

- Place the insertion point anywhere within the paragraph you want to format.
- Pull down the style list from the Style list box on the format toolbar.
- Choose the style you want to apply by double-clicking on the style name.

You also can choose a style from the Style dialog, available from the Format menu. I'll give you more details on using the Style dialog later in this chapter.

NOTE: Word paragraph styles are shown in boldface in the style list; character styles appear in normal text.

Word includes a number of paragraph styles, including several heading styles (Heading 1, Heading 2, Heading 3, and so on), Normal (the style used for the majority of body text), list styles, annotation styles, and more. Character styles include the Default Paragraph Font style, the Line Number style, and the Footnote Reference style.

When you start a new document with the Normal template, you are using the Normal style for the majority of the text. Normal is the default style for body text in the Normal template.

A style may include only a single setting, such as paragraph indenting, or how much extra space will be allowed before or after the paragraph break. Or, you can include typeface attributes, line spacing, margins, indenting, and more within a single style.

The Normal style is relatively complex and contains a number of character and paragraph settings and in general forms the basis for all other styles, ones included with Word and ones you create yourself. You don't have to base a new style on the Normal style, of course, but unless you specify otherwise, new Word styles are based on the Normal style.

You can use the Format, Style... command sequence to display the Style dialog to learn more about the Normal style. This dialog (see Figure 9.1) lets you view style settings, edit styles, create style shortcut keys, and create new styles.

To see what settings are associated with the Normal style, select Normal in the Styles: window on the left side of this dialog if it is not already selected. Click on Modify... to display the Modify dialog, shown in Figure 9.2.

Click on the Format button to pull down a list of additional dialogs you can use to view or change settings in the Normal style. These are dialogs you can use to set individual document attributes, but when you change them here you are setting

Figure 9.1 Style Dialog

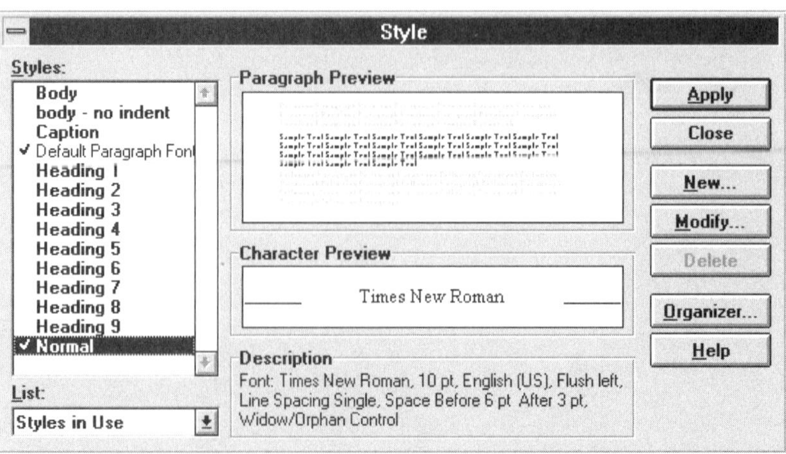

Figure 9.2 Modify Style Dialog

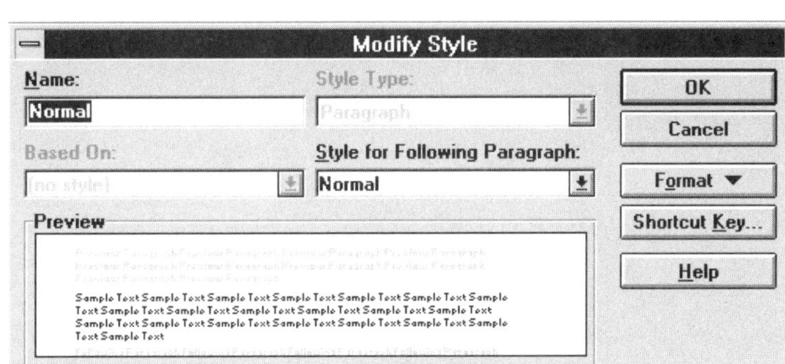

attributes for the style. The list in Table 9.1 shows the basic formatting included with the Normal style.

So, the settings in Table 9.1 are the ones you use most frequently with your Word documents, unless you have modified the default settings for the Normal template, or you use a different template for the majority of your documents.

Here's a simple exercise to show you how styles work.

- From the main Word screen click on File and choose New. The template dialog, shown in Figure 9.3, is displayed.
- Accept the default Normal template by clicking on OK or pressing Enter at this dialog. Word displays a blank editing screen with the Normal style selected. (Look at the style list box in the upper left corner of the screen, at the extreme left of the format toolbar.)
- Type at least two paragraphs of data. You can make something up, or "Greek" the text if you wish. (*Greeked* text is nonsense words you enter from the keyboard during document design just to test fonts, spacing, layout, and so on. Just type a series of characters with regular spaces to simulate words.)

Table 9.1 Normal Style Formatting

Attribute	*Setting*
Font	Times New Roman, 12 Point
Paragraph	Indentation: 0 Special: None Spacing (Before/After): 0 Line Spacing: Single Alignment: Left
Tabs	Default (every 0.5 inch)
Border	None with No Shading
Language	English (U.S.)
Frame	Text wrap around; auto height and width Horizontal Position: left, relative to column, 0.13″ from text Vertical Position: 0″ relative to paragraph
Numbering	Plain bullets with decimal numbers

Figure 9.3 New Dialog Showing Templates

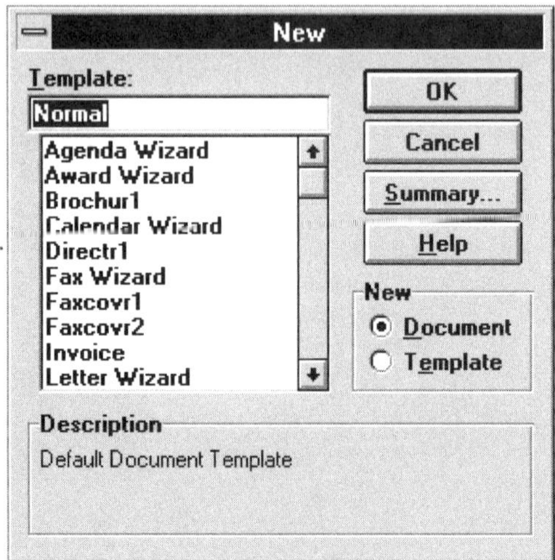

- Insert an extra line between the two paragraphs by positioning the cursor at the beginning of the second paragraph and pressing the Enter key.
- Type a heading for the second paragraph. Something like **Paragraph Two** will be fine.
- Pull down the list of styles from the format toolbar and choose Heading 1 as the style for this heading. You will see the font change and you will see the name of the style in the style box change to Heading 1.
- Move the cursor into the second paragraph. Notice that the Heading 1 style label is replaced by Normal when you position the cursor inside the paragraph.

That is the basics of styles. You have two paragraphs in this new document, both with Normal formatting, and you have one heading with the Heading 1 formatting. You can tell from looking at the document on the screen that the Heading 1 format is different from the Normal formatting. Word goes beyond simple screen appearance in using this difference in style. When you design a document with paragraph and heading styles, you can then create an outline or table of contents automatically. Word uses the different levels of heading style to create levels within the table of contents or within the outline.

Changing Styles

There is still another aspect of the style question. This sample document is very simple—two paragraphs and a single heading—but suppose the document were hundreds of pages long and included thousands of paragraphs? How are you going to change the font used in each of the paragraphs? Or suppose the editor or team director on the project decides hundreds of pages into the document that the initial line of all paragraphs should be indented?

By using styles, you can solve problems such as these quickly and easily. Using the sample document you have on the screen, let's demonstrate how both of these "problems" can be handled easily.

- Select Format and choose Style... from the main Word menu bar. The Style dialog you have seen before is displayed.

Figure 9.4 Font Dialog

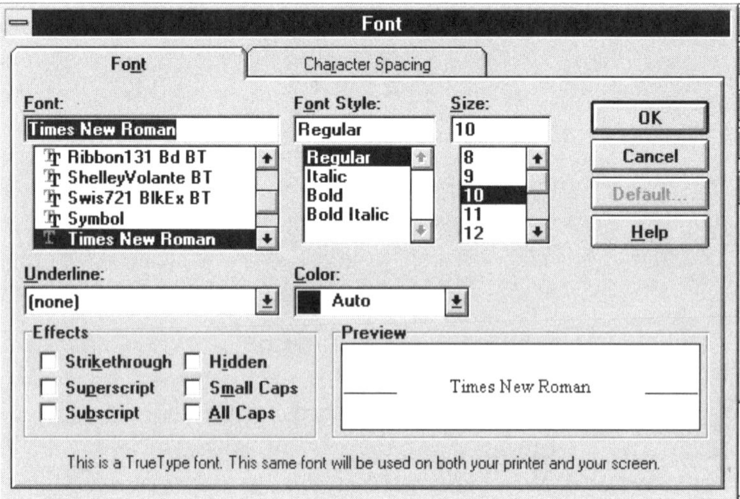

- Make sure the Normal style is highlighted in the left window of this dialog and click on Modify... to display the Modify Style dialog.
- Click on the Format button and choose Font from the pull-down list. The Font dialog, shown in Figure 9.4, is displayed. Notice that the default font, Times New Roman, and the default size, 10 point, are shown.
- Choose a font that is significantly different from Times New Roman. Arial Rounded MT Bold is a good choice.
- Choose a large font size, say 14 points.
- Click on OK to close the Font dialog and return to the Modify Style dialog.
- Click on Format again and choose Paragraph... from the pull-down list. The Paragraph dialog is displayed.
- Pull down the list of options under the Special: title and choose First Line. This tells Word to indent the first line of all paragraphs.
- Click on OK to close this dialog and return to the Modify Style dialog.

- Click on OK to close this dialog and return to the Style dialog.
- Click on Apply to apply this style to the current paragraph, close this dialog, and return to your document.

Notice what has happened. The Heading 1 font is the same as before, but the font used in both paragraphs has been changed to Arial Rounded MT Bold (or whatever font you chose when you were changing the style). In addition, the first line in each of the paragraphs is indented a single tab setting.

See the value in styles? This is a two-paragraph document, but if the document contained 1,000 paragraphs based on the Normal style, the result would have been the same. All of them would have been changed to match the new specification you chose from the Modify Style dialog.

Creating Style Shortcut Keys

There's another way of modifying styles that I find useful: shortcut keys. A *shortcut key* is a combination of keystrokes, usually a Ctrl+ or Alt+ key combination, that lets you conduct certain software operations quickly without going through menus.

I particularly like to specify shortcut keys for the heading styles so I can turn on heading formatting from the keyboard without having to pull down the style list on the format toolbar or use the Style dialog from the Format menu. Some shortcut keys already are defined within the Normal template. For example, you should be able to hold down the ctrl+alt+1 keys at the same time and turn on the Heading 1 style.

Try it. Did the style of the current paragraph change to Heading 1? If not, you can create this shortcut combination—or any other style shortcut you want—easily from the Modify Style dialog. Here's how:

- Select Format from the main Word menu and choose Style... to display the Style dialog.
- Choose the style for which you want to create a shortcut key from the list at the left of this dialog.
- Click on the Modify button (or use the Alt+m key combination) to display the Modify Style dialog.
- Click on the shortcut keys button to display the Customize dialog shown in Figure 9.5. This is a tabbed

Figure 9.5 Style Customize Dialog

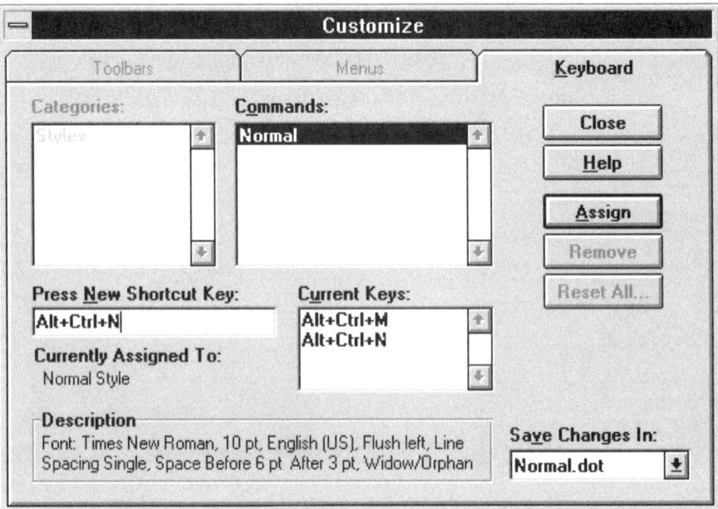

dialog; the Keyboard tab is on top and the cursor is positioned in the Press New Shortcut Key: field.

- Press the keyboard combination you want to use for this shortcut key. This should be a combination that is unlikely to be used in the normal course of typing a document and it should be one you can remember.

For example, to create a shortcut key for the Heading 4 style, you might use Ctrl+Alt+4. This is a fairly easy combination to enter with today's keyboards that generally have Alt and Ctrl keys on both sides of the keyboard. And the number 4 helps you remember that it is for heading style 4. Notice that Word tells you if the combination you specify has previously been assigned to another shortcut key. If you see "unassigned" below the shortcut key field, then that combination of keystrokes is not in use. Otherwise, you will see what that combination of keys is already programmed to do.

- When you have specified the shortcut key combination you want to use, click on the Assign button at the right of this dialog.

NOTE: Do not just click on Close without clicking on Assign. If you do, the shortcut key combination will not be assigned to the Word style.

- Click on Close to close the Customize dialog.
- Click on OK to close the Modify Style dialog and click on Apply to close the Style dialog, apply the style to the current paragraph, and return to your document.

NOTE: You can click on Close instead of Apply to save the setting without applying the style to the current paragraph.

Now you can use the newly specified shortcut key to turn on a specific style by placing the insertion point within the paragraph you want to format and pressing the correct keyboard combination.

NOTE: If Word tells you the shortcut key combination you specify is already assigned to another Word feature, you can either choose another keystroke combination, or elect to overwrite the existing definition with one of your own. Even when a previous assignment is noted, when you click on Assign in the Customize dialog, whatever shortcut key you specified will be assigned to the style you chose from the Style menu previously.

Modifying Styles in the Current Template

The style formats and changes I have shown to this point have applied only to the current document. Remember that when you start a new document based on the Normal template (or any other template) Word loads the specifications for that template and inserts them into the current document. Any changes you make to the document format apply just to this document.

There may be times, however, when you create a new style or change a style and you want those changes to apply to the underlying template whenever you use that template again. I find that the 10-point type is too small for my liking, for example, because I use 1,024 × 768 resolution. I prefer 12-point type, so I change the template to default to 12-point whenever I start a new document.

To do that, use the techniques I described previously to modify a style, then before you close the Modify Style dialog, click on the Add to Template check box in the lower lefthand corner of this dialog. That tells Word to apply the style changes to the current document, but also to make the same changes to the underlying template.

After you close the Style dialog the style you modified changes immediately within the current document, but the next time you start a new document, these changes also show up in the style you modified. Changes you save to the template appear in any new document you create with this same template.

Creating New Styles

Creating a new style in Word is almost as easy as changing an existing one. Let's assume you are working on a document that will include a number of lengthy quotes (longer than 8 or 10 lines). You can format quotes any way you want, but the *Chicago Manual of Style* suggests that long quotes should be set off from the rest of the text in some way to indicate clearly the difference between the current text and the quoted text. There are several ways to set off long quotes, including smaller type size, different alignment, different line spacing (sometimes called *leading*), indenting from the left and/or right, or some combination of these.

For this example, let's assume you will indent quoted material from the left and reduce the type size two points. Here's how to create a QUOTE style that you can use for any paragraph that is a long quote:

- Select Format and choose Style... to display the Style dialog.
- Click on New... (or press Alt+n) to display the New Style dialog, shown in Figure 9.6. Style1 is the default name highlighted in the Name: field of this dialog.
- Type the name of the new style.

  For our example, type **QUOTE** as the new style name. Note that the next field to the right shows the default is a Paragraph style. That's what we want for

Figure 9.6 New Style Dialog

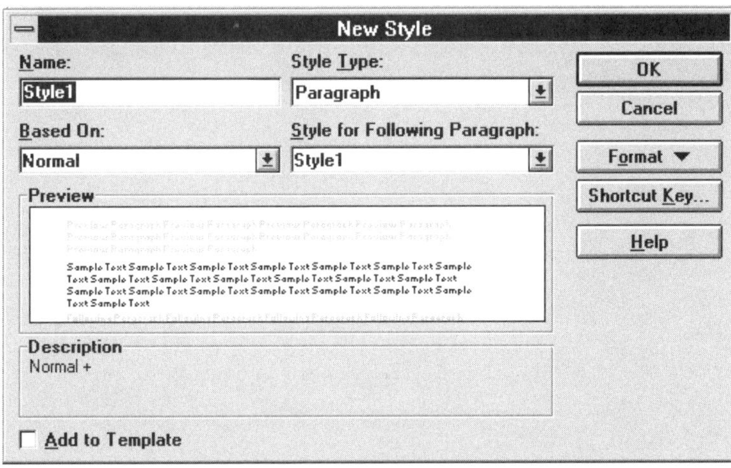

this example, so we won't change that, but you could pull down a list and choose Character instead, if you wanted.

- Accept the default of Normal in the Based On: field of this dialog.

  Normal is the default, but you can pull down a list of all available styles to base this one on something else if you wish. At the bottom of the dialog you can see how the style is taking place. Notice the Normal+ notation in the Description area of this dialog. As you add new features Word adds details to this notation.

- Choose Normal from the pull-down list associated with the Style for Following Paragraph: field.

  This field stores the style that Word will insert automatically when you press Enter after the paragraph formatted with QUOTE. The default is QUOTE, but we don't want to follow our new style with a repeat of the same style. We want to return to Normal after using QUOTE, so enter Normal in this field.

NOTE: You can move among the fields on this dialog by pressing Tab or Shift+Tab, or you can use the mouse to place the cursor where you want to add new data.

- Pull down the Format list and choose Paragraph.
- Enter **0.5** in the Left field in the Indention group of this dialog. You can type the number or use the up arrow key beside this field to specify the indention.
- If your Normal style is set for double spacing, then specify Single in the Line Spacing field of this dialog.
- Specify 6 points as the Spacing Before and 3 points as the Spacing After. You can specify additional spacing in this area if you want to offset the quoted material even further from the body text.
- Click on OK to close this dialog.
- Pull down the Format list again and choose Fonts.
- Specify a 10-point type, if you are using 12-point type for body text, or 8-point, if you are using Word's default of 10-point body type.
- Click on OK to close this dialog, then click on OK again to close the New Style dialog and return to the Style Dialog.
- Use the scroll bars if necessary to select the new QUOTE style you just created.

  Notice the description area of this dialog. Now you have a complete look at this new style. In addition, can you see from the list of available styles why I suggested that you enter the name of the new style in all uppercase? This makes your own styles stand out from those supplied with Word. Word's styles are listed in upper and lowercase, paragraph styles in boldface, and character styles in normal type. By entering your own styles in all uppercase you can spot them quickly and so can anyone else using your template, which might be the case if you have created a template for departmental or team use.
- Click on Close to close the Style dialog and return to your document.

Now try the new style. Enter a plain paragraph, using the default style (this should be Normal unless you have changed it), and introduce a quote. Press Enter to move the insertion point to the next line and pull down the list of styles in the Style list box on the format toolbar.

Choose the QUOTE style from the list, and type the text of the new paragraph. Note how the new text appears. It should be indented a half an inch and should appear in a typeface that is two points smaller than your body text.

Press Enter again to close this quote paragraph and return to the body of your document. Word should automatically revert to the Normal style, moving the text to the left margin and returning to the larger, default font.

NOTE: You could create a shortcut key for this new style if you wish. Use the Modify Style dialog as I described earlier to create a shortcut key. Alt+Ctrl+q, for example, would be a logical choice to turn on this style.

Create as many styles to support your particular document needs as you wish.

Organizer Dialog

Even with just the default styles included in Word it can be difficult to keep track of all the styles available, or to apply them as you wish. Two utilities—the Organizer and the Style Gallery—help you manage your styles. I'll discuss the Gallery in a moment. In this section I'll show you how to use the Organizer to help you manage Word styles.

The Organizer is a split-screen dialog that lets you copy styles from one document or template to another. This is useful if you have worked on a document, editing or creating styles, then you want to use one or more of those styles in a new document or document series.

To display the Organizer, select Format from the main Word menu, choose Style... to display the Style dialog, and click on the Organizer button to display the Organizer dialog, shown in Figure 9.7.

On the left side of this display is a list of styles available in the current document. On the right are the styles included in the Normal template. This dialog works left to right. You can copy any new styles you have created or style you have modified in the current document into the Normal template by

Figure 9.7 Style Organizer Dialog

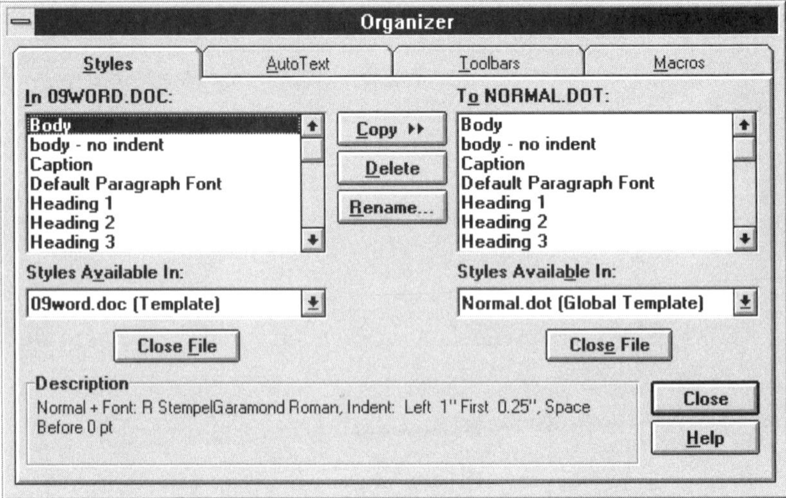

selecting the style you want to add to the Normal template and clicking the Copy button between the two windows.

Two other buttons provide additional control of the styles listed in the current document, Rename and Delete. These buttons apply to any style you have highlighted in the left window.

But suppose this isn't really what you want to do. Suppose there is an earlier document that contains a style you want to use in the current document. You can use the Organizer dialog to help you do this as well.

- Click on the Close File button on both sides of this dialog, closing the current document and the Normal template. The Close File buttons change to Open File.
- Click on Open File on the left side of this dialog and choose the file that contains existing styles you want to add to a later document from the file manager display.
- Click on Open File on the right side of this dialog and choose the file that will receive existing styles from the first document on the left side.

- Highlight the first style you want to add to the second document in the list on the left side of the dialog.
- Click on Copy to place a copy of the selected style into the document on the right side of this dialog.
- When you have copied all of the styles you want, click on the Close button to close this dialog.

Style Gallery

The Style Gallery provides still a different way of looking at your document styles. To display the gallery, select Format from the main Word menu and choose Style Gallery... to present the dialog shown in Figure 9.8.

The Style Gallery displays all Word templates and the styles available in each one. You can view a sample of each template in the Preview window at the right of this dialog. And you have three choices for viewing the results of choosing a specific template. You can have Word format the current document with the

Figure 9.8 Style Gallery Dialog

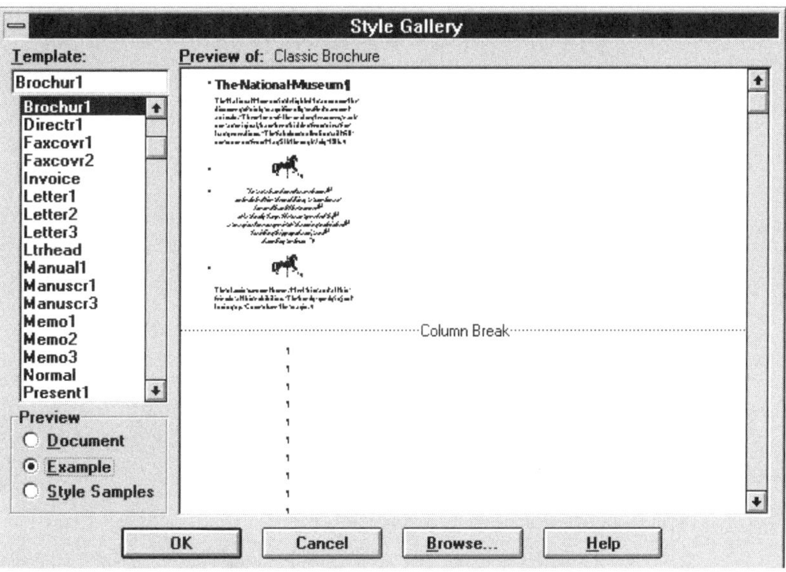

styles in the selected template (this is the default setting), you can display a sample document formatted with the selected template (an example), or you can display a sample document with all of the styles listed and with an example of each style.

The Style Gallery, as you can see, is really a template gallery, a way for you to experiment with different Word templates as they apply to your current document or to a sample document Word supplies for you.

When you have found a template you want to apply to the current document, click on OK to close the Style Gallery and return to your document with the specified template—and all of that template's styles—applied to the document.

The Style Gallery is an excellent tool for helping you understand what templates are available and what styles each of these contain.

Showing Styles in Use (The Style Area)

Normally as you work in a Word document, you aren't consciously aware of the styles in use, unless a particular style causes some really unusual formatting. You can tell what is the current style by looking at the style window on the format toolbar. But you have to move the cursor or insertion point into the paragraph or over the characters for which you want to check the style.

There's another way to view all of the styles in use in your document. Word maintains a hidden area to the left of each document page to display style names. If you want to open this display so you can view the style list, select Tools from the main Word menu and choose Options. The View tab should be on top of this multitabbed dialog. If it is not, click on View to bring this tab to the front.

Notice the Style Area Width field in the Window area at the lower left corner of this dialog. The Word default setting is zero, which hides the style name display. To display the names of all styles in use in your document, enter any number greater than zero in this field. About one half inch is a good choice. This is wide enough to display the style names without interfering greatly with normal document display. Figure 9.9 shows a document with the style area set to one-half inch.

Figure 9.9 Sample Document with 1/2-inch Style Area

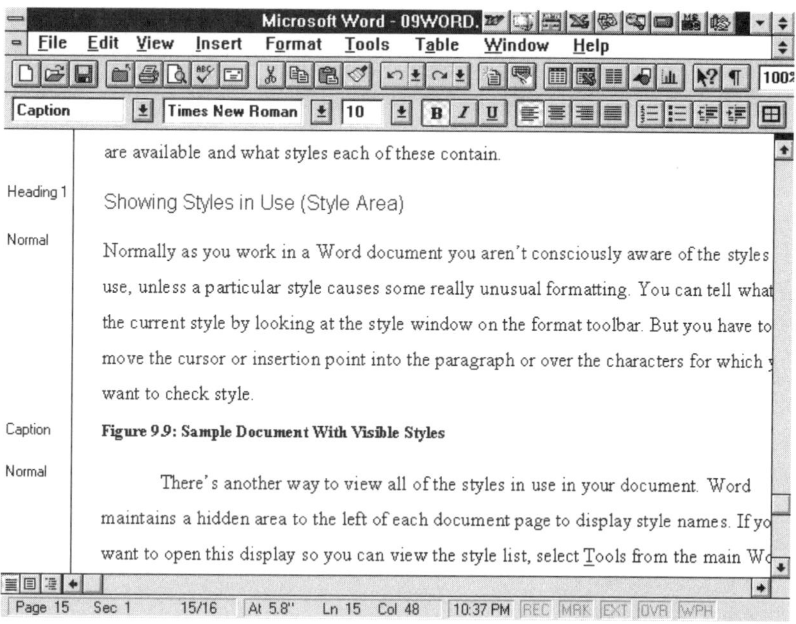

To remove (actually, to hide) the style list display, you can use the View tab on the Options menu to return the Style View width to zero. However, you also can hide the style name display with the mouse without calling up the Options dialog.

Simply grab the line that separates the document text from the style name display and drag the line to the left until the space is too narrow to display the style names. You can use this same technique to widen the style name display area if you want. You may need to do this if some style names are too long to be seen with the width you have chosen.

Summary

Word document styles are an important part of using Word successfully. Though it's true that you can do a lot with Word without ever using any but the Normal style (you have to use it because it is the basis of body text for the Normal template), if you experiment with using Word's default styles, and with modifying them or creating new styles of your own, you soon will see the value of this level of document formatting control. Styles are useful even if you are working alone, but you will really appreciate the flexibility styles offer as you work together with a group on a Word document project.

The best advice is to practice with styles before you really need them so that when you get into more involved document designs you will have at least been exposed to styles and the learning curve will be sharp.

Well, that's it. We've covered all the basics of Word 6. By now you should be fairly comfortable with this powerful and popular word processor.

In Appendix A I'll give you a brief tour of the CD-ROM included with this book. You'll learn how to install it, and I'll give you some hints on how to use it in conjunction with this book. Appendix B covers differences between Windows 3.x with Word 6.0 and Windows 95 with Word 7.

Appendix A

The Word CD

I feel extremely fortunate to have a working relationship with LearnKey, Inc. in St. George, Utah and AP PROFESSIONAL, in Chestnut Hill, Massachusetts. These liaisons combine into a powerful educational and marketing team that is responsible for bringing you this book.

I mentioned in the Introduction that this book is unusual. There aren't very many book-CD-video combinations available (in fact the AP PROFESSIONAL series is the only one I know of that is actually on the market). This book by itself offers a pretty good introduction to Microsoft Word for Windows 6.0. You can use the concepts I've offered here to learn how Microsoft has designed the product, how the basic screens are laid out, and how you use these basic tools.

I haven't covered everything you could do with Word in this book, and for a couple of very good reasons. For one thing, this is intended as an introductory book, something to make the transition to a full-featured word processing product easier, and a way to achieve comfort with basic Word functionality. The other reason for choosing the coverage I have for this book is to offer a range of topics that can also be covered reasonably on a CD-ROM video platform.

This book and the included CD-ROM work together to provide a complete learning solution. You can, and probably will, use either of these tools independently. However, it is the printed instructions coupled with the interactive voice and video on the CD-ROM that makes the most powerful and useful tool.

Why a CD?

This CD video actually has its beginnings in a 1992 book project with another major publisher. As I started writing this rather lengthy text, one of the editors on the project observed, "Now, Tom, you need to keep in mind that you are writing a book for an audience that really doesn't want to read books."

I found this seemingly simple statement surprising, thought provoking and not a little disturbing. At that point I had written somewhere in the neighborhood of 25 books and my entire career depended on continuing along the same track of producing four to six major books each year. What were the long-term implications, I wondered, of continuing a career track that was based on a product that the consumers of the product itself didn't really want?

Further research and introspection reassured me that books are still a quite viable product that millions of people do indeed want, thank you, but I also could see the need for alternative learning tools for people who are more interested in *using* the software or hardware I was writing about than in really *learning* about it. This new group of computer users were just that, users, not worshipers, of the technology.

So, I began drawing on a 10-year career of radio and television broadcasting and documentary film production to investigate other ways of sharing some of my hard-won knowledge of the computer field. During this research I stumbled across John Clemons and his crew of professionals at LearnKey. They were plowing new ground converting successful computer-industry books to video tape. They were working with writers to turn 300- or 400-page computer books into four to six hours of video tape.

I liked what I saw and started producing a few tapes to go along with the books I was writing. Then John's brother, Dave, started working with all these videos to convert them to interactive CD-ROM videos. The rest is history. It took a lot of sweat and tears to make it all work, but the CD-ROM interactive video you have in your hands is proof of the validity of the idea. The combination of book and CD makes a powerful learning tool that is easy to use. I believe it makes learning a potentially difficult subject a whole lot easier.

Besides, how many books have you bought where you could see the author, hear the author speak, and work interactively with the products the author writes about?

This combination is the beginning of a successful trend in publishing and education, I believe.

WHAT IS ON THE CD?

This CD stores somewhere around 600 megabytes of graphics, software, sound and video. In today's computer market where you can purchase a 1-gigabyte, IDE hard drive for under $300, this doesn't sound as impressive as it did just a couple of years ago. But it is still a lot of interactive data, in a format that can't be written over or erased.

There are three basic components to this CD. There is the video component, of course. This is where the programmers at LearnKey, Arizona, studied, tweaked and edited several hours of video and crunched it down to fit on this CD. You'll see me sitting in front of my PC discussing various aspects of Microsoft Word: what it is, how to use it, how to design documents with it.

Then there's the graphic component. This is where LearnKey programmers show you closeups of Word screens on video and use digital recordings from the Word software. These sections let you see in sharp detail how to manage Word facilities. You will see my video describe an operation, then you will see on the screen how the mouse moves and what keystrokes are used to accomplish the described task.

Finally, there is the interactive Word component. Through skillful programming, LearnKey has made it possible to keep the CD-based software running, launch Word from your local PC, and step you through interactive operations so you can try for yourself the techniques you saw demonstrated and discussed on the CD. When you are finished with the hands-on practice, you can jump right back into the video/graphics section of the CD for further instruction.

That's the format of the information on the CD. But what is the content? Basically what is covered in this book is covered with either more or less detail on the CD. I have taken some subjects a little further in the book than I had time to do on the CD, so you may want to work with the CD first, then expand your knowledge by reading the book for additional detail.

CD Hardware Requirements

You don't need a particularly sophisticated hardware platform to use this CD-ROM. You need a CD player, of course, and you'll be happier if yours is a quad speed drive. However, a dual speed drive will work OK, too.

Then you need a multimedia platform—speakers and a sound card—so you can hear the audio component of this CD. In addition, you should have at least 8 megabytes of RAM memory. This helps all Windows-based programs run faster. Of course, additional memory, say 16 MB or so, will speed things up as well.

And, you need enough hard disk space to install the software associated with this CD. You'll need about 1 megabyte of free disk space to install the software that comes with the CD-ROM.

CD Software Requirements

Software requirements also are modest. You'll need Microsoft Windows 3.0, 3.1, or Windows 95 to run this disk. That also says something about your hardware requirements. If you have enough memory to run Windows at an acceptable speed, for example, you have all that is absolutely required.

In addition to Windows and the underlying DOS software (unless you are running Windows 95), you will need any driver software required to run your CD-ROM player, your hard disk, and your audio (sound) card.

Installing the CD

Installing the Word CD-ROM video software is easy and predictable. If you have installed other Windows-based software, then installing this CD-ROM package should be straightforward. Here's how it works:

NOTE: In this section of this book I have used Windows 95 to demonstrate the installation of the LearnKey CD software in this environment. Operation in Windows 95 and Windows 3.x is the same. Some of the dialogs appear slightly different in the two environments, that's all.

- Insert the CD disk in your player.
- Use File, Run from the Program Manager screen and enter the path to your CD-ROM to run the program setup.

  If your CD player is on drive D, for example, you would enter **D:setup** on the File, Run dialog. Within a few seconds the opening screen shown in Figure A.1 appears.

Figure A.1 Opening Setup Screen

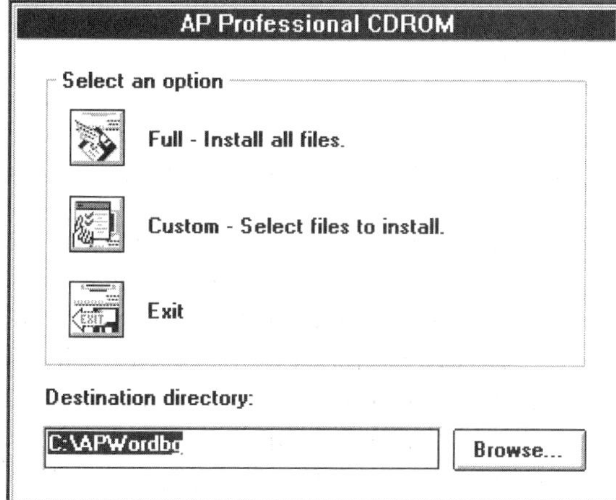

The setup routine suggests a directory for the LearnKey files. The default is c:\learnkey.

- To change the default directory, select the Destination directory field and enter the new path. To accept the suggested path, do nothing with the Destination information.

NOTE: You can click on the Browse button to scan available directories if you are not sure where you want to install the CD software.

- Click on Full-Install all Files to specify a full LearnKey installation. If you are concerned about available disk space, click on Custom install. However, I recommend a full install.

  When you click on Full-Install, the progress dialog shown in Figure A.2 is displayed.

  After a few seconds, the setup program asks if you want a Windows Program Manager group to be created. If you say no, you'll have to run the software with the File, Run command sequence. If you say yes, the dialog shown in Figure A.3 is created.

  Next, the setup routine tells you it is installing the video player software to allow your PC to play the video components of the CD. That screen is shown in Figure A.4.

Figure A.2 Install Progress Dialog

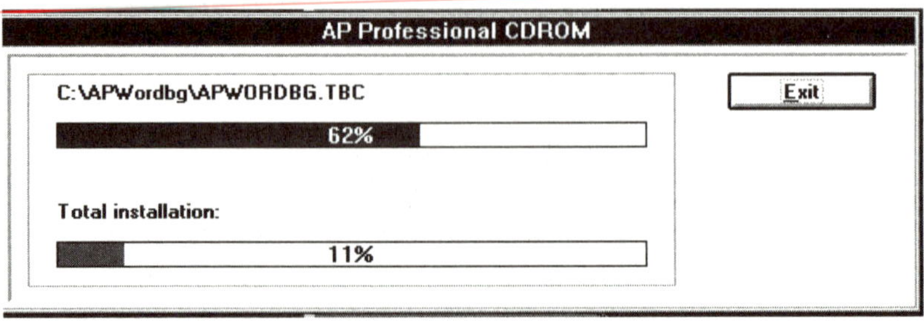

Figure A.3 LearnKey Program Manager Group

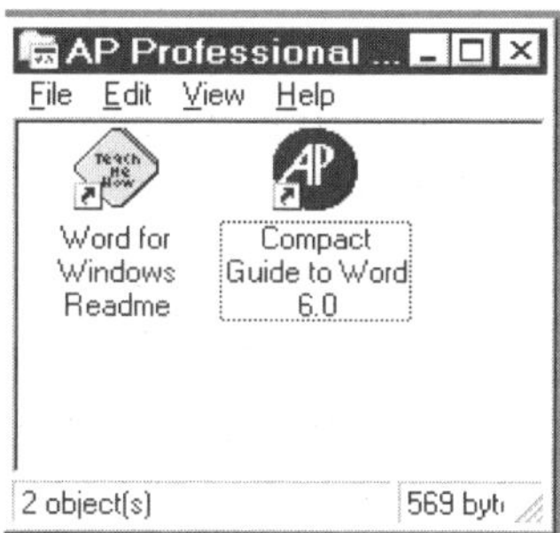

At the end of the installation, you have the necessary software on your hard drive, a Program Manager program group, and a CD that still contains the audio and video software. You are now ready to try the CD-ROM.

Figure A.4 Install Video Player Software Dialog

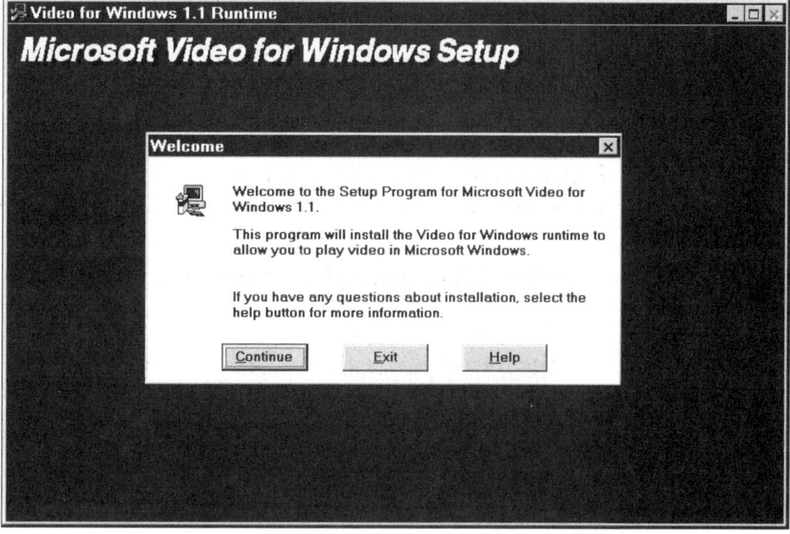

Using the CD

To launch the CD software, double-click on the Microsoft Word for Windows 6.0 icon in the LearnKey program group. The opening screen shown in Figure A.5 is displayed.

There are two choices on this dialog: Introduction and Directory. If you click on the Introduction button you will view a short introduction that includes a brief summary of the topics covered on the CD. One of the screens in this series is shown in Figure A.6.

When the introduction is over, the Directory screen, shown in Figure A.7, is displayed.

You can jump to the first item in the menu by clicking on the right arrow at the bottom of the display. Back up through topics with the left arrow. The screen in Figure A.8 is what you see when you click the right arrow.

Figure A.5 LearnKey CD Video Opening Screen

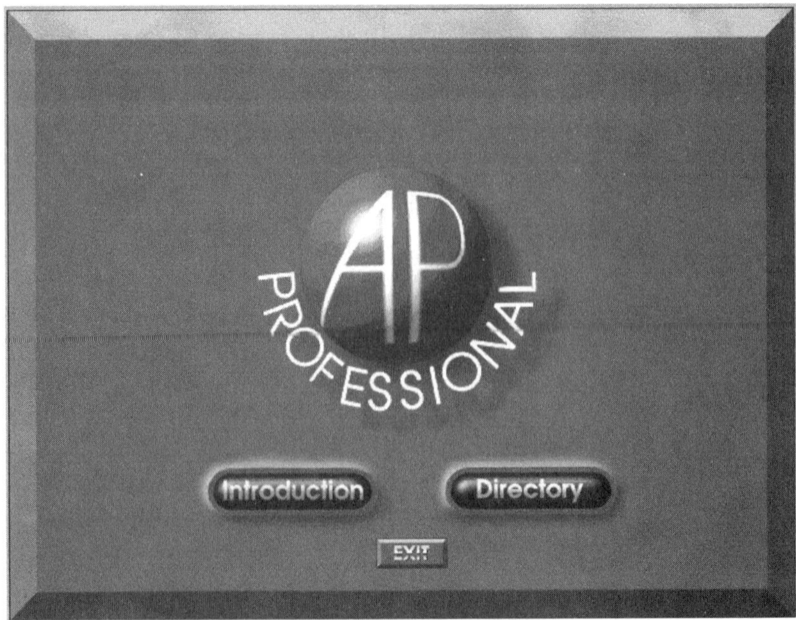

Figure A.6 LearnKey Introduction Sample Screen

Choose any of the topics on the Directory screen by clicking on the desired directory item. Each topic is slightly different, but in general you will see an opening video segment, then Word screens illustrating what I'm discussing, then in many cases a chance to interact with the section of Word discussed in the chosen segment.

Notice the four buttons to the right of the Directory dialog. You can use these to jump directly to some segments of the CD. On the Directory screen, for example, you have four choices, Help, Directory, Search, and Test.

Figure A.9 shows one of the screen segments from the Create a Document selection under Word 6.0 Basics.

Notice that the dialog changes once you enter one of the instructional areas. Now, instead of the large buttons for Directory, Search, and so on, you should see a series of smaller buttons in the upper right corner of the display that show the current topic being discussed on the video.

Figure A.7 LearnKey CD Directory Display

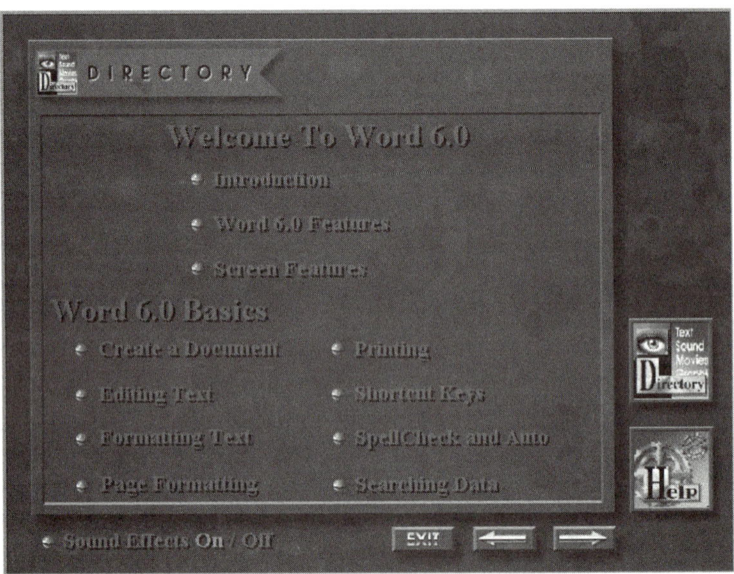

Figure A.8 Second Screen of the CD Video Directory

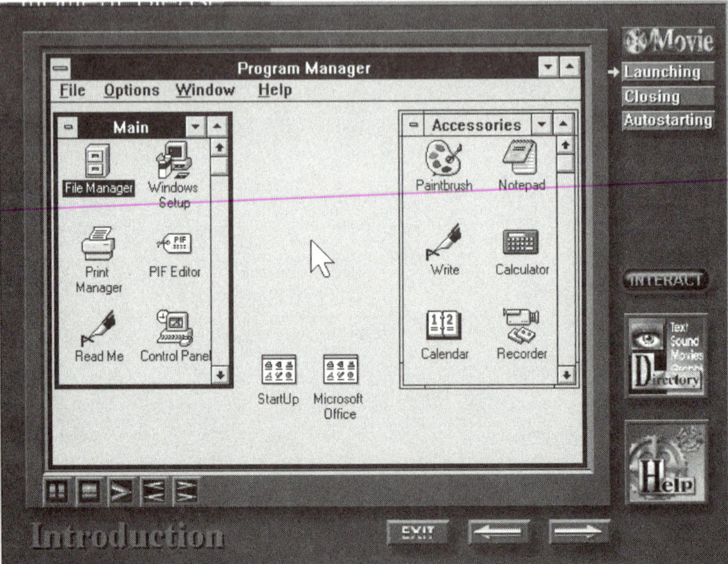

Figure A.9 Sample Create a Document Dialog

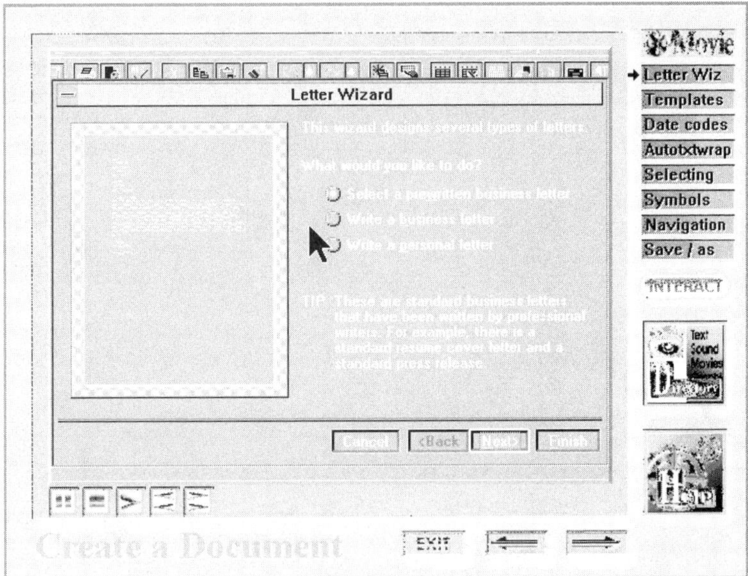

In Figure A.9, for example, the top button is Letter Wiz and there is an arrow pointing to it, indicating that it is the current topic. Beneath that button are others labeled Templates, Date Codes, Autotxtwrap, Selecting, Sumbols, Navigation, and Save/as. If you just let the video run, you'll see information on each of these topics in turn. Or, you can jump ahead to other topics by clicking on the appropriate button.

Notice the Interact button between the topic list at the top of the dialog and the Directory and Search buttons at the bottom. This is a way to suspend the video instruction and launch Word so you can interact directly with the software. This is one of the really powerful features of this CD. You can listen to the video discussion, you can watch as I demonstrate a process, then you can jump out of the CD software and into Word to try something for yourself.

When you choose the Interact button, you may be presented with a screen like the one in Figure A.10 asking which of the topics under discussion you want to try.

If Word is already running then the Word screen comes up very quickly. The first time you choose Interact, it will take a

Figure A.10 CD-ROM Interact Dialog

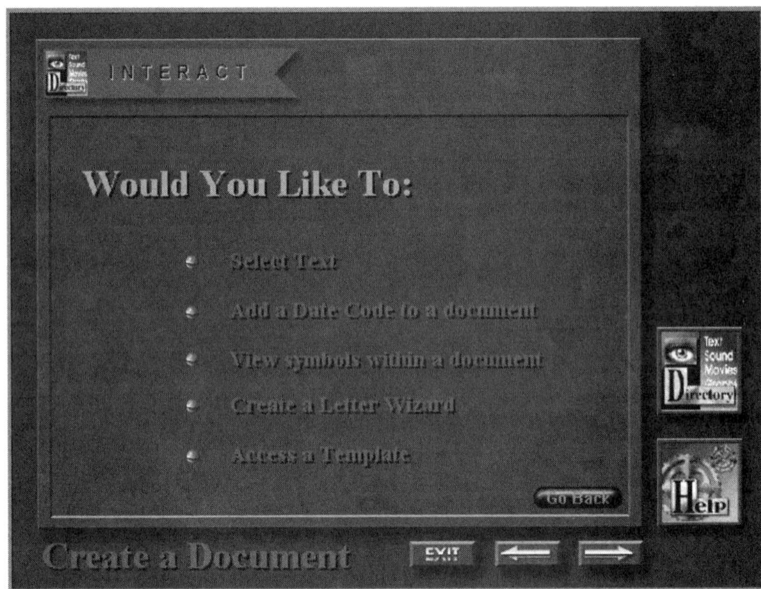

few seconds for the instruction software to locate the Word software and launch the program.

When you choose a topic from a dialog like the one in Figure A.10, Word is opened with an appropriate screen for the task you selected. You can return to the CD by closing Word and, if the CD software is not on the screen, selecting the icon from the Program Manager. You can toggle between Word and the CD by holding down the Alt key and pressing Tab until the application you want to access is displayed. You can also use Ctrl+Esc to display the task list. From this screen you can choose the CD or Word at your discretion.

Choosing Topics

With the interactive nature of the CD video screen, you can pick a topic from the Directory and jump straight to it. Choose

Figure A.11 CD Search Dialog

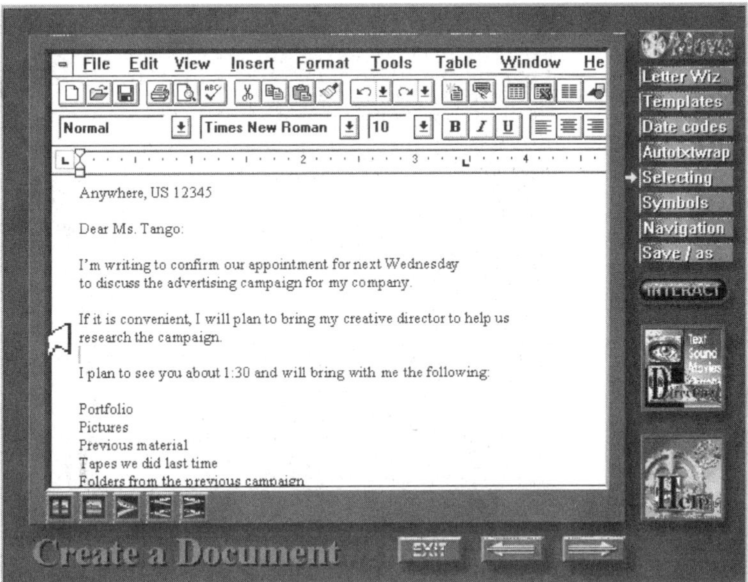

a subtopic from the first screen by clicking on a button on the right of the dialog. For example, you can click on the Selecting button (Figure A.11).

CD Help

Although this interactive CD should be easy to install and to use, you may need some pointers on some procedures. Online help is always available. Simply click on the large Help button that appears on most of the screens to display the dialog shown in Figure A.12.

Click on the topic button you want to explore to bring up help for that area. You will hear an audio description of the procedure, accompanied by graphics and text. For example, if you select the General Instructions button from the Help dialog in Figure A.12, you'll see the screen in Figure A.13.

Figure A.12 CD Help Dialog

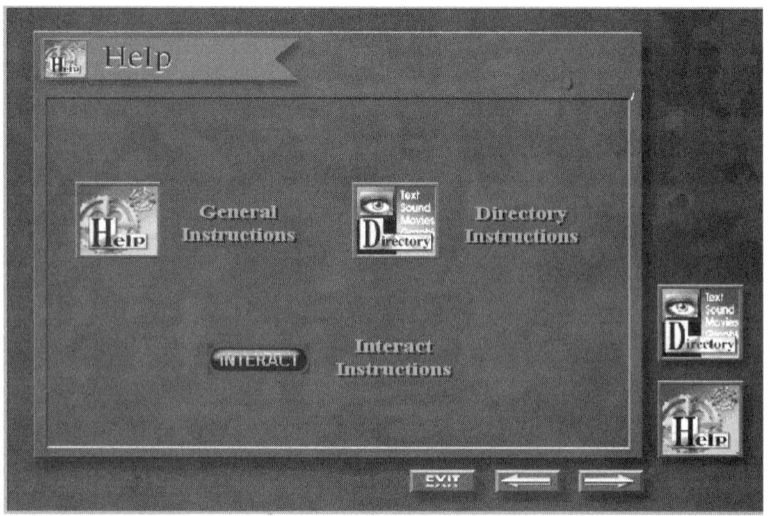

Figure A.13 General Help Dialog

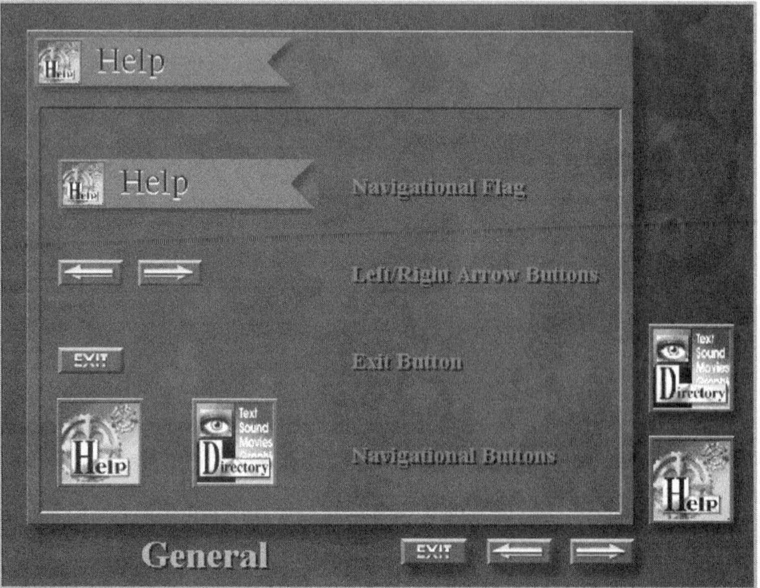

This screen displays a number of screen objects and topics. When you click on one of them, you hear an audio description of the chosen object.

SUMMARY

The Word CD that accompanies this book is intended to be intuitive and easy to learn and to use. Once you have the package installed, you should be able to step through the various features on the CD easily. After a few short sessions you'll understand the basic design conventions behind the package and moving deeper and deeper into the application should be easy.

Don't neglect the Help button. It provides audio and video help with the section you choose. Like the video CD itself, the help section is interactive so you can step through it to find the topic you want to know more about.

Also, consult Appendix B if you now have or are considering upgrading to Windows 95. Many of the features—in fact most—that I have shown in this book and that you see on the CD video apply equally to Windows 95. The screens and dialogs have a different appearance, and a few of the mouse and menu techniques are slightly different, but for the most part Word 7, which is the Windows 95 version, is very similar to Word 6.0.

Appendix B

Word and Windows 95

As this book is written Windows 3.x is the reigning operating environment for PC platforms, but Windows 95 enjoyed an extensive beta program and has now been released. From what I've seen—not just of the hype, but from several weeks of hands-on evaluation—Windows 95 will be a popular product. And, with the re-entrenchment of Windows, applications software written for it will follow close behind.

Microsoft released Office 95 concomitant to Windows 95. Office 95 includes PowerPoint 7, Excel 7, Schedule, Mail, and Word 7, the natural follow-on to Word 6.0. And, while Excel and PowerPoint underwent fairly deep changes in the Office 95 versions, Word 7 is only a modest upgrade from the previous versions, at least from the user perspective.

In this section I will provide a brief overview of Windows 95 and of Word 7. The data you find in the rest of this book as well as on the accompanying CD video is still valid. The basic concepts remain the same in this new version. However, you should be aware of the screen differences between Windows 3.x and Windows 95, because the applications that run with it, including Word 7, mirror this look.

Windows 95 Overview

Windows 95 is either the beginning of a new era in Intel-based computing, or a sad case of over-hype by America's giant among computer giants. Either way, it is destined to change the computer lifestyles of millions of people. If you're not using it now, you probably will be in the near future.

Windows 95 is a 32-bit operating system that includes a graphical user interface. It uses a folder motif to help you organize data, supports multitasking, and includes some user-oriented enhancements and changes that make it easier to learn and use. For one thing, Windows 95 is designed to let you install software and even hardware with a minimum of personal intervention. This "plug and play" concept has eluded computer users for years (although the Apple Macintosh has been closer than PCs for some time), but today's hardware and software is getting us closer to this reality.

As I mentioned, with Word you won't see quite as many changes between Windows 3.x and Windows 95, but as you broaden your software experience under Windows 95 the differences will become more apparent.

The first difference you will see between these two operating environments is the opening desktop display. In Windows 3.x the Program Manager is the basic operating environment. The Program Manager is composed of program groups that hold icons that represent individual programs. Figure B.1 shows a typical Program Manager desktop.

Windows 95, on the other hand, uses a series of icons that represent programs, disk drives, directories, and other objects. You can make this display relatively simple, or you can put everything you're likely to need as you work with your computer on the Windows 95 desktop. Figure B.2 shows a typical Windows 95 desktop.

In addition, notice that Windows 95 includes a status and control bar at the bottom of the screen. You use this bar to switch among running programs and to control some program features, such as the loudness of the sound system, if one is installed.

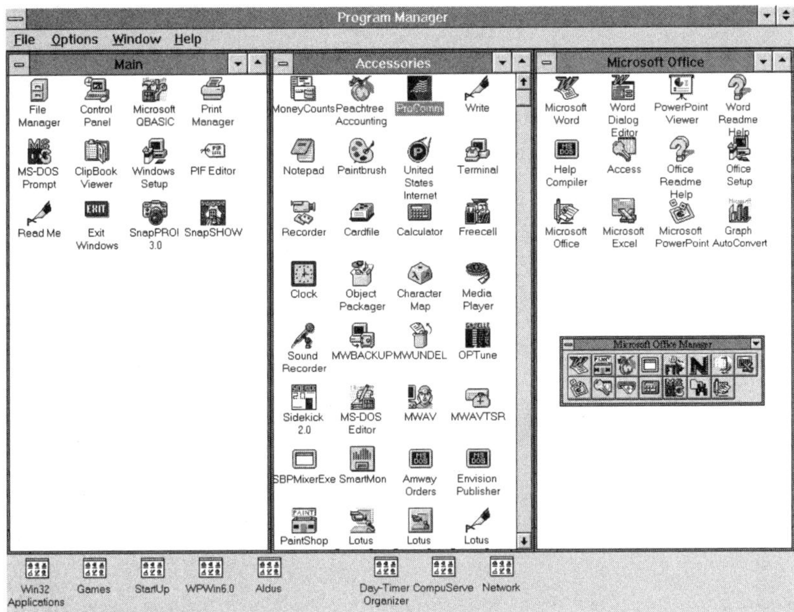

Figure B.1 Typical Windows 3.x Program Manager Desktop Screen

In Windows 3.x you would press Ctrl+Esc, for example, to display the task list, which shows what programs are running. You can switch to another program by double-clicking on the program you want to bring to the front (See Figure B.3 for a typical Windows 3.x Task List).

In Windows 95, however, the currently running programs are shown on the bar at the bottom of the screen. To bring one of them to the forefront you simply click on the button that represents the program you want to use.

There are some other obvious differences on the Windows 95 desktop. Notice the absence of a menu bar at the top of the screen. To run a specific program you use the Start button at the bottom. Click on Start and a list of available programs pops up, like the sample in Figure B.4.

Figure B.2 Typical Windows 95 Desktop

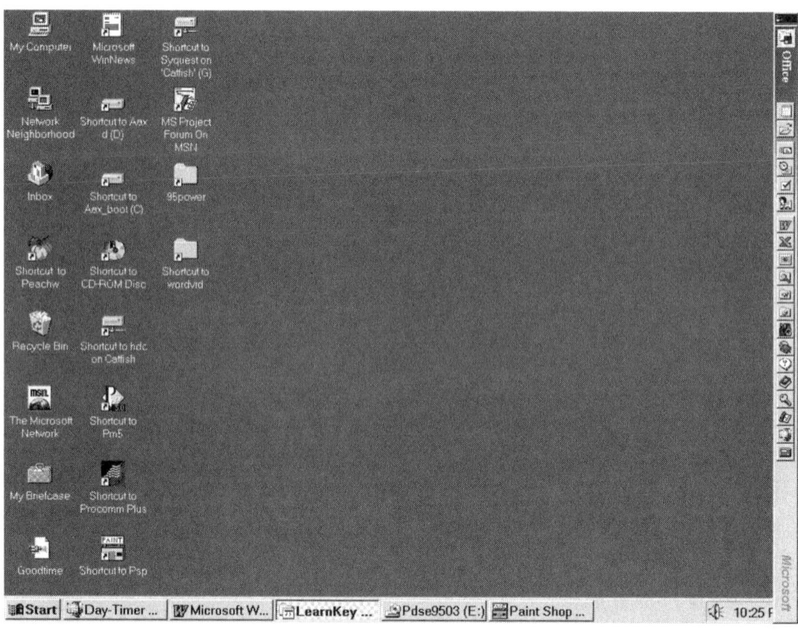

Figure B.3 Typical Windows 3.x Task List

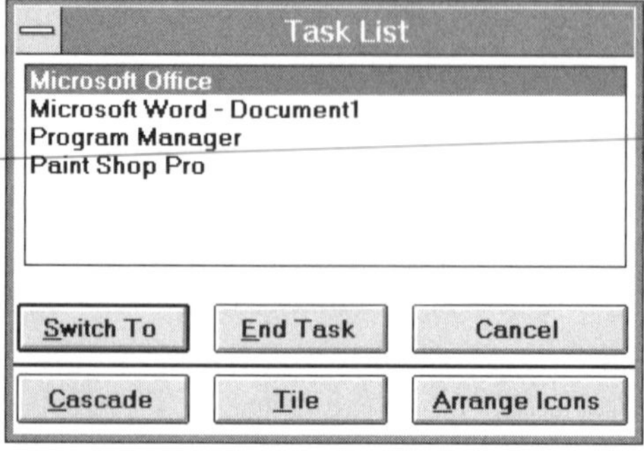

Figure B.4 Typical Windows 95 Start Program Pop-Up

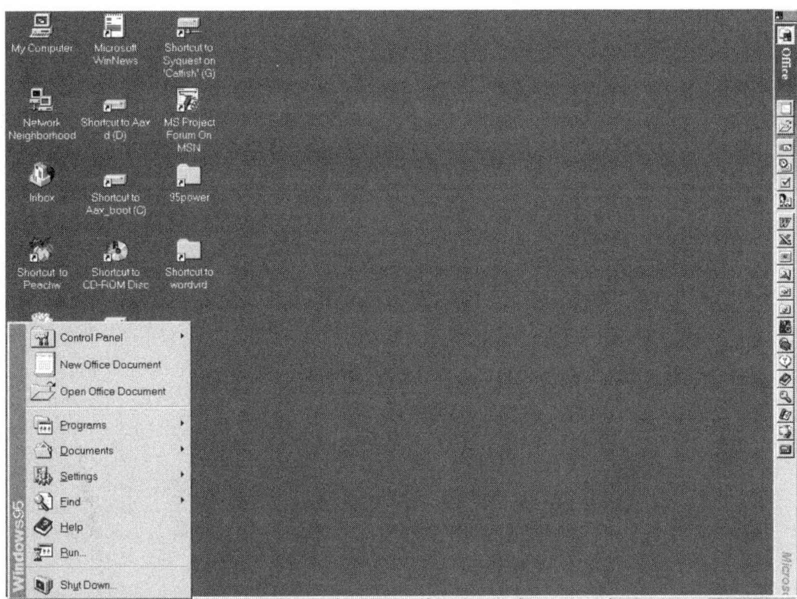

You can view available programs from this pop-up by dragging the highlight cursor up the Start bar. As you do, additional pop-up menus appear, as shown in Figure B.5.

To launch one of the programs on the secondary list, you move the cursor over to the secondary menu and pull the highlight down the list to the program you want, holding down the left mouse button. When you release the left mouse button, the program launches. You can also move the highlight over the program list without holding down the mouse button. That's one of the differences between Windows 3.x and Windows 95. You can actually cause additional menus to pop up without holding down a button. If you have selected a program without a button pressed, you'll need to click on the program you want to launch.

Figure B.5 Start Program Bar with Second Pop-Up Menu

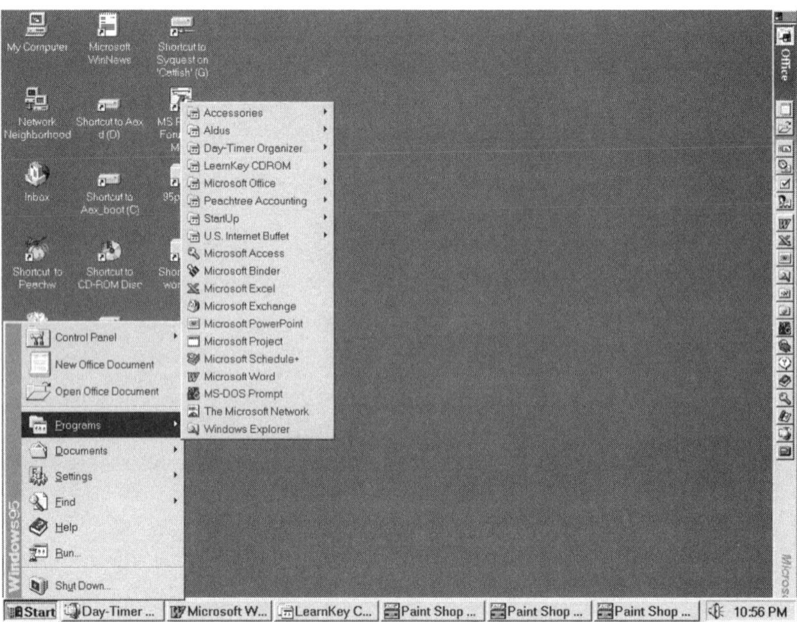

Windows 95 and Microsoft Word

Within each program, Windows 95 also offers some differences. Notice the Word 7 screen shown in Figure B.6. It shows the basic Word menu and toolbar, but there are a few differences.

Notice, for example, the upper right corner of the Word 7 screen. In Windows 3.x there are two buttons in this location, a Restore button (up-facing arrow) and a Minimize button (a down-facing button). In Windows 95 there are three icons. The one at the left of the group, an ellipsis, is the Minimize button, the two overlapping screens in the middle represent the Maximize (Restore) button, and the X icon on the right closes the program.

These same icons appear at the top of document windows. You can shrink a document to an icon, expand (restore) a document, or close it with these icons.

Figure B.6 Word 7 Main Screen

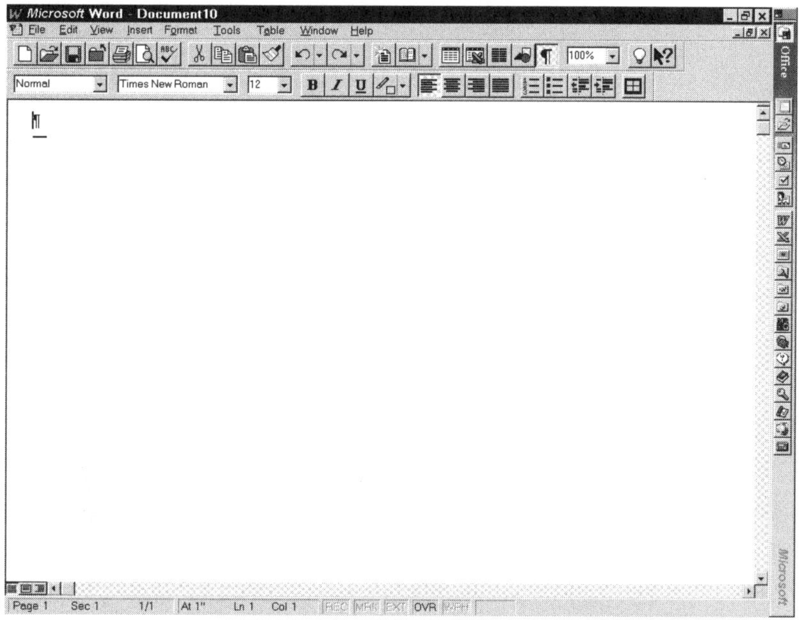

Word 7 also has some additional features that are useful and interesting. I've mentioned the enhanced AutoCorrect feature. This facility was available in Word 6, but the new version can do more.

Word 7 also includes an address book feature, really an interface to Microsoft Mail. This lets you store and access the contact information you need. The advantage of having this type of feature built into a word processor is that you don't need to close one application and open another to conduct a task that is quite common in a business environment. And if you are like many word processor users, Word is the program you use the most—perhaps all day every day—so it is convenient to have this type of addition built in.

A simple but really useful little utility is the Word highlighter. You know how you read a document and your hand automatically reaches for a familiar yellow highlight marker to

Figure B.7 Pull-Down Highlighter Color List

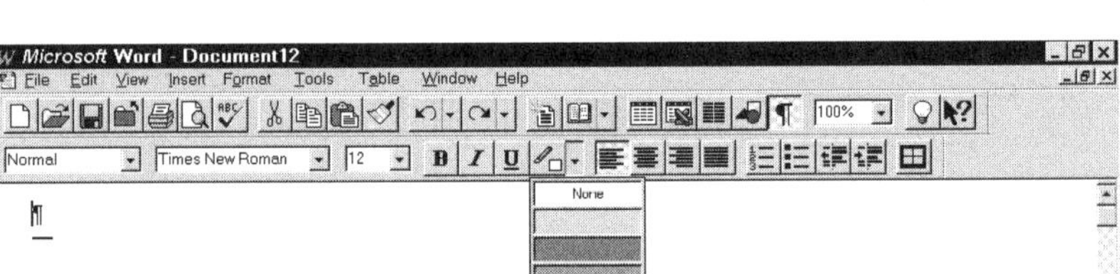

highlight something you want to find easily later? Word 7 has this feature built in with multiple colors. You can grab the highlighter icon from the toolbar, swipe the text you want to mark, and you have highlighted text. This is useful when several people may be reading or commenting on your documents. Each person can read, highlight, and comment as the document makes its electronic rounds over your local network.

The highlighter is intelligent in the same sense as the character attributes markers. Mark one word, drag the pointer right or left and Word automatically marks the next word. You can unmark text by choosing None from the pull-down color list on the toolbar (see Figure B.7).

As with Windows 95 there also are some behind-the-scenes features that won't be immediately obvious but which you will come across as you use Word 7.

Summary

There's no substitute for putting your hands on a new piece of software as a path toward understanding it. However, I hope this short overview can at least get you started and help you understand the differences between Word 6 and Word 7. Actually, if you decide to upgrade to Windows 95 and thence to Word 7, the transition should be really easy.

I find the Windows 95 interface even easier to use than earlier versions, and Word 7 looks and feels enough like earlier releases that you should have no problems with the upgrade. Just remember not to get lost in the mechanics and remember the basic concepts that make for successful documents.

INDEX

LIMITED WARRANTY AND DISCLAIMER OF LIABILITY

LearnKey CD-ROM Product Line

Novell Perfect Office
WordPerfect 6.1 - Beginning $49.95, #8131
WordPerfect 6.1 - Intermediate $49.95, #8132
WordPerfect 6.1 - Advanced $49.95, #8133
All three WordPerfect 6.1 CDs for only $129.95, #8130

Presentations 3.0 - Essentials $49.95, #8711
Presentations 3.0 - Advanced Tips & Tricks $49.95, #8712
Both Presentations 3.0 CDs only $89.95, #8710

GroupWise 4.0 - Essentials $49.95, #8911
GroupWise 4.0 - PowerTools $49.95, #8912
Both GroupWise 4.0 CDs only $89.95, #8910

Quattro Pro 6.0 - Beginning $49.95, #8311
Quattro Pro 6.0 - Intermediate $49.95, #8312
Quattro Pro 6.0 - Advanced $49.95, #8313
All three Quattro Pro 6.0 CDs only $129.95, #8310

Envoy 1.0 - Essentials $49.95, #8001
InfoCentral 1.1 - Essentials $49.95, #8011
PerfectOffice Integration - $49.95, #8035

Other Novell Products
WordPerfect 6.0 Windows - Beginning $49.95, #8151
WordPerfect DOS 6.0 - Beginning $49.95, #8101
WordPerfect DOS 6.0 - Intermediate $49.95, #8102
WordPerfect DOS 6.0 - Advanced $49.95, #8103
Quattro Pro 5.0 - Beginning $49.95, #8301

Windows
Intro to Windows '95 $29.95, #8051
Intro and Applications for Windows 3.1 $49.95, #8066

Microsoft Office Professional
Word 6.0 - Beginning $49.95, #8151
Word 6.0 - Intermediate $49.95, #8152
Word 6.0 - Advanced $49.95, #8153
Access 2.0 - Beginning $49.95, #8541
Access 2.0 - Intermediate $49.95, #8542
Access 2.0 - Advanced $49.95, (product number unavailable)
Excel 5.0 - Beginning $49.95, #8351

Lotus Products
1-2-3 4.0 - Beginning $49.95, #8391

ClarisWorks
ClarisWorks 3.0 $49.95, #8061

Internet Series (product numbers unavailable)
Executive Intro to the Internet
Doing Business on the Internet

Notes on Using the CD-ROM

See Appendix A for installation instructions.

The programs will not run without 256 colors. If you attempt to run the programs and the video looks grainy, then your system is probably set to less than 256 colors. If this is the case you will need to change the color setting to 256. Your system's graphics card may come with a utility to change the color setting. If that is not the case, then you will need to go to the main group in the Program Manager and open the Windows Setup icon. Select Options, then select Change System Settings. Pick a 256 color option. It may be necessary to use the Windows 3.1 disks to get the driver. If you can find the Microsoft 256 color super VGA driver, use it!